CLIL Essentials

for Secondary School Teachers

Peeter Mehisto with Y. L. Teresa Ting

CAMBRIDGE
UNIVERSITY PRESS

CAMBRIDGE
UNIVERSITY PRESS

University Printing House, Cambridge CB2 8BS, United Kingdom

One Liberty Plaza, 20th Floor, New York, NY 10006, USA

477 Williamstown Road, Port Melbourne, VIC 3207, Australia

314–321, 3rd Floor, Plot 3, Splendor Forum, Jasola District Centre, New Delhi – 110025, India

79 Anson Road, #06–04/06, Singapore 079906

Cambridge University Press is part of the University of Cambridge.

It furthers the University's mission by disseminating knowledge in the pursuit of education, learning and research at the highest international levels of excellence.

www.cambridge.org
Information on this title: www.cambridge.org/9781108400848

First published 2017

20 19 18 17 16 15 14 13 12 11 10 9 8 7 6 5 4 3 2 1

Printed in Great Britain by CPI Group (UK) Ltd, Croydon CR0 4YY

A catalogue record for this publication is available from the British Library

ISBN 978-1-10840084-8 Paperback

Contents

Foreword

Diane J. Tedick

After completing an undergraduate degree in Spanish and Education in the late 1970s, I was convinced I would never teach language. Teaching language through grammar did not inspire me (or the high school students I was trained to teach). Lacking other options, I moved to Spain where (ironically) my only work opportunity was to teach English. I was hired by individuals who needed English for specific purposes – for example, to read Biology texts for an undergraduate degree or to interact with academics internationally in the field of agronomy. As I gained experience, I had an epiphany – *that's* how language should be taught – through content that is meaningful to students! Little did I know that this content-based approach to language teaching (CBLT) had surfaced 15–20 years earlier in the form of French immersion education in Canada and bilingual education in the US and that it would become the focus of my academic career. I have worked as a teacher, teacher educator and researcher in the field of CBLT/CLIL/language immersion education for nearly four decades, and it is with this experience that I come to Mehisto's *CLIL Essentials for Secondary School Teachers*, written in cooperation with Y. L. Teresa Ting.

I first met Peeter Mehisto in 2014 while giving a week-long workshop with a colleague in Estonia. We had been invited to work with educators who were planning to implement two-way immersion (Estonian/Russian) programmes. Mehisto took part for the entire week, and I recall how impressed I was by his knowledge, insights, creativity and ability to explain complex concepts with clarity and ease. He brings these attributes to *CLIL Essentials*.

Much has changed in the field of language education since I had my first encounter with CBLT in the 1970s. CBLT/CLIL – a large umbrella that encompasses many types of programmes wherein a second or foreign language is used as the vehicle to teach subject matter content – has grown exponentially around the globe. This growth is due in part to research that has demonstrated that CBLT/CLIL programmes are more effective at developing second/foreign language proficiency than programmes that teach language traditionally (i.e. through a grammatical approach).

Despite these positive research findings and the increasing popularity of CBLT/CLIL programmes, studies have also shown that these programmes may not be reaching their language teaching potential. CLBT/CLIL students' language typically lacks grammatical accuracy, and lexical specificity, and learners in these settings struggle to develop a command of academic language. Scholars argue that much more systematic attention to language development within these programmes is critical; this is especially the case at the secondary level where the cognitive and linguistic demands of content learning are so significant. Both content and language teachers in CLIL programmes need to learn how better to integrate language and content as they develop curriculum, design classroom activities, provide instruction and assess learning. *CLIL Essentials* masterfully and artfully addresses these needs. This book is impressive for its quality and clarity of writing, depth of content, and precise articulation of theory and practice connections.

Mehisto's approach to *CLIL Essentials* is refreshingly non-prescriptive. Instead, the author invites teachers to explore new ideas, try them on, and reflect on their enactment; indeed, the author provides rubrics for content and language teachers to facilitate self-reflection. Mehisto draws broadly on learning theory and research, and applies their insights to CLIL teaching. After the Introduction, each of the seven content-rich chapters is organised to facilitate navigation, with advance organisers and descriptions of how the chapter connects to other concepts in the book. The chapters are brimming with practical ideas that are grounded in research and learning theory; they offer helpful graphics and are replete with outstanding, concrete examples to illustrate new concepts.

Many of the examples are extensive, and offer readers step-by-step descriptions of how to implement the concepts being introduced. For example, Chapter 3: *The Language Teacher's Perspective* walks readers through an extensive instructional sequence to demonstrate how a language teacher can focus on a biography of a famous person using a text that aligns with content being studied in a CLIL Biology class. Chapter 8: *Learning Progressions* presents an adaptation of a unit on the human heart that was developed by Mehisto's co-collaborator on the book, Y. L. Teresa Ting. Most interesting about the detailed description is the inclusion of an analysis that displays how the learning tasks and materials exemplify best practices in CLIL teaching.

Examples also appear throughout the book in the form of *View from the Field* insets contributed by educators from around the world and references to others engaged in implementing CLIL. Through these examples, Mehisto reveals his international reach and, most importantly, illustrates that the text is not filled with pie-in-the-sky ideals but rather with activities and strategies that are feasible and being applied by actual CLIL practitioners – from South Korea to Mexico, the UK and beyond.

Readers of this text will find that it also has strong social justice underpinnings. Drawing upon recent work by scholars such as Cammarata, Cummins and Reagan, Mehisto assists readers in seeing the important relationships among critical pedagogy, enquiry-based learning and critical thinking skills, and makes a strong case for these approaches. Moreover, Mehisto devotes an entire chapter to culture and intercultural competence in CLIL. In doing so, he demonstrates that CLIL is not just about content and language learning but can also serve as a mechanism for helping young people approach difference with curiosity and openness instead of fear and contempt; for aiding them in developing and respecting diverse perspectives; and for encouraging them to see that how we use language, how we think and how we act matters. It's hard to imagine more important understandings, skills and attitudes for today's world.

Quite simply, *CLIL Essentials* represents state-of-the-art thinking with regard to language, content and culture integration for secondary school teachers. Mehisto is to be congratulated for writing a book that is pedagogically visionary and that, in concrete ways, unpacks the complex concept that is academic language, demonstrates how language and content can be integrated in both instruction and assessment with appropriate strategies and scaffolds, and invites readers to explore the far-reaching potential of CLIL.

Diane J. Tedick
Professor, Second Language Education,
University of Minnesota

Acknowledgements

We dedicate this book to the many CLIL students and teachers who have taught us much about CLIL, and who have chosen to walk the 'different' and potentially powerful path that is CLIL.

In addition, we thank former CLIL teacher, school principal and current CLIL trainer Tuula Asikainen for her insightful comments and advice. A thank you to David Marsh as well, for his helpful suggestions.

The thoughtful and supportive Helen Imam, who gave this book its spark of life, is deserving of a very special thank you.

About the authors

Peeter Mehisto, University College London Institute of Education, specialises in CLIL (Content and Language Integrated Learning). He has worked with a wide variety of stakeholders to support the development of CLIL programmes at the primary, secondary and university levels. This includes substantial hands-on experience in learning materials development. Peeter has also delivered professional development for teachers and other CLIL stakeholders in countries as diverse as Brazil, Canada, Estonia, Finland, Germany, Kazakhstan, Italy, Malaysia, Mexico, Spain, South Korea, the United Arab Emirates and Vietnam.

He has won several awards for his work. He has also taught at the secondary and university levels. He is the lead author of the awarding-winning book *Uncovering CLIL: Content and Language Integrated Learning in Bilingual and Multilingual Education* (Macmillan). More recently he has written *Excellence in Bilingual Education: A guide for School Principals* (CUP), and *Building Bilingual Education Systems: Forces, Mechanisms and Counterweights* (CUP), co-written with Fred Genesee and others.

Y. L. Teresa Ting, university of Calabria, holds BSci Degrees in Biology and Psychology, a PhD in Neurobiology studying animal models of learning and memory (Kent State University, Ohio, USA), an MA Ed. with a thesis comparing quantitative versus qualitative methodologies in education research (University of East Anglia, UK), and is currently Assistant Professor of English Applied Linguistics at the University of Calabria. She has been involved in CLIL teacher training courses and ministerial-level workshops in Austria, Belgium, Italy, Spain and the UK, as well as for the European Language Council and the British Council. She was a member of the ECML (European Centre for Modern Languages) 2012–2015 project on CLIL and Literacies.

Her secondary CLIL materials, some of which have been adapted in this book, received the Macmillan Education Innovative Writing Award at the British Council ELTons in 2013. She collaborates extensively with schools and teachers to 'field-test' her materials and teachers' guides.

1 Introduction

Welcome to *CLIL Essentials for Secondary School Teachers*!

This book explores the core drivers of CLIL (Content and Language Integrated Learning). *CLIL Essentials* is not prescriptive in nature, as its title might suggest. Instead, it covers what could be considered the essentials for having a wide-ranging and in-depth discussion about what is at the core of CLIL.

Above all, *CLIL Essentials* aims to offer in parallel two different sets of ideas to explore CLIL. First, there is a thorough discussion of some key constructs that can drive learning in CLIL contexts. That discussion is meant to spark teaching and learning ideas. Second, there is a substantial storehouse of practical ideas for adaptation by the reader. In the real world of teaching, no one could be expected to apply all of their own ideas sparked by the key constructs, let alone take on board all the practical ideas proposed in the book, but everyone could try out a few of these.

Ericsson and Pool (2016), who research how all of us can achieve extraordinary things, argue that even high performers gradually deteriorate if they do not make deliberate efforts to improve – if they do not regularly aim just a little higher. One of their mottos is not just to try harder, but to 'try differently'. That can mean integrating something completely 'new' into one's practice. Or, why not try something old, which is tried and true, with a 'new' twist to give it even greater power? Many of the ideas in this book, be they theoretical or practical, have been shown to have a high positive impact on student learning. They are offered for perusal, possible selection, reflection, and implementation and adaptation to the reader's context – one reflective step at a time in order to enhance teaching practice and CLIL student learning.

In this introductory chapter, we define CLIL and sketch out all the chapters in the book. The definition of CLIL is offered as a vision of what can be achieved. Although the definition constitutes a high expectation – a key characteristic of effective CLIL programmes – this definition does not suggest that if one does not meet all of these parameters that one is not doing CLIL. Each and every context offers its own constraints and possibilities. Whatever the CLIL context, the ideal vision embedded in this definition is meant to serve as a source of inspiration, but not to undermine what is possible in a given context.

In the ideal, CLIL is a dual-focused teaching and learning approach in which the L1[1] and one or more additional languages are used for promoting both content mastery and language acquisition to pre-defined levels.[2] At least two languages including the L1 are used to teach different high-status content subjects such as Mathematics and History. CLIL educators largely separate the L1 and L2 by teaching a given subject primarily through one or the other language. However, the L1 is used sparingly and judiciously by teachers teaching through the students' L2 and vice versa, thereby taking into account the fact that the L1 and L2 continually interact in the learner's mind. Concomitantly, content and language learning are systematically supported in both content and language classes. In the short and long term, CLIL aims to support students from diverse socio-economic backgrounds in developing age- and grade-appropriate levels of:

- L1 competence in reading, writing, speaking and listening comprehension
- advanced functional proficiency in L2 reading, writing, speaking and listening comprehension
- academic achievement in all school content subjects, such as Mathematics and Science taught primarily through the L2 and in those taught primarily through the L1
- understanding and appreciation of the culture(s) of the L1 group(s), and of the L2 group(s);

At the same time, CLIL aims to promote:

- capacity for and interest in intercultural communication; and

---

1 The term 'L1' refers to a student's first and strongest language. For simplicity's sake, when referring to a situation in general, it is assumed that the L1 is also the society's dominant language. At the same time, it is recognised that for individual students from immigrant or minority backgrounds the L1 can be their second (L2) or even third language (L3).

2 If these levels of language proficiency have not been defined in a regional or a national curriculum, various language proficiency guidelines can be used as a point of departure for their articulation (see page 259).

- the cognitive and social skills and habits required for success in an ever-changing world.

This definition builds on earlier definitions of immersion (Genesee, 2005) and CLIL (Coyle, Hood and Marsh, 2010; Marsh et al., 2010, referring to Maljers et al., 2007). The referenced CLIL definitions are useful in getting an understanding of the core concept of CLIL. However, they offer limited 'measurables' that could guide educators, administrators and researchers in either co-constructing programmes or in measuring progress in CLIL programme development. In contrast, the above definition seeks to offer more tangible 'measurables'.

By referring to both classes taught through the L1 and the L2, the above definition speaks to the reality that CLIL classes are part of a larger ecology of an entire school. The implied stance is that CLIL does not undermine classes taught through the school's L1 and that the L1 classes do not undermine CLIL. CLIL is presented as a value-added option. A reference is made to high-status subjects and by implication the need to manage the status of both languages.

In addition, the definition draws out the need to systematically support content and language learning in both content and language classes. As discussed in Chapters 2 and 3, this is not without its challenges, but the integration of content and language is at the heart of CLIL.

The above definition of CLIL expressly includes a mention of socio-economic background. This invites those implementing CLIL to avoid establishing elitist programmes. This is a realistic goal. In the four Canadian provinces of Quebec, Manitoba, Saskatchewan and British Columbia, there is 'no real difference in the average family background of immersion and non-immersion students' (Statistics Canada, 2010). Genesee and Fortune (2014) report that students with high socio-economic need tend to do at least as well in bilingual programmes as they do in monolingual programmes. Even more limited forms of bilingual instruction appear to be suitable for students from diverse backgrounds (Whittaker and Llinares, 2009; Van de Craen, Ceuleers and Mondt, 2007).

Finally, the above definition integrates one of the key elements of bilingualism and plurilingualism, which is intercultural communication (see Chapter 6). It draws out culture and intercultural communication as one of the pillars of CLIL (see also Coyle et al., 2010). Because the meaning of the term 'culture' is highly debated, if the above culture-related goal is taken on board, it is important for a community to agree on a working definition so it can decide on what cultural content will be taught and how learning thereof will be measured. By clearly stating that CLIL aims to build students' capacity for and interest in intercultural communication, this definition of CLIL invites regional and national authorities to reflect this goal by including key intercultural competences in curricula and initiatives that support curriculum implementation (see Chapter 6).

What the definition does not address is the amount of time spent learning through the L1 or L2. It allows for multiple options (see Mehisto, 2012, for an overview of some of the programme types that can be grouped under the term 'CLIL'). It is important to understand the implications of each option and how to take into account and build a context suitable for CLIL (see Genesee and Hamayan, 2016). In order for key stakeholders to understand the option chosen, it is also helpful to report on: the baseline knowledge of students entering the CLIL programme/class; the number of hours of instruction provided in and through a given language; the socio-economic background of the students; language use in the classroom; language use outside of the classroom; core teaching and learning practices, and other contextual factors.

Although grounded in research evidence about education in general and CLIL, this book does not offer a review of the CLIL professional literature. That can be found in a large number of other sources. To name but a few, these include: The National Academies of Sciences, Engineering and Medicine, 2017; Ruiz de Zarobe, 2015; Tedick and Wesely, 2015; Valentino and Reardon, 2014; Thomas and Collier, 2012; Lindholm-Leary and Borsato, 2006; Johnstone 2002; Lindholm-Leary, 2001; Swain and Lapkin, 1982; and Lambert and Tucker, 1972.

As stated, this book concentrates instead on core constructs that drive CLIL, and on practical teaching and learning strategies. More specifically, **Chapter 2:** *The Content Teacher's Perspective* – discusses why general best practices in teaching and learning are essential in CLIL contexts. Stressing the need for the thorough teaching of core concepts and big ideas, the chapter argues for taking a language-sensitive approach towards content teaching. This promises to lead to greater content learning. The chapter also explores language use and translanguaging. It discusses the value of setting and discussing intended content and language learning outcomes, and offers an extensive list of generic language learning outcomes.

Chapter 3: *The Language Teacher's Perspective* – takes as a reference point Cenoz's (2015) argument that when it comes to 'their essential properties', there is no difference between CLIL and CBI (content-based instruction).

The chapter argues for a content-based approach in CLIL language classes, that encourages critical thinking. Critical thinking is defined. Practical ideas are offered for integrating content learning and critical thinking into language lessons. It is argued that this will improve language learning. Content and language teacher cooperation is also discussed.

Chapter 4: *Academic Language* – defines academic language. It explains why academic language is important, including how it is tied to academic literacy. Key components of academic language and ways of teaching this language are drawn out. In addition, the chapter explores ways of determining what academic language students need to learn.

Chapter 5: *Scaffolding Content and Language Input and Output* – defines scaffolding and related concepts. It explains why scaffolding is indispensible in CLIL. It stresses the role of affect and cognitive load, both of which need to be managed with additional care in CLIL contexts. In addition, the chapter provides a repertoire of content and language scaffolding strategies. Part of this repertoire includes a detailing of language learning skills.

Chapter 6: *Culture and Intercultural Competence* – fleshes out the link between language and culture. It explores definitions of culture and offers a substantial list of cultural elements worthy of study. The chapter also draws out inter- or cross-cultural competences, and suggests ways of teaching culture and fostering the development of intercultural competence.

Chapter 7: *Assessment* – explores assessment through a CLIL lens. It outlines the foci of assessment in CLIL and analyses how testing and marking are adapted in CLIL contexts. The chapter provides a repertoire of high-impact formative assessment strategies. As effective feedback regarding content and language learning are central to moving forward the learning of each, the chapter details the characteristics of effective feedback, how teachers can increase student uptake or incorporation of their feedback, and how they can get feedback from students. The chapter concludes with an introductory CLIL lesson suitable for several subjects. The lesson includes multiple feedback loops.

Chapter 8: *Learning Progressions: Bringing it all Together* – shows how good CLIL practice can guide the development of a complete learning progression of one short unit. It provides the reader with the option of stepping into the students' shoes to experience a CLIL learning progression. In addition to providing a series of tasks and related materials, the chapter provides an explanation of their use and an analysis of how these tasks and materials support learning in a CLIL context.

Finally the book offers appendices that break down the academic language of Geography, History, Maths and Science.

2 The content teacher's perspective

Pupils can't learn to think like scientists in a meaningful sense unless they actually engage with scientific content. Pupils can't become successful readers without the vocabulary and background knowledge that is commonly referred to in most [academic] texts. (Christodoulou, 2016)

INTRODUCTION AND CHAPTER NAVIGATOR

Content teachers are first and foremost interested in teaching students their subject, be that Computer Programming, Geography, Maths, Physical Education or Science. Subject-matter knowledge and accepted disciplinary practices such as using the scientific method are fundamental to being able to think critically about content. Learning skills are also important, but these are usually best learned whilst working with meaningful content. Meaningful content is and shall remain at the heart of education. This does not change in CLIL.

In CLIL, however, it becomes particularly important for content teachers to identify and teach core content concepts and 'big ideas' thoroughly. Core concepts and big ideas provide the foundations for future learning in any discipline. Furthermore, by using best practices in pedagogy that lead students to deeply engage with these core concepts and big ideas, content learning is likely to become better anchored in long-term memory in the form of solid subject-related cognitive schemata[1] or mental models. Having easy access to these cognitive schemata frees up short-term memory, through which all learning must pass, so it can concentrate on new learning.

1 Baddeley, Eysenck and Anderson (2015) define a cognitive schema as 'a well-integrated chunk of knowledge about the world, events, people, or actions'. Schema includes both frames and sequences.

In CLIL, L2 academic language is also a gateway to the knowledge and skills of any given content subject. The CLIL content teacher faces the challenging fact that students almost inevitably need help to navigate and learn the L2 academic language of the given subject. If CLIL students are systematically helped not only to engage deeply with the content concepts and big ideas and to build on these, but also to notice the related academic language and to use this language several times for meaningful tasks over a period of time, they are likely to recall it when needed. Once that language has been solidly stored in long-term memory, short-term memory can concentrate on new learning and not have to struggle with recalling language that has only been used on rare occasions.

Taking account of the above principles, this chapter explores some key aspects of the CLIL content teacher's role. It discusses core concepts and big ideas that drive learning when teaching through an L2. In particular, the chapter:

- discusses why general best practices in teaching and learning are essential in CLIL contexts
- examines the need to favour the thorough teaching of core concepts and big ideas
- defines communication awareness and suggests which common patterns of communication to approach with caution and which ones to favour
- defines language awareness and discusses why CLIL content teachers and students need to be language aware
- discusses L2 versus L1 language use and offers principles and guidelines for effective translanguaging
- explores the setting of content and language outcomes/objectives which serve as tools for planning and assessing learning
- offers a tool for content teachers to determine where they are in their journey as they take on board a CLIL ethos and adopt CLIL practices.

GENERAL BEST PRACTICES IN TEACHING AND LEARNING

CLIL does not operate in a vacuum. Before discussing powerful pedagogies used in CLIL, it is essential to be aware of what works best in education in general. This knowledge has a vital role to play in supporting learning in the challenging environment that is CLIL. John Hattie (2009) and his team initially synthesised over 800 meta-studies in education with the aim of determining what works best in teaching and learning. By 2015, they had synthesised over 1200 meta-studies analysing 195 influences on learning (Hattie 2012, 2015a). These influences can be categorised as focusing on six different domains: the student; the home; the school; the curriculum; the teacher; and teaching and learning approaches.

Know thy impact!

Analysing your own assignments is one of the most effective ways of determining what you believe your students are capable of doing (Fisher et al., 2016). Your beliefs and expectations are likely to drive or thwart student learning. For example, asking students to interrogate ideas, create concept maps, and/or develop and follow a line of enquiry are likely to encourage deep thinking and learning. In contrast, assignments that simply ask students to find existing answers in a text are likely to do the opposite.

Many influences on learning that regularly receive a great deal of attention in a wide number of nations have a low impact on student learning. These include reducing class size, establishing charter schools, matching teaching and learning styles, teaching test-taking, concentrating on problem-based learning and changing school calendars. This does not mean that these have no influence; it is just that there are many other influences on student learning that are much more powerful, and which tend to have a much greater positive effect on student learning. Equally importantly, the influence of the home is often referred to as being powerful. Hattie has found it to be powerful, but he has also found over 50 other more powerful influences that schools can draw on to support students even if their home circumstances are not ideal.

Hattie calculates the 'effect size' (magnitude of impact) of these 195 influences on student learning.[2] An effect size shows the relative impact of each of the 195 influences on student achievement. These are particularly important in the demanding CLIL context, as they direct teachers to the most powerful influences on student learning, including powerful teaching and learning strategies. They also highlight those often-used strategies that have a relatively modest influence on student learning. Currently Hattie's effect sizes range from -0.42 (student depression) to 1.62 (teacher estimates of student achievement). An effect size of less

2 An 'effect size' is calculated using the difference in the pre-test and post-test mean or average scores for a group of students. This figure is then divided by the average spread of student scores. This provides the average standard deviation (i.e. deviation from the mean). Student scores on a pre-test (pre-intervention) and post-test (post-intervention) are compared. Typically in education research, the results of a comparable control group and an experimental group are compared. The experimental group has received an intervention, and the control group has not.

than 0.0 has a negative effect on learning while an effect size above 0.0 has a positive effect on learning. The vast majority of educational interventions have a positive effect on learning. Hattie suggests the average gain students get from schooling translates into an effect size of 0.40 per annum. Therefore, he suggests that if teachers wish to have an above-average, positive effect on student learning, they need to concentrate on using those strategies with an effect size of 0.40 or more. An effect size of 0.50 is the equivalent of a one-grade improvement in a mark (e.g. from a C to a B) while an effect size of 1.00 is the equivalent of a two-grade improvement (e.g. from a C to an A).

Some of the greatest influences on student learning are those that help build learner autonomy. For example, self-reported grades and students' own high expectations have an effect size of 1.33. As students develop an understanding of success criteria and build their capacity to assess their own work, they are more likely to understand how to improve it. They are more likely to set themselves new and higher expectations. Feedback that is focused on helping students to move forward has an effect size of 0.73 and formative assessment of 0.68 (see **Chapter 7:** *Assessment*). Teacher estimates of student achievement stand at 1.62, implying that teacher beliefs regarding what students are able to do drive what students actually accomplish in a given class. Throughout this book we will return to these important influences on student learning and discuss how these can be used in CLIL contexts to enhance student learning of both content and language. However, before that we discuss Hattie's primary conclusion, which is that in order to help students to learn, teachers above all need to reflect on their own practices and examine their own influence on student learning.

Based on his research, John Hattie (2015b) argues that in order to support student learning teachers and schools need to focus on the impact they are having on students' learning: 'Know thy impact!' A prerequisite to knowing thy impact is to be able first to define what constitutes high-quality, average or low-quality student work. Teachers need a strong understanding of the criteria for judging the quality of student work. Moreover, students need to be aware of and understand these criteria. They need to know what is expected of them and how they can judge their own work and how their work will be judged. Students need feedback on how to improve their work. They need support in setting new and higher targets for themselves.

Hattie goes on to stress that teachers need to become expert at evaluating their own work and the impact that it is having on student learning. In particular, the following teacher actions tend to lead to very substantial improvements in student learning:

- working together to evaluate their [the teachers'] impact (0.93);
- moving from what students know now towards explicit success criteria (0.77);
- building trust and welcoming errors as opportunities to learn (0.72);
- getting maximum feedback from others about their effect (0.72);
- getting the proportions of surface to deep learning correct (0.71);
- using the Goldilocks principles of challenge (the challenges must be not too big, not too small but just right); and
- using deliberate practice to attain these challenges (0.60).

(Hattie, 2015b)

The above points imply that there is a great deal of knowledge in schools about best practices, but in order to access that knowledge, teachers need to cooperate with one another. Hattie (2015b) adds that 'to get these effects requires listening to the learning happening in the classroom. It requires less talk by teachers and more listening to student dialogue; it requires more evaluation of surface and deep understanding and knowing when to move from one to the other; and it requires teaching that builds on a deep understanding of what students already know.'

It also requires that the quality of teaching and in particular student learning move to the top of the policy and meeting agendas in schools in order to ensure that the school is first and foremost a 'learning powered institution' (Claxton et al., 2011). School leaders have a particular role to play by using meeting time to focus on the core business of schools, which is helping students learn. Learning-powered schools are usually professional learning communities. Professional learning communities are a major vehicle for improving teacher and student learning (Stoll and Louis, 2007). They assume collective responsibility for student learning, they engage in open and frank debate, teachers are focused on their own as well as student learning, and there is a climate of 'reflective professional inquiry' (Bolam et al., 2005). Professional inquiry would involve subjecting assumptions, terminology, plans and practices to a rigorous process of critical thought and analysis, in order to build a common vision and goals. It would involve being open to and seeking out new learning.

As previously stated, all of the above applies to CLIL as well. High-impact strategies can be used to optimise learning and to help students better meet the extra challenge of learning through an L2.

CORE CONCEPTS AND BIG IDEAS VERSUS DETAILS

Knowledge in all school subjects is constructed on and around core concepts and big ideas (i.e. critical information/underlying principles/ways of understanding). Once students have engaged deeply in meaningful tasks that help them to use the related language to articulate on multiple occasions in diverse ways their learning of a given core concept or big idea, the core concept or big idea hopefully forms part of their cognitive architecture – the cognitive schemata or mental models for storing learning. Once students have these cognitive schemata or mental models securely constructed in their long-term memory along with the related language, these provide a framework for organising and storing additional related details. In other words, once the elements of the core concepts and big ideas have been well constructed in memory (i.e. organised, understood and well learnt), students are able to more effectively navigate additional related details and language, and go deeper in their learning. Ideally, the new details are integrated with the core concept or big idea, leading to a richer understanding of what has become 'a single [more complex] idea' (Hattie and Yates, 2014).

For example, in **Chapter 8:** *Learning Progressions*, we present material on the human heart. The big idea or critical information in these materials is that the human heart pumps blood in one direction through the blood vessels of the circulatory system and does so in a manner that ensures that oxygenated and deoxygenated blood never mix. There are many details associated with the anatomy and the physiology of the heart that make one-directional blood flow possible. The presence of one-way valves is a case in point. The CLIL learning materials initially mention the bicuspid and tricuspid valves as they help students understand the core principle of one-way blood flow. Once the core idea and related language have been understood and learned, then that learning can be enhanced with additional details through additional tasks such as working with further reading on the matter.

The same would be case with a core concept used in Civics or History such as freedom of the press – *the freedom of opinion and the right to express that opinion through diverse media without interference or censorship by the government*. First, the basic concept can be explored through an analysis of its key characteristics and related constraints such as liable and national interest. Then, one can move on to investigate additional important details such as erosion of freedom of the press through an analysis of international statistics on journalists' deaths and detentions or the rise of 'fake news'. Eventually students would be expected to integrate their understanding of freedom of the press with other concepts such a democracy, civil liberties, government, transparency and a given economic order.

It is essential in CLIL classrooms to focus on the learning of core subject concepts and big ideas along with related academic language as these are the foundation for future learning. Once this has been accomplished the students will be better placed to learn additional details.

COMMUNICATION AWARENESS

Some communication patterns are more effective at supporting learning than others, whilst some patterns are known to undermine learning. The quality of communication is particularly pertinent to CLIL teachers, as student communication through the L2 may primarily be restricted to classroom use. Thus, the limited opportunity for communication through the L2 needs to be used as effectively as possible. Communication systems in classrooms are in large part set up by teachers. CLIL teachers with a high degree of communication awareness – an understanding of the systems/patterns that operate when people communicate – are better placed to build more effective learning environments.

Communication systems/patterns shape the role that students play in the classroom by influencing how and to what extent students engage in learning. For example, if teacher talk dominates lessons, students often find it difficult to remain engaged (Yair, 2000). In contrast, students report greater levels of mental engagement when they are afforded meaningful and cognitively challenging opportunities for communication in groups. Furthermore, many teachers use 'teacherese', a register of language whose dominant functions are associated with 'management and control, and to encourage reasoning', but not dialogue (Hopwood and Gallaway, 1999).

Yet it is difficult for a student to become proficient at developing a line of reasoning without rich opportunities to work through, by way of a dialogic process, his or her thoughts about what is being taught.

The 'initiation-response-feedback (IRF) pattern' – asking a question, listening to a response and providing some form of feedback/evaluation – is another form of communication that dominates many classrooms (Sinclair and Coulthard, 1975). Often IRF exchanges are focused on recalling something that has been taught. Mercer and Dawes (2008) argue that teachers over- and mis-use this pattern. These exchanges are also common in CLIL (Lyster, 2007). Although IRF exchanges can be used as a dialogic tool to build a narrative leading to a common understanding of intended learning, they can also demotivate and disempower students. This is the case, if they imply that only teachers ask questions when they wish to do so and only teachers evaluate student answers (Mercer and Dawes, 2008). Such situations also undermine learner autonomy.

AN IRF EXCHANGE

Teacher: What is the capital of Nigeria?

Student: Abuja

Teacher: Excellent. What is the capital of Djibouti?

Barnes and Mercer offer another useful construct for analysing classroom talk. They argue that classroom talk can be divided into different **types of talk**:

- exploratory talk (sense of shared purpose, aimed at achieving agreement – see below for a more detailed explanation) (Barnes, 2008)
- cumulative talk (all ideas are collected, but not evaluated) (Mercer, 2008)
- disputational talk (competitive rather than cooperative; no pooling of resources to reach a common understanding) (Mercer, 2008)
- presentational talk (a final view 'for display and evaluation' focused on the content and language expectations of the audience) (Barnes, 2008).

Barnes (2008), discussing education delivered through the dominant societal language, sees the value in presentational talk and writing, but feels teachers often move too quickly to this stage. **Teachers need first to direct students' attention to core facts, and** provide access to core content knowledge. In CLIL, this also means helping students notice, use and learn the required academic language. Barnes proposes that teachers increase the use of exploratory talk and writing where the focus

> **A DIALOGIC EXCHANGE**
> ***Exploratory talk***
>
> *Teacher (T): So do we have 100% agreement for your definition of power?*
>
> *T: Mmm. No one? Talk with your partner. What is missing from the definition?*
>
> **Students (S) speak with one another.**
>
> *T: Sarah and Antonio?*
>
> *S: The positive.*
>
> *T: Help me understand what you mean.*
>
> *S: That definition. It's about people misusing power, right?*
>
> *T: For example?*
>
> *S: They can also help poor people.*
>
> *T. Does someone want to build on that using some concrete examples?*

is on the student 'sorting out his or her own thoughts'; that is to say, on 're-arranging' and developing his or her thoughts in relation to the content that is being taught. This process is often referred to as the core element in dialogic teaching and learning. Dialogic learning leads to deeper engagement with concepts and ideas. Dialogic learning helps students (and the teacher and peers) to explore, and thereby discover and overcome gaps in student understanding of subject content and their thinking about that content. Exploratory talk and writing, core elements of dialogic learning, also call on students to search for and use language to express their rearranged and/or new thoughts. Exploratory talk and writing can reveal gaps in language knowledge to students and teachers. This may help students develop a better understanding of their language needs and motivate them to seek out and learn that language.

Alexander (2010) states that teaching is 'dialogic' when it seeks 'to exploit the true potential of talk' and when classroom practice is:

- collective (teachers and students work together)
- reciprocal (teachers and students listen to each other and share ideas)
- supportive (free of fear)
- cumulative (builds on each other's ideas to create a common line of reasoning/inquiry – a common understanding), and
- purposeful (focused on meeting visible intended learning outcomes).

Teachers can (building on Mercer and Dawes, 2008) foster exploratory talk by:

- increasing the wait time after asking a question and before picking a student to answer it (in order to encourage greater levels of engagement and give students time to reflect)
- allowing (during whole class discussion) a series of student answers before any evaluations are made

- giving students a few moments to reflect on some aspect of a topic and/or at key moments having them write out some of their reflections before beginning/continuing a class discussion
- having all students prepare an answer to a question with a 'learning/talk partner' for 30 seconds to 2 minutes before answering
- encouraging students to ask questions of each other
- asking students to explain their reasoning (e.g. instead of asking for the answer to a Maths question, having students first explain how they solved the problem, and then asking if someone has used another way to solve it)
- linking the teacher's definitive explanation to the students' previous explanations
- discussing how work took place and asking students to suggest new ways of or rules for working
- having students choose who will speak.

In summary, if teachers are doing most of the talking, it is difficult for students to remain interested in the lesson and be focused on achieving the intended learning outcomes. Learning is likely to become less meaningful. By contrast, if students' thoughts are given greater public space, those thoughts and student-produced oral and written language are given greater status. They are valued by the teacher and hence by the students. In CLIL, where student L2 use may largely be limited to the classroom, offering students rich opportunities to summarise their thinking about content through exploratory talk and writing takes on a particular importance. If students are being supported in re-arranging their thoughts in relation to intended new learning (of content and language), additional learning needs will become apparent and eventually new learning is likely to become better integrated into memory. It is more likely to be recalled when and as needed.

LANGUAGE AWARENESS

Language awareness is the ability to step back from oral or written language in a manner that allows one to become consciously aware of and sensitive to:

- the nature of language

- the role language plays in communication and learning.
  (James and Garrett, 1991)

In this section we focus on one aspect of language awareness – student awareness of and sensitivity toward the correct use of language. We do not address the social and cultural role of language. Traditionally, schools sought to raise student linguistic awareness by teaching grammar in language classes. CLIL has arisen in part in response to the fact that traditional approaches to language teaching and learning generally speaking have not led to high levels of L2 proficiency among students. However, teaching content through an L2 does not mean that language classes are no longer necessary. Neither does it mean that language teachers no longer teach grammar or that content teachers do not draw attention to the correct use of language. Grammar is still taught in language classes. At the same time, correct language usage needs to be reinforced in content classes while students are speaking, reading and writing about something that they consider meaningful. By reinforcement we mean that content teachers draw student attention to key terms, phraseology, language patterns and grammatical conventions that students are expected to use. It would also involve prompting students to correct language errors. Without doing this in content classes, students are less likely to value the correct and precise use of language.

However, in addition to reinforcing the correct use of language in general, content teachers have a special responsibility to make visible to students the language of the given discipline, and to support students in using this language. After all, in each discipline CLIL content teachers are likely to be those people in the school that have the strongest command of the academic language of their discipline including in the L2. An entire chapter of this book, **Chapter 4:** *Academic Language*, is dedicated to discussing what academic language is and how to teach it. In addition, examples of how to teach academic language are offered in other chapters including in **Chapter 5:** *Scaffolding Content and Language Input and Output* and **Chapter 8:** *Learning Progressions.*

In addition to engaging with those chapters, the raising of teacher and student language awareness can begin with a **language analysis** prior to or shortly after the start of a CLIL class. This is a way of determining: (1) what the student can do using their L2 when they listen, speak, read and write, (2) what they have to be able to do (understand, say, read, write) by the end of a unit or course, (3) what they want to be able do, and (4) what support students will need to overcome any gap between what they currently can do and what they need to and want to be able to do. In the ideal, a language analysis is conducted by content teachers working in co-operation with language teachers. Not only are language teachers skilled at noticing elements of language that may need teaching, but after such cooperation they would also be better placed to teach or reinforce some of that language in their own classes.

To determine what learners must do, a teacher can review short- and long-term intended learning outcomes and materials, as well as lesson plans. The focus is on deciding what new language (e.g. structures, terminology, phrases, sets of phrases) students need to understand and above all use to meet those intended learning outcomes. This would also involve analysing learning materials and planned in-class and out-of-class tasks and assignments. In addition, samples of writing and recorded lessons can be analysed to identify language that was not used, but that would ideally have been used. It would be important to create a record of the language students need to learn. Furthermore, students can be asked to explain in writing in their L1 what language they feel they need to learn in the L2. This can be particularly effective when done in relation to a concrete assignment that students have just begun or when they are asked to reflect on a major upcoming term project. Without undertaking a language analysis, it is difficult to plan lessons that address students' language learning needs. With the analysis, it becomes easier to choose appropriate material and decide on how to scaffold input and student output in order to maximise student engagement.

Finally, language awareness among CLIL content teachers is a prerequisite for developing realistic and well-defined high expectations regarding language learning. As discussed in the above section entitled *General Best Practices in Teaching and Learning*, high teacher and student expectations are potentially amongst the most powerful positive influences on learning. In contrast, in classes where content teachers have low expectations regarding language learning, language learning is likely to slow down or stop. This is especially the case once students reach a level where they can communicate in the CLIL target language with relative ease. In these circumstances, not only does language learning slow down or stop, certain language errors become engrained or fossilised (see page 219 for further details on this matter).

LANGUAGE USE AND TRANSLANGUAGING

In the past it was generally argued that in dual-language programmes it was important to keep the two languages apart (Genesee and Hamayan, 2016; Heugh, 2016). Teachers teaching through the L2 were expected to teach 100% through the L2. However, in practice teachers may have been more flexible often using as much L2 as possible and as little L1 as necessary. In practical terms, Canadian CLIL trainers Olga Little and Lynda Boynton (2004) report that if students have trouble understanding an L2 term, a phrase or a concept, and if repeated explanations do not bring clarity, then a student can be asked to provide a short translation or summary in the L1 so learning can continue through the L2. If CLIL students are silent during group work that is supposed to take place in the L2, teachers can instead allow the students to use the L1, but have students report on their group work results through their L2. Later, teachers can scaffold the conducting of group work partly through the L2.

Currently, CLIL experts no longer suggest that teachers teaching through the L2 should never or almost never use the students' L1. There is an increasing recognition that languages are interdependent (Cummins, 2000) and that it is normal to mix languages when speaking in informal contexts, but essential to be able to separate languages when producing written academic work (Heugh, 2016). This does not mean that more than one language cannot be used in the process of creating academic work even if the final product is only in one language. The thoughtful use of more than one language for learning in one and the same class is often referred to as 'translanguaging' (Williams, 1996). More specifically, translanguaging involves speaking, listening, reading and/or writing about a topic in one language, and then speaking or writing about it in another. See Kathleen Heugh's *View from the Field* on page 23 for a more thorough exploration of the definition of translanguaging and for suggestions about how translanguaging can be systematically applied in CLIL contexts.

In translanguaging, 'both languages are used in an integrated and coherent way to organise and mediate learning' (Baker, 2011). The focus of translanguaging is on meaning-making and gaining a deeper understanding of subject-matter content through two languages. This involves a thoughtful and purposeful use of two languages, which is aimed at deeper level processing of both content and language. It avoids any overuse of the L1 in CLIL classes that might in the long-term undermine L2 use.

Although more research is required on the matter, initial indications are that translanguaging may:

- lead to deeper conceptual understanding of a topic
- help students to better encode learning in memory
- allow for easier retrieval of learning from memory.

(Baker, 2011)

Similarly, Genesee and Hamayan (2016 referring to Cummins 2007; García and Wei 2014; Genesee and Geva 2006; Hornberger and Link 2012) put forth that:

- Cross-linguistic connections create meaning.
- Learning in and about one language supports learning in and about another language.
- Making the two languages an integral part of lessons reflects the value and high status of both languages.
- Discussing concepts in more than one language helps to better encode knowledge in the brain for later use.

Translanguaging is also a strategy used by some teachers who feel their language skills are as of yet insufficient to teach fully through the L2. This is particularly the case in jurisdictions where teachers are required to teach through the students' L2 despite feeling their language skills are not yet up to the task. Whilst working on improving their language skills, many of these teachers use L2 learning materials, but discuss the materials in the students' L1. Students hand in written work in their L2. In order to mark and/or provide feedback on language, these content teachers partner with a language teacher. They provide feedback on content issues in the L1.

What follows is a series of practical suggestions for translanguaging in diverse contexts. The application of many of these suggestions would also require support for students in processing content and language input as well as content and language output.

Students:

- listen to a talk, a short lecture or watch a video in one language and take notes in another.

The talk, lecture or video can be stopped, restarted, and/or replayed to give the students time to think and summarise what they have heard.

- analyse a graphic organiser that has been written in one language and summarise it in another language.

  If there is considerable new language involved some of this might be provided in a scaffold that simply lists in an organised way key phrases that students might find helpful for the task.

- draft an outline of an essay or a report in their L1. They get feedback from the teacher in their L2, and write the essay/report in their L2.

  This is particularly helpful for reducing the affective filter. It gets students started on an essay, which is often the most difficult part of the writing process.

- work through a content matter text on one topic where one paragraph is in the L1 and the next is in the L2.
- read content compatible material in the language that is not used to teach the given class.

  For example, if students are studying Geography in their L2 and the topic under study is the effects of the latest Ice Age on the landscape, then the students might read a text in their L1 about how scientists determined the existence of the Ice Age and its effects. This would be discussed in the L2.

- brainstorm in one language, and write and organise the points in another language.
- conduct an enquiry that requires them to use L1 and L2 sources when doing their research.
- listen to a text in their L1. They are tasked with identifying and writing down in their L2 the five key points from that text.

  As a follow up, students are given an L2 version of the text, which is used to improve their work. This creates the opportunity for students to assess their own work, and gives them an authentic purpose for working with the L2 text.

- do cross-curricular projects partly in one language partly in another.

  For example, reading a piece of science fiction in an L1 Language class, and comparing and contrasting that with what is being learnt about the similar topic in L2 Science class. The language could be checked by the Language teacher and the content by the Science teacher. Alternatively, in L1 Civics discussing the United Nation's Declaration of the Rights of the Child and in L2 Mathematics analysing health, education and labour statistics in five nations, and relating the results to the rights of the child.

- produce an L2 leaflet or poster about a topic for peers or younger learners.

  This requires shifting from one register of language to another. Students need to reprocess what they have learned in simple and clear language that a novice can understand. This helps students understand the nature of academic language.

- write a school newspaper article in their L2 about a topic that has been studied in the L1.

  Newspaper articles use the structure of first presenting a headline summarising the most important information, and following it with evidence and additional facts. This helps students identify the critical information, and work through how this can be expressed in the L2.

- write an academic text for publication bilingually in the school newspaper.

  This can help raise meta-linguistic awareness in reference to the L1 and the L2.

- do a science experiment in one language, but write the laboratory report about it in another.

- analyse three texts in two (or if possible three) different languages about an historical event such as the 100th anniversary of Australian independence.

  For example, this could include having students analyse a summary of aboriginal community views compared with a summary of diverse settler community views. Students then compare their analysis with what they read in a highly respected foreign press report that seeks to offer a balanced overview.

- build, step-by step, complex sentences in the L2 and the L1 in parallel to show differences and similarities.

  For example, one can begin with a simple sentence and then continue to build a longer more complex and dense sentence – Kazakhstan has pursued a foreign policy. Kazakhstan has pursued a <u>balanced</u> foreign policy. Kazakhstan has pursued a balanced foreign policy and worked to develop its economy. Kazakhstan has pursued a balanced foreign policy and worked to develop its economy, especially its hydrocarbon industry. ... *which finally leads to a complex compound sentence* – Since becoming independent in 1991, Kazakhstan has pursued a balanced foreign policy and worked to develop its economy, especially its hydrocarbon industry).

- work in groups to suggest assessment criteria in their L1 for an assignment that they will eventually complete in their L2. The criteria are then finalised as a whole class using the L2.

  This should help ensure that students deeply process the assessment criteria.

In addition, students who speak a home language other than the languages of schooling can research a topic in their home language and report on that in one of the two languages of schooling.

VIEW FROM THE FIELD:
Translanguaging as an opportunity to expand and strengthen students' bi-/multilingual repertoires

Kathleen Heugh, University of South Australia

Recently, the term 'translanguaging' has become popularised in the literature of bilingual and multilingual education, with linguists agreeing that it has the potential to benefit learning. However, there are some controversies about what the term means and if it means much more than other well-known terms associated with bi-/multilingual practices (e.g. codemixing, code-switching) or explicit use of translation in teaching the second/target language. My purpose here is to show that translanguaging can be used in a purposeful way in bilingual programmes, such as those based on CLIL. To do this, I distinguish between two different understandings and usages of translanguaging because teachers need to be clear about when and why they might focus on one rather than another, if they are to achieve their pedagogical purpose.

In the first use of the term, we notice that translanguaging is regarded as an important pedagogy for developing high levels of language expertise in two languages (i.e. vertical bilingual development) to prepare students for opportunities to access higher education and future career advancement. In the

(continued over page)

second use of the term we notice an emphasis on the horizontal use of bilingual and multilingual expertise to establish collaborative empathy among peers and to reduce potential inequities in the classroom. I suggest that these two purposes are not mutually exclusive, and that a third way is to know how to use translanguaging strategically to establish learning environments that reduce inequities and value the linguistic repertoires that diverse students bring into classrooms, and that also build on these to achieve high-level bilingual proficiency.

Translanguaging *as introduced by Cen Williams (1996)*

Cen Williams first used the term (in English) in 1996 to explain a design feature of a particular Welsh-English bilingual programme. Translanguaging, in this programme, involves the deliberate use of Welsh for part of the lesson and deliberate use of English for another part. Sometimes this means that the teacher will teach a component of a lesson while speaking in Welsh, and the students are then expected to follow this with a writing task in English, or vice versa. Translanguaging in this sense involves listening and understanding in one language, and engaging in a metacognitive process of interpreting this information from one language to another language. This metacognitive and linguistic information is then converted into a written text in the second/target language. This involves a series of highly complex metacognitive and metalinguistic processes and capabilities. Because these occur inside the brain, and they are neither audible nor visible, they may not be obvious to a monolingual speaker.

Translanguaging *as discussed by Ofelia García and Li Wei (2014)*

The second use of the term 'translanguaging' is substantially different from how Williams used it, and it is important for teachers to understand the differences between the two interpretations. A growing number of applied and educational linguists, notably Ofelia García and Li Wei (2014), have adopted the term from the Welsh context and used it to refer to fluid linguistic practices rather than deliberate alternation between two clearly demarcated standard languages (such as English and Welsh). Translanguaging from the second perspective is understood to include authentic, often informal (horizontal), communicative exchanges that take place among multilingual people outside of formal education. The emphasis in this interpretation of the term is on how bi-/multilingual people transgress (go beyond/cross) linguistic boundaries in their normal everyday encounters. It is also on how teachers and students can use these transgressive practices (including codemixing and code-switching) in formal school classrooms to welcome and value the knowledge and language repertoires that diverse students bring.

Over the last few years there have been several qualitative classroom studies that indicate that where teachers explicitly encourage students to use their linguistic repertoires as fluid resources, students engage productively with diversity, and their self-esteem and confidence grow. This is particularly important in classrooms where it is obvious that there are socio-economic, cultural, epistemological and linguistic differences, and where there is risk of marginality.

What we can do in bilingual education/CLIL classrooms

Recent classroom-based research that I have been conducting in an Australian university indicates that students gain confidence, find their 'voice', and develop strong academic bilingual expertise when teachers develop a focused pedagogy that includes the following considerations:

- building on and encouraging students' linguistic and knowledge repertoires, in both spoken and written contexts
- recognising that developing bilingual proficiency involves metacognitive and metalinguistic processing (transferring meaning and knowledge back and forth between languages)
- understanding writing as a process in which language mixing and code-switching are valued when students are learning and developing their repertoire in a second or additional language
- understanding that this is not enough to achieve social justice, equity, or high-level learning outcomes
- adopting a deliberative or purposive approach towards developing expertise in translating written information back and forth between two languages over time.

These considerations can be implemented in structured learning activities and assessment tasks. Below I show an example (not a template) of how translanguaging can be purposefully designed to include both horizontal and vertical dimensions of building bilingual expertise in a classroom.

(continued over page)

What does this imply for teaching, learning and assessment?

<table>
<tr><th>Student awareness of</th><th>Systematic translanguaging</th></tr>
<tr><td>• their linguistic repertoires (academic proficiency in L1 & L2)
• their epistemological (knowledge) repertoires</td><td rowspan="3">• Formative task built into each summative assessment
e.g. 1 task in primary language built into each assignment
• Translation requirement in each task: L1 to L2 and/or L2 to L1
• Academic sources:
Students read and draw from academic sources in both L1 and L2 for summative tasks
• Reflective/research dimension
To enhance student metalinguistic and metacognitive awareness of bilingual learning
• Students draw on full linguistic repertoires in group work (mixing, code-switching, interpreting, etc.)</td></tr>
<tr><td>Student expertise</td></tr>
<tr><td>• in translanguaging
- language mixing
- code-switching
- translation
- interpreting
• as language-brokers
- in tutorials/peer learning</td></tr>
</table>

I encourage students to work through drafts of essays in which they are free to 'mix' their languages in ways they find useful, and through various re-drafting stages, to move towards offering translations of specific terms, phrases and expressions, where appropriate, and then towards closer proximity to 'standard' versions of the target language/s (e.g. Heugh, Li and Song, 2017).

Conclusion:

Translanguaging, when used purposefully, can enrich bilingual programmes including CLIL. The value of translanguaging in contexts that exhibit high levels of linguistic and other diversities (e.g. Africa, South and South-East Asia, and increasingly also in Europe because of recent migration), is likely to be amplified if it can deliver both horizontal and vertical expertise in or between two or more languages.

VIEW FROM THE FIELD:
10 tips for CLIL

Dulce Allen and Judith Woodfield, United Kingdom

Dulce Allen and Judith Woodfield are two school head teachers who have respectively taught Science and Geography through French to their Year 7 and 8 students in the UK. In Year 7, they only teach some topics through the L2 not all topics in a given course. In Year 8, Geography is taught entirely through the L2. The vast majority of their students speak a language other than English at home. They report a significant rise in CLIL student achievement in all subjects including those taught through their L1.

1. **Be methodical** – Develop a research methodology which can be used to monitor the effectiveness of learning. Looking at student achievement data (content and language learning) in CLIL along with motivation and attitude surveys can help you refine and develop what really works in the classroom. Having concrete proof that CLIL works helps counter any possible negativity.
2. **Plan in detail and thoughtfully** – CLIL lessons are content-driven so first decide on your intended content outcomes. Next, decide on the activities that will ensure pupils engage with the core concepts so they can achieve the outcomes. You also need to consider the language needed (both core – language they need to achieve the outcomes – and peripheral – the classroom language they need to do the tasks) (Teacher, Claire Fazilleau).
3. **Embed learning skills into teaching** – CLIL allows pupils to develop transferable learning skills and to learn Science/Geography through the medium of the target language. Design your lessons to include thinking skills, risk-taking and problem-solving activities.
4. **Don't duplicate content** – Select some aspects of the Science curriculum for teaching in the target language and don't teach them again in the L1. Design your L1 assessment including exams to test student learning of the topics they studied through their L2. Our analysis of student attainment shows that their achievement in topics taught through the L2 is in line with that in other topics taught through their L1. There are no significant differences in achievement.

(continued over page)

5 **Have high expectations** – Expect students to engage with L2 texts with the same level of detail as is the case with the L1 learning resources they use. Expect students to tackle concepts with the same level of difficulty in their L2 as they do in their L1.

6 **Emphasise meta-cognition** – Help students to become aware of their own and other students' learning processes and strategies so they become confident in applying these transferable learning strategies to their work in other subjects.

7 **Use authentic texts** – Only use resources in the target language during the CLIL lessons. Combine original L2 resources from other countries with translations of British curriculum resources (ask your language colleagues for help). Strategies to help students access these texts include playing word-hunting games or simply asking them to underline every cognate in a text. Avoid watering down the content by using simplistic L2 texts or videos.

8 **Run the lessons fully in the target language** – All activities, worksheets and presentation materials should be in the target language, including discussions. Don't give any English translations; instead use visual clues to aid understanding. Accept all answers in the L1 or a combination of the L1 and L2. Recast any L1 answers in the L2. Expect all written work to be in the L2; do not ask students to write L1 translations of their work.

9 **Be an actor** – Reinforce content learning through the use of visuals. Use a combination of diagrams, gestures, mime, models and practical demonstrations.

10 **Build up the vocabulary** – Design each unit so the students are learning the vocabulary in a step-by-step manner. Always finish with a written assignment where students use the words and phrases used throughout the unit. Expect students to produce work of the same standard as they would if studying the topic through their L1; however, provide scaffolding to help them write their assignments.

CONTENT AND LANGUAGE OUTCOMES

The well-known American CLIL expert Myriam Met (2014) argues that if you are about to go on a journey and you only have a vague notion of where you will be travelling to and what you are going to do when you get there, it is hard to prepare for that trip. Similarly, without clearly stating intended content and language learning outcomes (i.e. what a learner will know and be able to do by the end of a lesson, unit or course), it is difficult for teachers and students to plan for and undertake needed learning. Clear intended content and language learning outcomes not only provide a focus for planning lessons, but they also facilitate course development and the choice, adaptation and/or creation of learning resources. Outcomes also provide an important reference point for assessment of learning and for course evaluation.

On the affective level, intended learning outcomes can give a personal focus to learning by helping students to set their own learning targets, and feel a sense of accomplishment as they meet those targets. Outcomes/ objectives/targets/goals[3] are considered fundamental to building and maintaining learner motivation (Gardner, 1985; MacIntyre, 2002). On a political level, outcomes can make teaching and learning intentions visible to partners in education – be those parents or local authorities. Making targets visible to these partners helps to reduce speculation about a CLIL programme. It reduces concerns and makes it possible to better manage expectations.

Cloud, Genesee and Hamayan (2000) stress that in CLIL intended learning outcomes also need to be challenging. Several researchers in the field argue that maintaining high expectations in reference to both content and language learning is essential (Baker, 2006, Cloud et al., 2000). By contrast, if this is not done, it can lead to impoverished learning environments. Cloud et al. (2000) also emphasise that intended learning outcomes and how their achievement will be measured need to be shared and discussed with students to ensure they are understood. In addition, intended learning outcomes must be set for both the short and long-term. Helping students see how short-term goals link to long-term

---

3 **Learning objectives** define the demonstrable skills and knowledge that a student is expected to acquire by the end of a lesson, unit or course; **learning outcomes** define what a learner will know and be able to do by the end of a lesson, unit or course. The terms 'learning outcomes', 'learning objectives' and 'learning goals' are often used interchangeably both in the professional literature and in public discourse.

goals is thought to help them understand the usefulness of what is being learned in the short-term. Finally, progress in achieving outcomes needs to be discussed regularly. Hattie (2009) suggests that classroom discussion about learning and the learning process in reference to goals and their achievement significantly fosters learning.

This discussion about learning outcomes does not imply that learning should be turned into a mechanical process that is rigidly driven by predetermined intended learning outcomes. Outcomes are an often-used tool for building effective learning environments. At the same time, effective teachers also operate in the 'here and now', adapting the learning process as they get feedback from learners and as they see a need to adjust their plans and the intended learning outcomes. In addition, sometimes there is benefit to outcomes being rather general so that each student can interpret them in his or her own way, such as when developing a cross-curricular project. Some content lessons in any subject may simply begin with a good enquiry question that aligns with the given topic under study and that triggers student interest by inspiring them to research the answer. For example, in Geography when studying the causes and effects of the latest Ice Age, how do we know there have been Ice Ages?

Next the **common characteristics of effective content and language outcomes** are discussed. This is followed by examples of unclear versus clear content outcomes. Finally, the nature of language outcomes is explored and a wide range of language outcomes suitable for use in many subjects are offered for consideration.

The field of education has adopted the acronym SMART, originally used in the world of business, in order to define the key criteria or characteristics of effective intended learning outcomes or objectives (Doran, 1981). The acronym stands for Specific, Measurable, Achievable, Realistic and Time-bound. All outcomes are not expected to meet all of these criteria. Over the years, the acronym has been built upon in several ways. For example, some use the acronym SMARTER (Specific, Measurable, Achievable, Realistic, Time-bound, Engaging/Energising, Relevant) as a guide for writing outcomes.

Writing an outcome that makes clear to the students what they are expected to be able to do at the end of a lesson, unit or term is particularly challenging. On the left-hand side of the table below are lesson or unit content outcomes teachers were dissatisfied with because they did not provide students with sufficient clarity about what they would be expected to do. For example, some of the unclear outcomes constitute an activity on simply list topics as opposed to a concrete result students are expected to achieve. Others are focused on knowing or understanding, but provide no indication of what the student will have to be able to do in order to demonstrate knowing and understanding. One is so complex that it is difficult to grasp. On the right-hand side are revised content outcomes that teachers felt students would find more helpful. They are more helpful because they are clearer, more specific and measurable. The students get a better sense of what they must be able to do.

Increasing the clarity of intended learning outcomes:

Before	After
Chemistry	
You* can label electron arrangements.	You will be able to label and discuss electron arrangement by energy levels, sub-levels and orbitals in atoms of small and big periods.
Civics	
You can evaluate the allocation of government funding to Planned Parenthood in the US.	You can evaluate from a moral, economic and socio-political perspective the allocation of government funding to the Planned Parenthood programme in the US.
Emergency Medicine for Paramedics (vocational CLIL)	
Students will know: • the injuries caused by cold (signs and symptoms** of hypothermia) • the assessment and treatment of a hypothermic patient • the materials related with the treatment of a hypothermic patient.	Students will be able to assess and treat a patient with hypothermia. This includes: • describing the signs and symptoms caused by hypothermia • listing the materials used for treating a hypothermic patient and explaining why these materials are used • proposing in writing a logical step-by-step treatment for the patient • demonstrating through role-play their knowledge of the treatment of hypothermia.
Food Sciences (vocational CLIL)	
You can create a new dish.	You can create a new dish and evaluate it from a client perspective based on price, appearance and taste.

* **You** in the outcomes statements refers to the student.

** A **symptom** is any subjective evidence of disease, while a **sign** is any objective evidence of disease.

Computer Sciences (vocational CLIL)	
Types of connectors Types of transmission mediums Local network devices	You will be able to: • explain the key characteristics of different types of cables and connectors • instruct in detail a new employee in how to mount a Local Area Network (LAN) • build a LAN that meets client specifications.
Geography	
You will understand and be able to write about deforestation.	You will be able to discuss: • 5 major causes of deforestations, and • how deforestation may affect the sustainability of human life on the planet.
History	
You can create a timeline showing 10 major events in 20th century Japan.	You can create a timeline showing what you consider to be the 10 most significant political/military events in 20th century Japan, and can justify your choices using facts and examples.
Mathematics	
You can successfully use quadratic functions.	You can successfully use quadratic functions such as $y = a(x-p)^2 + q$, including the concepts: vertex; intercepts; domain and range; and axis of symmetry.
Physical education	
You can judge a dance.	You can judge a dance based on: • choreography (originality and style) • execution (timing, coordination, projection) • audience impact.
Science	
You can discuss the validity of any particular data being used as evidence by explaining (a) the reliability and (b) the relevance of the evidence by: • making a claim, and • giving an explanation to back up the claim.	You will be able to explain the difference between validity and reliability using examples.
You will be able to analyse water samples.	You will be able to identify parameters that can be used to evaluate the quality of a specific water supply, and justify your choice of parameters.
You will be able to explain how temperature affects bacteria and algae.	You will be able to design (using the scientific method) an experiment to determine how temperature influences the growth rate of cyanobacteria or aerobic algae.

Writing intended language outcomes is particularly challenging. If no language outcomes are set for content classes, then teachers are implying to students that language learning is an incidental and a secondary process in CLIL. Without reflecting on and setting language outcomes, content teachers are less likely to plan for language learning. As a result, students are less likely to set language learning targets and plan for their achievement. Less language learning is likely to take place.

All of the content outcomes listed above involve language; however, the emphasis in those outcomes is primarily on content learning. Language outcomes primarily focus on one or more of the following four aspects of language:

- **Language awareness:** These outcomes focus on the use of academic *versus* social language and on grammatical conventions.

  For example:

  - *You can use a rich diversity of language to elaborate and clarify.*

- **Communication awareness:** These outcomes focus on the nature of communication such as whether students are using short answers *versus* a well-developed line of reasoning, and the richness or paucity of language being used.

  For example:

  - *You can support your opinion with a two-point explanation.*

- **Language learning skills:** These outcomes are focused on developing meta-cognitive and meta-linguistic awareness that allow students to take better charge of their own language learning.

  For example:

  - *You are able to read a text for different purposes (e.g. consistent flow of ideas, grammar, spelling).*

- **Intercultural communication:** These outcomes focus on intercultural competence with a particular focus on knowledge, skills, attitudes and values that favour intercultural communication.

  For example:

  - *You can suspend immediate judgement whilst analysing unfamiliar situations when reading about X people.*

A list of intended language learning outcomes that content teachers have identified as useful in helping them to prepare lessons is offered below. In addition, teachers found that these can help students plan for and take greater responsibility for their own language learning. The suggested outcomes are a random collection of options. They are not listed in any particular order. They are not presented as an integral whole. We stress that students would need to see exemplars of the types of language-use described below in order to achieve these outcomes. They may also need to see evaluation criteria and require scaffolding. Many of the proposed outcomes are generic, and thus suitable for use in a wide range of subjects.

Language awareness

You will be able to:

- plan the structure of an essay or a lab report
- organise a written report under the following headings:
  - purpose of the experiment
  - hypothesis
  - variables and constants
  - equipment
  - method
  - findings
  - conclusion
- recognise and defend against the use of emotional language
- use the language of chronology, temporality and period
- paraphrase (put in your own words) what a historian/scientist/researcher has stated
- write an essay primarily in the passive voice
- correctly use the phraseology and terminology for this unit found in the class language bank
- use consistently and precisely high-frequency IT terminology (see class databank)
- write an unbiased newspaper report of an historical event
- write a biased newspaper article presenting two or more points of view
- maintain a consistent and precise use of terminology and other scientific vocabulary throughout a written text

- analyse a graphic organiser that has been written in the L1 and summarise your findings in the L2
- explain the differences and similarities in the writing of L1 *versus* L2 business letters
- identify the language of subjectivity
- explain causes and consequences using correct verb forms
- distinguish opinion from fact, and justify your categorisations
- write an evidence-based conclusion (e.g. drawing on data and explaining its limitations).

Communication awareness

You will be able to:

- partake actively in classroom discussions and group work using the L2
- manage your voice (volume, intonation, enunciation, tone) when making a presentation
- present an opinion/conclusion and support it with an example
- disagree and negotiate politely and effectively with fellow students using a variety of language
- create concise and easy-to-follow instructions for conducting diverse tasks (e.g. an experiment, a line of enquiry)
- explain in a logical and well-structured step-by-step sequence a process or an argument
- write concise and clear definitions, and support your definitions with examples
- create a short and concise PowerPoint presentation and present it persuasively
- develop a line of argument on an abstract historical or social concept/ issue
- ask for clarification and/or additional information
- provide clarification and/or additional information
- back up your claims with examples, with details or with evidence
- build upon or challenge another student's ideas
- read the body language of your negotiating partner in order to readjust your negotiating strategy

- recognise leading questions and explain how they are being used.

Learning skills

You will be able to:

- use an L2 thesaurus to enrich language use in your written work
- skim long (and complex) texts to decide whether a source is suitable for further study
- make research notes in an organised fashion that allows you later to find relevant information quickly
- a) create successive draft versions of a text; b) test the intelligibility of your text based on the reactions of others; and c) use what you have learned to correct and improve your text
- identify and state the main ideas in a text/the main idea in a paragraph
- a) create a databank containing new terminology and phraseology you learned while viewing this week's videos; and b) use that 'new' language in your summaries
- summarise texts or discussions.

Intercultural awareness

You will be able to:

- use formulae of politeness appropriately
- analyse your own attitude regarding the L1 and L2, and how that may be influencing your learning of these languages
- identify and analyse misunderstandings arising from cultural differences
- compare your own non-verbal communication practices with those of people from other cultures
- demonstrate deep-order perspective-taking (based on Candelier et al., 2012, and Deardorff, 2013).

In order to stress the importance of language outcomes/objectives, some CLIL schools **pick one language objective for two weeks that all teachers in a given Grade or Year emphasise**, and pursue this objective sometimes in both classes taught through the L2 and the L1. For example, if students are tending to only provide short answers to teacher or student questions, then if all teachers in one Grade/Year set the same target – having students back up their opinions/conclusions with a two-point explanation and examples – it is more likely that students will achieve this objective.

A SELF-REFLECTION TOOL FOR CONTENT TEACHERS ON THE INTEGRATION OF CONTENT AND LANGUAGE[4]

This tool is intended for CLIL content educators who are teaching their subject through the students' L2.

In order to improve practice, it is often helpful to begin by reflecting on and declaring what one believes and where one currently stands on a particular issue. Once we shed light on our thinking, feelings and practices, we can move from the abstract to the concrete. This allows us to: (1) deepen our own analysis; (2) discuss education and best CLIL practice with our colleagues; and (3) hopefully improve our practice.

This self-reflection tool for content educators is divided into four levels or stages from *CLIL novice* to *expert CLIL practitioner.* Level one describes the possible beliefs, understandings and practices of someone who has started doing CLIL by simply switching the language of instruction. Level four describes the possible beliefs, understandings and practices of someone who systematically integrates the teaching of content and language. The statements within each category have been collected over the years from CLIL teachers and their colleagues. We do not assume that all the comments in each category would apply to all teachers.

Each level is divided into three columns. The **first column** – *My beliefs and understandings* – describe where someone is in their thinking about CLIL. Decision-making is driven by beliefs and understandings. Without explicitly stating them, it is difficult to foster growth in beliefs, understandings and related practices. The **second column** – *What is visible to others* – describes practices reported by CLIL teachers and trainers. These are examples of tangible practices that either do or do not support best practice in CLIL. The **third column** – *What others can hear* – represents comments that have been heard from content educators at each of the four levels or stages of their CLIL professional development. They are offered as reference points in order to support teachers in reflecting on their own practice.

It is important to note that this tool is intended for teacher self-reflection. It is not suitable for CLIL teacher evaluation.

---

4 Inspired by the work of Stoddart et al. (2002).

Level 1: CLIL novice

No integration: I have just switched the language of instruction		
My beliefs and understandings	What is visible to others	What colleagues can hear
I am responsible for the content. The language teacher is responsible for teaching the language before the students come to my class. I am interested in CLIL but have not yet started reading about it. I am very familiar with my content curriculum, but not at all with the language curriculum. I should teach entirely in the L2. I should at least initially do most of the speaking in order to model the language students need to learn.	... me working as before without any particular plan for integrating content and language ... me not attending professional development on CLIL ... me pointing to the language teacher for the students' lack of language knowledge ... me engaging in professional dialogue about the integration of content and language ... me working only with content colleagues, not language colleagues ... me speaking much more than my students	Does anyone have an article on or book about CLIL that I could read? It's not my job to teach language. I teach History. The language teacher hasn't done her job. The students haven't been prepared properly to learn through the second language. I can't be expected to get them to learn if they can't speak the language properly.

Level 2: CLIL beginner

First steps on the road to integration		
My beliefs and understandings	What is visible to others	What colleagues can hear
I recognise the importance of integrating content and language. I accept the need for changing some of my practices. I wish to have more ideas for how to integrate content and language. I have taken a look at the language curriculum. I believe I need to find ways of supporting students in using the L2.	...me describing the teaching of content and language as separate steps in the learning/teaching process ...me referring to articles or presentations on the integration of content and language ...me struggling with the integration of language teaching into my lessons ...me asking for help with the integration of content and language ... me scaffolding student L2 output	I know that the language is important, but I don't see how one can take the time away from content teaching. Does anyone have any good ideas about how to support language learning in content classes? Does anyone have any learning materials they have adapted? How do you scaffold the language so you can mostly concentrate on the content?

Level 3: Proficient CLIL practitioner

Considerable integration is occurring		
My beliefs and understandings	What is visible to others	What colleagues can hear
I recognise the need to provide language support when students are learning challenging new content. I seek out and use ways of integrating content and language. I want to learn more about integrating content and language. Most of the time, I first teach any new language I think students need to understand the content, and then I teach the content. I am aware of some key components of the curriculum in other subjects and occasionally create cross-curricular learning opportunities for students. I sometimes have students use L1 materials that we discuss in the L2.	... me talking about CLIL with other colleagues ... me asking for CLIL-related professional literature ... me exploring ways of supporting language learning and its impact on content learning ...me usually focusing either on content or language, as opposed to both at the same time ... me occasionally sharing and discussing language outcomes with students ... me sometimes co-operating with a language colleague ... me sometimes providing students feedback on how to improve language use ... me not getting nervous if students use L1 sources or the L1 for group work	I used to try to first teach the language I thought the students might not know and then the content. Now, I sometimes do both at the same time. I do still worry that language learning is taking too much time. Anybody have any ideas on how to speed up the language support process? Let's form a working group to tackle this issue. The texts I need to use in class next week contain lots of verbs in the conditional tenses. I see you are going to teach the conditional in two weeks. Any chance you could teach it this week instead? I asked my students to tell me what sort of help they need with learning the language of my subject. They told me that ...

Level 4: Expert CLIL practitioner

Integration is the norm		
My beliefs and understandings	What is visible to others	What colleagues can hear
Students will learn more content if I help unpack the academic language of my subject(s). I believe it is not only possible, but essential that I teach content and language at the same time. I understand that content learning is incomplete if students do not also learn 'the language of that content'.	... me richly scaffolding both content and language input and output ... me discussing intended language outcomes with students and measuring progress in achieving them ... students getting and giving feedback on both content and language ... me drawing students' attention to the nature of academic language	My students speaking more and generally being more active and doing 'more work' than me during the lesson. (speaking to the content and/ or language teacher) *Let's build a joint inventory of language learning skills.* *Can we agree on ways of teaching language learning skills?*

My students and I need to discuss progress made in achieving content and language outcomes. Where possible, I work with my language colleagues to see if we can develop an integrated curriculum (e.g. suggesting concepts and materials that could be integrated into their language lessons). I create cross-curricular learning opportunities for students which include working in cooperation with content and language teachers. I believe that as students expand their repertoire of learning skills they become more effective learners of content and language. I believe that if students occasionally translanguage then this can deepen their understanding of what they need to learn.	... me and my students using exploratory talk to help students draw out their thinking (lines of reasoning) my students and I reflecting on and solving language problems as they arise ... me helping students develop language learning skills ... me co-operating weekly with the language teacher(s) to plan for the integration of content and language, as well as the sequencing of language learning ... me often referring to the integration of content and language in my professional discussions with colleagues ... me partaking in professional development in CLIL ... me having students research a topic using two languages, but reporting on it in the L2 ... my students sometimes writing a draft in their L1, but the final paper in their L2	*Can we agree on some common language objectives/ outcomes for the Year I students?* *The language teacher and I try to meet once a week to co-ordinate our planning. I let her/him know what I am doing and what language the students need, and I share ideas about how s/he could integrate content from my subject into her/ his classes.* *In addition to encouraging students to think critically about the content, I am now also encouraging them to improve their use of language.* *I used to see content and language learning as sequential – first you teach the language then the content. Now, I think it is more important to teach both at the same time.* *I think a limited use of the L1 can help students to better learn both the content and the L2.*

CONCLUSION

By taking into account well-synthesised knowledge from meta-studies in education about influences on student learning, and by reflecting on one's own impact on student learning, CLIL content teachers can help students to significantly improve their depth and scope of content learning. In CLIL, that content learning has to go through the gateway of L2 academic language. Consequently, the CLIL content teacher is faced with the practical reality that their students need support in navigating and learning the L2 academic language of the given subject. In particular, a step-by-step approach, which includes the thorough teaching of core content concepts and big ideas in digestible chunks of content and language, is key to freeing up the cognitive resources required for students to learn new content and language. Also, communication awareness can help content teachers and students to learn. In particular, it has been suggested that by increasing the use of exploratory talk and writing, where the focus is on students 'sorting out' their thoughts in relation to the content that is being taught, teachers can help students to not only deeply process new learning, but make visible remaining content and language learning needs. Finally, in order to set high expectations with reference to both content and language learning, and in order to systematically plan for both, teachers are encouraged to create and discuss with students 'SMARTER' intended content and language learning outcomes.

3 The language teacher's perspective

Connections

How this chapter connects to other concepts in the book:

Exploratory talk

Exploratory talk helps move learning, including the learning of both content and language to a deeper level – that is to say, beyond the simple recall and reporting of facts and language. Exploratory talk gives students rich opportunities to explore and organise their thinking about content. It also requires the use of a wide range of academic language, and draws out any shortcomings in students' thinking and language use that need to be addressed. Importantly, exploratory talk also has the potential of increasing learner engagement.

Critical thinking

First and foremost, critical thinking is fundamental to learning (Moon, 2008). Secondly, critical thinking is key to the recall of learning.

Students are more likely to recall details from a cognitively challenging problem than an easy one (Baddeley, 2004). In dual-language education, Lindholm-Leary (2001) found that 'students were no more likely to incorrectly answer a high-order question than a lower-order one' and suggests teachers concentrate on asking challenging questions.

Affect

In order to get 'learners to engage willingly with content [and language] in meaningful and cognitively challenging ways, [teachers] will need to nurture learners' [belief in their own capacity to learn and their] desire to want to know more, ask questions, explore, and inquire within and beyond the walls of the language classroom' (Cammarata, 2016).

Learning outcomes

Having clear intended content learning outcomes in language classes are a prerequisite to building a rich language learning environment.

As students work to understand and use new content, the related language also becomes more meaningful to them and thus more likely to be recalled.

Culture

Developing language proficiency implies that a student is able to 'take part in intercultural action' (Council of Europe, 2007). Students require support in noticing and developing the knowledge, skills and attitudes required for effective intercultural communication.

Moreover, in an era of globalisation, in-depth knowledge of more than one culture is considered a vital part of the cognitive development of young people (Eccles and Gootman, 2002).

INTRODUCTION AND CHAPTER NAVIGATOR

In CLIL, students, parents and content teachers all have increased expectations when it comes to learning the L2. Moreover, students have an immediate need to use their L2 to navigate, to think critically about and to learn content. This need for content learning drives student language learning. In addition to placing extra responsibility for language learning on CLIL students and content teachers, this need places substantial additional responsibility on the language teacher. In language classes, CLIL students likely wish and definitely need to learn language that is of practical use in their content classes. Hence, CLIL language classes ideally adapt by teaching elements of language in a sequence that takes into account the language demands students are faced with in their CLIL content classes.

At the very least, CLIL calls on language teachers to focus on the 'language forms and functions' students need for learning in CLIL content classes (Brinton, Snow and Wesche, 2011). In addition, in the ideal, CLIL language classes also model the best practices in education discussed in **Chapter 2:** *The Content Teacher's Perspective*, as these have a very high positive impact on student and teacher learning. They help students to substantially improve learning and manage the added cognitive load of working through their L2. Equally importantly, in the ideal, CLIL language classes also exemplify the CLIL best practice of integrating both content and language. This means that language classes use meaningful and authentic content that is new to the students in order to teach both that new content and the related language.

This chapter will draw out how the role of language classes changes in CLIL contexts. More specifically, this chapter:

- draws out the key parameters of CLIL language classes. This includes a definition of critical thinking and an exploration of its purpose
- provides a rationale for content-based learning in CLIL language classes
- discusses in practical terms how content and critical thinking are integrated into language lessons
- explores how language and content teachers can cooperate and what the focus of that cooperation can be
- offers a tool for language teachers to determine where they are in their journey of taking on board a CLIL ethos and adopting CLIL practices.

KEY PARAMETERS PARTICULAR TO CLIL LANGUAGE CLASSES

A CLIL or content-based approach to language instruction involves, first and foremost, a **triple-focus on content, critical thinking and language**. The content and the critical thinking are at the forefront of the learning process, including the language learning process. Importantly, in language classes, content learning is not simply focused on acquiring facts and related language, but is also 'a means to help learners to develop cognitively' (Martel, 2016; see also Coyle et al., 2010).

In other words, CLIL language teachers are advised not to treat content as an afterthought or simply as a vehicle that is creating a language learning opportunity. An effective CLIL language class is not 'a thinking-light subject' focused primarily on the learning of grammatical structures: language teachers must choose content and tasks that are 'thought-provoking' (Martel, 2016). At the same time planning for 'intellectual quality' in a curriculum requires a relentless double focus on building a 'high-challenge, high-support' learning environment (Gibbons, 2009). This means that the content and related tasks are engaging, intellectually challenging and considered meaningful by the students, while the students are supported in understanding the input and producing linguistically rich output that also demonstrates critical thinking.

But **what constitutes critical thinking**? Definitions abound. Two are offered below in a slightly adapted form:

- '(C)ritical thinking involves the use of information, experience and world knowledge in ways which allow learners to seek alternatives, make inferences, pose questions and solve problems, thereby signalling [deeper order] understanding in a variety of complex ways' (Liaw, 2007).
- 'Critical thinking is that mode of thinking – about any subject, content, [language] or problem – in which the thinker improves the quality of his or her thinking by skilfully taking charge of the structures inherent in thinking and imposing intellectual standards upon them' (Paul and Elder, 2001).

We infer that critical thinking can operate in schools at two levels. First, it would involve engaging students with received world knowledge in and across disciplines so that students are supported in thinking like a geographer, historian and/or scientist. Among other points, this would involve the synchronous and asynchronous processing of information and the analysis of experiences through meaningful tasks where students explore and evaluate diverse solutions, make inferences, and suggest possible solutions to problems. This implies deep-order engagement with both the curricular content and language. Second, critical thinking is focused on taking greater charge of one's own thinking. That calls for meta-cognition – thinking about thinking, including the strategies[1] we use to think. Critical thinking is 'the awakening of the intellect to the study of itself' (Critical Thinking Community, 2008). Autonomous thinkers seek to identify their own and other people's thinking processes, analyse them, and consciously decide when and how to use meta-cognitive strategies to improve their own thinking and work.

Moseley et al. (2005) go further. They argue that the **primary purpose of critical thinking** is to take control of and responsibility for one's own thinking in order to participate effectively as a member of a democratic society. That implies that students are able to test assumptions and information, as well as resist falsehoods and being duped by others. It also implies that students are given a voice, that they become 'knowledgeable and collaborative' actors in the learning process who take an active role in decision-making (Thiessen and Cook-Sather, 2007). To do so they would need to understand their rights and limits, and be supported in reflecting on these and the learning process. This would involve students taking a stance whilst contributing to 'the well-being of self and others' as they move to achieve their own and the class's learning targets and prepare for the future (OECD, 2016).

Reagan suggests language teachers apply **critical pedagogy** in language classes – a pedagogy focused on reducing inequalities and injustices. Equality and justice are at the foundations of democracy. Reagan (2016, citing Wink, 2000) proposes that content-based language classes are well placed to have teachers and students jointly explore 'fundamental questions about knowledge, justice, equity in their own classroom, school, family and community'. Reagan (2016) contends that by having students engage with 'understanding their place and responsibility within' the world in order to improve it, they become truly engaged with thinking critically about content and language that reaches beyond the walls of the classroom. He sees critical pedagogy as a way of making content and language learning 'count' and thus memorable.

Despite maintaining a focus on critical thinking and the integration of 'non-language' content into language classes, it remains paramount for

---

1 See pages 169–182 for a discussion of learning skills.

language teachers to **continue to explicitly teach language**. 'Cognition and language create each other' (Ellis and Robinson, 2008). This means that deeper order thinking and meaning-making are also dependent 'on the development of advanced literacy skills' (Cammarata, Tedick and Osborn, 2016). In a context where students are being 'taught academic content in a language they are still [in the process of] learning', this co-dependency takes on a particular relevance (Lightbown, 2014). CLIL language teachers can above all teach language by acting as the mediator between the content and the L2 (Donato, 2016). They are expected to support students in understanding the content and language input, and thinking, speaking, reading and writing about the content (the output) in a manner that leads to the learning of both the content and language, while also building the students' capacity to think critically about both.

Similarly, Lyster (2016) suggests that one of the most effective ways of drawing students' 'attention to language is in the context of meaningful interaction about content. It is during such teachable moments that students are motivated to use the language and so are well positioned to notice how otherwise hard-to-notice language features play an important role in making meaning.' Lyster (2007) is a proponent of a counterbalanced approach where student attention is regularly drawn to both language use and the content without overemphasising either. In addition, Lyster (2016) proposes using both a 'reactive' and a 'proactive' approach. A reactive approach involves responding to language learning opportunities as they arise naturally while working on content. Through a reactive approach a teacher seeks to 'increase both the quantity and quality of student output' and to use corrective feedback focused on negotiating 'both form and meaning' (Lyster, 2016). Through a *proactive approach, teachers* plan 'for noticing and awareness activities followed by opportunities for both guided and autonomous practice. Planning for content and language integration in this way involves shifting learners' attention to language in the context of content instruction in cases where they would not otherwise process the language at the same time as the content (Lyster, 2016, referring to Lyster, 2007; see also Cumming and Lyster, 2016).'

In addition to developing language awareness, CLIL teachers are advised to develop their own and students' communication awareness. This is because thinking does not simply occur in a vacuum, but requires input from and interaction with others. Common understandings and knowledge are created through a process of 'socially shared cognition' (Kasper, 2008). Moreover, language and communication are also central to honing thinking (Vygotsky, 1978). (For a more detailed discussion of language and communication awareness see the previous chapter.)

Finally, moving to a content-based approach in CLIL language classrooms is likely to constitute a major shift in practice. It is best to assume that this major change will not be self-evident to all students, their parents, language teachers, content teachers or school administrators. Students, other staff and parents likely need their attention drawn to the fact that CLIL language classes support not only language learning, but content learning and critical thinking, and that students need to maintain a triple focus in language classes on language, content and critical thinking. This will require additional effort from and the use of effective learning strategies by students. Finally, this shift also calls for cooperation with content teachers and a language-sensitive approach to teaching in content classes (Wolff, 2008).

Next, the rationale for content-based learning in language classes is explained. This will be followed with a more detailed explanation of the role of language classes in CLIL and how some of the key parameters discussed in this section could be applied in daily classroom practices.

RATIONALE FOR CONTENT-BASED LEARNING IN LANGUAGE CLASSES

When content and tasks in language classes are not simply used to teach language, but are also focused on the 'acquisition of new knowledge as well as the completion of specifically targeted tasks designed to deepen students' understanding', capacity to think critically and learning of 'non-linguistic content', students and even teachers have much to gain (Cammarata, 2016). Some of the benefits of using a CLIL or a content-based approach in language classes follow.

Students are exposed to a richer range of language (input). This includes a richer variety of genres, topics, vocabulary (including terminology and phraseology), tenses, registers, structures and functions. The diversity of topics implies that this language will be suitable for use in a wider range of contexts than would be the case in a standard language class.

Students build their capacity to produce a deeper and wider range of language (output) (Cumming and Lyster, 2016). Working with content subject concepts in language classes requires students to use a richer variety of language than would be the case in a standard language class.

Students are likely exposed to and practice using the general academic language that is needed in several content subjects. The language, associated with core academic functions such as hypothesising, enquiring collaboratively, synthesising and verifying, is common to many content subjects (see page 110 for a more comprehensive list).

Students learn additional valuable content and become more adept at speaking, reading and writing about it.

Learning is likely to be more meaningful. Integrating content from subjects such as Science or History carries its own meaning above and beyond language. If that content is used in meaningful ways, this creates 'a genuine immediate need to learn the language', which in turn engages and motivates students to learn language (Lightbown and Spada, 2013).

Teaching may be more meaningful and motivating (Davison and Williams, 2001). Language teachers have reported to us over several decades that despite the hard work involved in preparing CLIL lessons, the resulting increase in student engagement, motivation and learning is inspirational.

Learner motivation, engagement and confidence in using the L2 are likely to increase. The meaningful nature of the content in CLIL language classes gives greater purpose to language learning. In addition, as language classes use content and tasks that are useful in CLIL content classes, this helps raise the value of what students are learning in language classes. As students use their emerging L2 knowledge and skills to create meaningful output, they experience success in their ability to use and learn the L2. As a by-product, anxiety related to language use and learning is usually reduced.

Students become more effective critical thinkers in reference to both content and language. CLIL reinforces the expectation that students and teachers think deeply about both content and language learning. Thereby, CLIL language classes can also make an important contribution to the development of students' intellectual autonomy.

Students planning to undertake post-secondary education in the L2 are likely to be better equipped with the language and language learning skills needed for further education.

Language teachers have **an opportunity** to benefit from cooperation with content teachers on several levels. They can **raise awareness**

about the importance of supporting language learning in all subjects across the curriculum. On a personal level, they can expand their knowledge base as they learn new content along with their students, and enjoy the benefits of working in an interdisciplinary team.

INTEGRATING CONTENT AND CRITICAL THINKING INTO LANGUAGE LESSONS

CLIL is based on the premise that when students learn new, meaningful and memorable content, they simultaneously learn a wider range of language, and they learn that language more deeply. Even in language classes, students are expected to obtain 'two for one' – the learning of both new content and language (Wesche, 1993). From the CLIL language teacher's perspective, that means integrating the learning of some new and meaningful content into their lessons. This content can be directly compatible with (that is, related in some way to) the content in CLIL subject-matter classes (e.g. Art, Biology, Economics, Geography, History). Alternatively, the new content may simply call on students to undertake common functions, such as developing a line of reasoning, that are compatible with functions undertaken in content subjects. Under such circumstances, the generic academic language being taught with the new content would also be applicable in CLIL content classes. From the students' perspective, in CLIL language classes, they concurrently use and learn not just the L2 but some new meaningful content. That content may or may not be directly related to the content in CLIL subject matter classes (e.g. Chemistry, Economics, History). However, the generic academic language they are learning with the new content would be applicable in content classes, as would the common functions students are undertaking in language classes, such as analysing causes and consequences. It is noteworthy that language is still taught, and language teachers draw particular attention to grammar and other elements of language, but this is done in a context where students are also learning new content.

A series of suggestions about how to bring meaningful content into language classes follows. First, various ways of integrating content and critical thinking about that content into language classes are listed. These various ways do not constitute completely distinct categories: considerable overlap exists between them. Second, each category is explored in greater detail.

Broadly speaking, meaningful new content can be integrated into language classes by:

- introducing and using topics and material that are compatible with what is being taught in content subjects
- developing critical pedagogy
- encouraging enquiry-based learning
- using cross-curricular projects
- using a theme-based approach
- focusing on common functions
- undertaking cultural studies.

The final point is discussed in **Chapter 6:** *Culture and Intercultural Competence*. Finally, in this chapter, we discuss language and content teacher cooperation, which is a hallmark of effective CLIL practice, before presenting a self-reflection tool for language teachers.

CONTENT-COMPATIBLE TOPICS AND MATERIAL

CLIL language teachers can use topics and materials in language classes that are compatible with what is being learned in content classes. However, this content-compatible material is not essential for students to meet the intended content learning outcomes of their content classes. The content-compatible topics and materials are often best suggested by a content teacher with whom a language teacher is cooperating. The content teacher may also need to suggest background reading for the language teacher to ensure he or she feels comfortable with using the material.

The content-compatible topics and materials are likely to be of interest to the students as they have an opportunity to learn more about topics being studied in other classes. These can support learner engagement and reinforce some language being used in content classes. In addition, these topics and materials are likely to introduce 'content-compatible language (language that can be taught naturally within the context of a particular subject matter and that students require additional practice with)' (Snow, Met and Genesee, 1989). In order to meet their language curriculum requirements, language teachers may need to adapt the content-compatible material to highlight the language they need to teach.

One option successfully used by CLIL language teachers for integrating content into their lessons is having students focus on the lives and inspiring accomplishments of famous people. In the field of Mathematics these might include Srinivasa Ramanujan of India, who in his short life with little formal education became a leading influence in the field, or Hypatia the female professor who taught advanced geometry and algebra at the University of Aleksandria in the 5th century, or Pythagoras of Greece, who was also an Olympic wrestler. Students could read about or research famous people in other fields such as the scientist Jocelyn Bell Burnell, who discovered pulsars but saw her adviser get the Nobel prize in part for her work. The lives of rival Antarctic explorers Robert Scott of the UK and Roald Amundsen of Norway and their preparations to reach the South Pole is another fascinating story that helps students see the value of critical thinking, thorough planning and cooperation, whilst also learning geographical content.

Understanding the circumstances, including the obstacles, that these famous people faced and overcame, as well as their setbacks and successes, can lead to a greater personal connection with and understanding of the content being learned in content classes. Many of the famous people listed below have fought for justice and equality, which creates opportunities for engagement with critical pedagogy. Researching these people can also make visible important personal qualities associated with overcoming adversity and achieving success. At the same time, speaking and writing about these people can be used to teach and reinforce elements from the language curriculum. In the interest of demonstrating the interconnected nature of the world and building intellectual quality, it is important for students to investigate famous people from several nations and to make certain they include both men and women. To make this point a wide range of examples follows: Mary Anning (self-educated palaeontologist), Hillary Clinton, Thomas Edison (self-educated inventor), Albert Einstein, Alexander Fleming (discoverer of penicillin), Bill Gates, Caroline Herschel (astronomer), Muhammad al-Idrisi (geographer), Nelson Mandela (South African anti-apartheid revolutionary, politician and philanthropist), Konosuke Matsushita (industrialist and management guru), Lise Meitner (identifier of nuclear fission), Golda Meir (politician), Elon Musk (South African-born Canadian-American business magnate and inventor), Queen Nzinga (anti-colonial who fought to stop the seventeenth-century slave trade), Sacajawea (explorer supporting Lewis and Clark), Sun Tzu (military strategist and philosopher), Desmond Tutu (Nobel Peace Prize winner), David Unaipon (Indigenous Australian inventor and writer), Juan Vucetich (Croatian-born Argentine pioneer of fingerprinting), Simón Bolívar (military and political leader), Chien-Shiung Wu (Chinese-American nuclear physicist who played an important role in the development of the atomic bomb), Al-Zahrawi (one of the fathers of surgery who over a thousand years ago wrote a thirty-volume encyclopedia of medical practices), and Mark Zuckerburg (founder of Facebook). Content teachers are well placed to suggest whom the students might research.

What follows is an example of a how Grade 11 (aged 17–18) students in two or three one-hour language lessons can focus on a biography of a famous person, using a text where the content is compatible with what is being studied in the CLIL Biology while still working to fulfil the language curriculum requirements. In Biology, the students are working through their L2 on creating an experiment to consider how some bacteria are able to grow, whilst others are not, in the presence of high levels of acidity or antibiotics. They are also practicing writing up their results and how to safely clean up after an experiment. In the language class students are focused on writing biographical summaries.

These Grade 11 language class activities are offered in the form of key instructions and questions in *italics*, followed by explanations.

1. *What do you know about stomach ulcers – signs, symptoms, causes and treatments/cures? Individually take a minute or two to write down everything you recall.* The title of the topic and the sub-headings are already on the board. The subheadings are intended to scaffold recall and provide a structure for organising what students remember.

2. *What have you come up with? Could I have two volunteers to help us capture on the board what you all have to say about ulcers? I will help the volunteers to do this.* The teacher's offer of help to the volunteers is likely to lead to more students taking on this role. The summary on the board makes visible what the students know, their possible misconceptions, and the language they know and still need to learn. Some of the language errors can be corrected immediately.

3. *We will return to the content after we have learned more about ulcers so you can compare what you know now with what you will learn in the next*

few classes. This is a moment for **content and language teacher cooperation**. The language teacher can take a picture of these student answers and send it to the content teacher for his or her input.

4. *Over the next two (or three) lessons we will be learning about two scientists who researched ulcers and bacteria. When they found a cure for most ulcers, they had trouble convincing others of their discovery. You are also going to look at other scientists who have faced similar obstacles. Here are the intended learning outcomes for the next two or three lessons. Read them. What is unclear? What do you want to ask about?*

   Intended content outcome

   You will be able to:

   - explain the personal qualities/characteristics and actions of famous people that have helped them to make their discoveries.

   Intended language outcomes

   You will be able to:

   - summarise precisely and accurately key points from your readings
   - correctly use the auxiliary verb 'would'.

   Intended learning skills outcome

   You will be able to:

   - name a personal quality/characteristic that you will seek to develop in yourself and how you plan to do it.

   The outcomes should help bring clarity to what students are expected to achieve over the next lessons.

5. *Get in pairs and place these scrambled sentences in a logical order. Here is a clue. The text ends in a question. Please also answer that question.* To differentiate, the first pairs to complete the two tasks can be directed to write the answers to the question on the board. This initial exercise requires all students to be actively engaged. It scaffolds working with the longer text by introducing key terms, phraseology and a key grammar point (e.g. 'peptic ulcer', 'treated with antibiotics', 'it was commonly believed that' and 'would take'). The text seeks to pique students' interest.

A peptic ulcer is an open sore often, but not always, caused by a bacterial infection.

It can be located either on the inside of the stomach lining or in the upper part of the small intestine.

It can cause great pain, cause cancer, and even lead to death.

Until 1994, it was commonly believed that peptic ulcers were caused by stress.

However, long before that, two individuals in two different countries had learned to successfully treat ulcers with antibiotics.

Unfortunately, it would take many years before the medical community would accept their results.

Why might this have happened?

6. *Alright, what do you have as a first sentence? Does anyone disagree? Why? Can someone tell me which ideas and words are linking one sentence to the next?*

   You might want to use those sentence stems on the board to answer that question. For example, 'X refers back to ...', 'The transition word x links with ...'.

7. *So, what do you think? Why was it so hard for these doctors to convince others? There are already some reasons on the board. Can someone add to these? OK, thanks for that. We will return to these after you have worked through a text on this topic so you can compare your thinking with what actually happened.*

8. *But before you read about how a cure was found for the majority of cases of peptic ulcers you are going to take a short survey about your own personal qualities. The characteristics are in bold. These can play an important role in success both in education and the workplace. Can you scan the text for any unfamiliar words? Anyone find one? Alright, complete the survey* (see next page).

9. *Can someone share a personal quality that is not in the survey? Can you give us an example?* Additional qualities are listed on the board, along with definitions. The survey seeks to personalise the subject matter and hence make it more meaningful. The provision of both the noun and the adjective for each personal quality/characteristic helps direct student attention to language. The survey also acts as a scaffold for reflecting on the personal qualities of the people discussed in the main text entitled 'Giving yourself a peptic ulcer'.

Some personal qualities/characteristics: self-assessment

<table>
<tr><th>Noun</th><th>Adjective</th><th>Definition</th></tr>
<tr><td>cooperation</td><td>cooperative</td><td>The act of working together for a common purpose.</td></tr>
<tr><td colspan="3">0 1 2 3 4 5 6 7 8 9 10
not at all somewhat often very much so</td></tr>
<tr><td>goal-orientation</td><td>goal-oriented</td><td>The tendency to be focused on self-development through the setting of goals.</td></tr>
<tr><td colspan="3">0 1 2 3 4 5 6 7 8 9 10
not at all somewhat often very much so</td></tr>
<tr><td>hard work</td><td>hard-working</td><td>The tendency to work with energy and commitment.</td></tr>
<tr><td colspan="3">0 1 2 3 4 5 6 7 8 9 10
not at all somewhat often very much so</td></tr>
<tr><td>persistence</td><td>persistent</td><td>The ability to continue with an opinion or a course of action despite difficulty or opposition.</td></tr>
<tr><td colspan="3">0 1 2 3 4 5 6 7 8 9 10
not at all somewhat often very much so</td></tr>
<tr><td>resilience</td><td>resilient</td><td>The ability to recover quickly from difficulties.</td></tr>
<tr><td colspan="3">0 1 2 3 4 5 6 7 8 9 10
not at all somewhat often very much so</td></tr>
<tr><td>self-confidence</td><td>self-confident</td><td>A belief or trust in one's abilities, qualities and judgement.</td></tr>
<tr><td colspan="3">0 1 2 3 4 5 6 7 8 9 10
not at all somewhat often very much so</td></tr>
<tr><td>self-discipline</td><td>self-disciplined</td><td>The ability to make yourself do things you know you should do even when you do not want to.</td></tr>
<tr><td colspan="3">Name personal qualities you think you have that are not listed above:</td></tr>
</table>

10. *Please scan the text 'Giving yourself a peptic ulcer'. Are there any unfamiliar words or turns of phrase?* This activity is a way of reinforcing the learning skill of scanning a text for unfamiliar words and then looking them up in order to facilitate reading.

11. *Before you read the whole text, please read the questions. Do any of them need to be made clearer?* The review of the questions, which are located at the start of the text, is intended to give the students a clear focus for reading the text.

12. *Alright, now please read the whole text.* The reading of the text shown below has been scaffolded through the explanation of three new terms. There are few compound sentences. Many terms and phrases are repeated several times to increase student exposure to this language – e.g. 'medical community', 'published in a medical journal'. A synonym is provided in parentheses for the verb 'disappeared'. Furthermore, students can also be encouraged to consult quietly with each other if they need help with understanding the text.

13. *Individually, please write answers to the questions.*

14. *Now, compare your answers with those of another student.* The answers to the questions are not directly stated in the text, requiring instead that students make inferences. This is intended to foster critical thinking. The text also reinforces language and ideas being used that week in Biology – for example the term 'Petri dish', and the process of growing bacterial cultures. For those who find the text too long, it could be shortened by removing the second paragraph and the word 'too' from the third paragraph.

Giving yourself a peptic ulcer[1]

* ostracised	=	being rejected by a group
* pathologist	=	a doctor/scientist who studies the causes and effects of diseases
* disposal	=	the action or process of getting rid of something

(continued over page)

1 The text was created based on an account of this case written by Gary Klein (2014).

Questions you will need to answer about the text:

- What personal characteristics did Barry Marshall have that helped him succeed?
- What is your evidence?
- What assumptions did he and others make?
- What is the primary conclusion you draw from reading the text?

Until 1994, it was commonly believed that peptic ulcers were usually caused by stress. The most common treatments were surgery or antacid medication. Surgery involved the removal of the lower third of the stomach.

Remarkably, in 1958, a Greek doctor John Lykoudis successfully treated his own peptic ulcer with antibiotics. The doctor would later successfully treat thousands of patients with peptic ulcers. He could not get his findings published in any medical journal. The medical community would not accept his findings.

In 1982, Australian physician Barry Marshall discovered that a chronic infection causes ulcers. His findings too were initially rejected by the medical community. Marshall would be **ostracised** *by much of the medical community for over a decade before his findings were widely accepted.*

In the previous year, Marshall worked with a **pathologist** *Robin Warren. Warren had noticed that some 20 patients with chronic stomach pain had a bacterial infection – Helicobacter pylori, commonly known as H. pylori. In another coincidence, one of the 20 patients – a man who did not qualify for surgery – was given antibiotics. Two weeks later his stomach pains disappeared [were gone].*

In 1982, Marshall and Warren would conduct a study to see if people with ulcers had H. pylori. Initially they found none. Later there was a backlog of work in the laboratory testing for the bacteria. Instead of letting cultures grow in Petri dishes for two days before **disposal** *they grew for five days. Marshall and Warren learned that H. pylori grew more slowly than other bacteria. They also found a strong connection between H. pylori and stomach ulcers. They were initially unable to get their work published in a medical journal.*

In order to gain further evidence, Marshall swallowed the contents of a Petri dish to infect himself with H. plyori. He then cured himself with antibiotics. Although they published an article in a medical journal about their findings, it would take a decade before their conclusions were widely accepted. Only in 1994, once they published their story in the popular press in the United States, did the medical community begin to accept Marshall and Warren's findings. In 2005, Marshall and Warren won the Nobel Prize for Medicine for their work on the cause of ulcers. Today ulcers are routinely treated with antibiotics.

15. *So what is the main issue discussed in the text? What did Marshall discover? What problems did he have in convincing others? What are Marshall's personal qualities or characteristics? What is your evidence for that? What conclusions have you drawn?* The answers can be written on chart paper, or on a computer and displayed on the screen, and polished until the class is satisfied with them. The answers are then displayed on the wall next to a picture of Marshall and under the following headings: (1) Explanation of the issue (setting the stage), (2) The key discovery, (3) Problems faced in convincing others, (4) Personal qualities and evidence, (5) Conclusions. The displayed texts are meant to serve as an exemplar for how students will report on their research about other famous people.

16. *Let's reflect on language. What is the purpose of the introductory paragraph? Which words are used for bridging the paragraphs? What is the function of the auxiliary verb 'would'?*

17. *Shall we go back and look at your initial speculations about why there was resistance to the discovery about how to treat Peptic ulcers? Which speculations were true and which ones were not?* This allows students to get feedback on their initial assumptions/logic.

18. *Find a partner. Have a look at the pictures of practitioners and scientists on the back wall. They have all shown among other qualities great perseverance. Choose one person you will research by taking one of the two folders I have prepared containing short texts about each famous person on display.* On the wall, each picture is accompanied with one key fact; for example, Edward Jenner – English doctor and scientist who discovered a vaccine against smallpox; Wangari Maathai – Kenyan environmentalist and Nobel Prize winner who founded the Green Belt Movement in Kenya to restore local ecosystems and improve well-being; Walter Reid – American who discovered the cause of yellow fever; Ignaz Semmelweis – Hungarian national who greatly reduced infant mortality rates through hand-washing in hospitals; Gao Yaojie – Chinese gynaecologist who is

committed to AIDS prevention. Each picture of the famous people also has five headings next to it: (1) Explanation of the issue (setting the stage), (2) The key discovery or understanding, (3) Problems faced in convincing others, (4) Personal qualities and evidence, (5) Conclusions.

19. *Your task is to work through the material in the folder in order to summarise key information under the five headings displayed on the wall. The folder also contains assessment criteria. Please review those.* The criteria state that the typed answers must have a point size of 24. Their texts should be accurate, concise and pertinent. They need to use the auxiliary verb 'would' at least twice. Spelling and grammar needs to be correct. Evidence must be offered where required. The conclusion must be logical. The headings and criteria provide structure for the work. The fact that two pairs will research the same individual creates an opportunity for formative assessment. The use of such a diverse mix of famous people will bring much new language into the class. Some choice was allowed with the intention that this would increase the likelihood that the students will find the object of research of interest.

20. *Finished? Exchange papers with the other two students researching the same person. Check their work against the criteria. Now, take one of the two texts and polish it.* Students are called to reflect on their work and that of their peers. In other words, they are first expected to be self- and peer-reliant, and only then to ask for help from the teacher.

21. *Ready? Please display your work under the appropriate headings.*

22. *Go and read what your fellow students have come up with. Keep an eye out for commonalities and differences in the personal qualities of these famous people.* If there is a language error that needs correcting, the teacher can mark off that sentence with a coloured dot and students could also be asked to think about how to correct it. The coloured dots prompt self- and peer-correction of language.

23. *So what characteristics or qualities did you find in common? Which qualities were unique to some individuals? What are your conclusions? Is there a quality we have discussed that you would like to further develop yourself? Over the next few days we will develop your plans further. For now, write a note to yourself.* The plan is something that will need to be returned to and developed over an extended period of time if it is likely to be implemented.

24. *Shall we go back to what you said about ulcers on the first day? What is true, and what is not? What have you learned?*

25. *What about the intended outcomes? What have we achieved? What do we still need to work on? What do you need my help with? What can you do?*

26. *For homework, can you imagine a major discovery you will make in 20 years from now? Use the same five headings we used in class today to tell that story.*

Other ideas for integrating content-compatible material into language classes whilst also maintaining a focus on language include students include:

- watching an L1 or L2 video on a content topic and writing up a summary of the key points (Sherris, 2008).

  The students could also be required to use certain grammatical features that are being learned.

- working with newspaper or magazine articles that are related to a topic being discussed in a content class.

  For example, if ecosystems are being investigated in Biology, then in language class, an article can be read about how an invasive species such as a plant, animal or fish is changing an ecosystem.

- analysing how shapes they are studying in Geometry can be found in art, architecture, in the classroom or in consumer products.

  Students can cooperate to see if they can generate 100 such items.

- working in pairs with each student having a slightly different text about a content-compatible topic. Each text contains some factual differences, some of which are content errors. Each text includes some different language errors.

- Without looking at each other's texts, students need to find the errors and write a correct version of the text, which they can then compare with a correct version provided by the teacher (drawing on Sherris, 2008).

- working in pairs with a content-compatible text that has been written in social language and rewriting it in academic language or vice versa.

  (See Chapters 5 and 8 for examples.)

- working in pairs to correct language errors that have been integrated into a content-compatible text.
- occasionally making 'use of functional grammar strategies [... to] engage students in extended conversation about the meaning of the texts they read' (Schleppegrell, Greer and Taylor, 2008).

Schleppegrell et al. (2008) report how teacher Sarah Taylor guides her students in answering the question 'What were the internal weaknesses of the Roman Empire?' The students were given a text that was discussed in detail by breaking up and analysing sentence fragments and their relationship to each other. For example, Taylor broke the following two sentences into four chunks and asked her students to analyse them: 'To finance Rome's huge armies, its citizens had to pay heavy taxes. These taxes hurt the economy and drove many people into poverty.' Schleppegrell et al.'s (2008) detailed explanation of what the teacher did follows:

Issues that challenge students' comprehension of the meaning in each clause are presented in parentheses below the analysis:

To finance Rome's huge armies,

Actor/ Participant (nouns)	**Action/ Process (verbs)**	**Receiver/Goal:** *Who or What?*
???	to finance	Rome's huge armies

(Here the Actor in the clause, the historical participant who *financed* the armies, is not presented in the text until the beginning of the next clause (*its citizens*). Students are challenged to recognize the historical agency.)

its citizens had to pay heavy taxes.

Actor/ Participant (nouns)	**Action/ Process (verbs)**	**Receiver/Goal:** *Who or What?*
its citizens	had to pay	heavy taxes

(The reference device (pronoun) its has to be linked back to Rome in the phrase *Rome's huge armies* in the previous clause to recognize who had to pay.)

These taxes hurt the economy ...

Actor/ Participant (nouns)	**Action/ Process (verbs)**	**Receiver/Goal:** *Who or What?*
These taxes	hurt	the economy

(Again a reference device (*these*) has to be linked to the heavy taxes in the previous clause if students are to understand which taxes the text is talking about. The taxes are a non-human Actor and the economy is an abstraction; students can discuss how taxes can hurt and who is hurt; who the real human participants are behind the economy (the Roman citizens mentioned in the previous clauses.)

and drove many people into poverty.

Actor/ Participant (nouns)	**Action/ Process (verbs)**	**Receiver/Goal:** *Who or What?*
???	drove	many people into poverty

(Here students need to recognise the participant that is not repeated in this clause, the Actor *these taxes*. How *taxes* would drive people into poverty and the metaphor 'drive' into poverty can be discussed.)

CRITICAL PEDAGOGY

As previously stated, critical pedagogy is focused on issues of equity and equality. By integrating issues of social justice into language classes, it is argued that students are likely to find learning more meaningful and memorable.

The challenge is that these issues are difficult to navigate. Teachers need to be well informed about a given topic, and structure the learning environment so that students are in the habit of active enquiry and research that demonstrates rigour, scepticism and care. This helps ensure that any line of reasoning the students develop is on solid ground, and that their opinions are informed. At the same time, students need to be able to maintain humility with respect to their own opinions, while still having the courage and skill to defend them. They also need to engage constructively with others to carefully weigh opinions and have the courage and skill to challenge and learn from others. Ideally, they need to work towards achieving consensus and proposing and implementing constructive solutions. These would be considered principles of good pedagogy.

Reagan (2016) reports on a secondary school Spanish language teacher who used the following text to engage American students in critical discussion about their country's involvement in the overthrow of a democratically elected government. The students had studied Spanish in language classes for a total of 13 months. During the lesson students spoke almost entirely in their L2, as did the teacher, except when they discussed grammar points. The teacher's primary goal seemed be to provoke student interest and discussion. In addition 'she used the text [below] to review a number of Spanish grammatical features (gender, noun-adjective agreement, - *ar* verbs, etc.)' (ibid.).

The other 9/11

When Americans think about the date 9/11 (September 11, 2001), we usually think about the attack on the World Trade Centre [and the Pentagon]. There was already another important 9/11, though – September 11, 1973. In Chile Dr. Salvador Allende was elected president in a democratic election in 1970. He began many social and economic reforms. On September 11, 1973, President Allende and his government were overthrown by a military coup supported by the United States CIA. From 1973 to 1990, Chile's leader was Augusto Pinochet, who headed a very brutal dictatorship in which 28,000 people were tortured and at least 3,200 murders and 'disappearances' took place.

After discussing the above text, the students' homework was to learn as much about the coup as possible and use that learning to evaluate the accuracy of the text. To further encourage and structure critical thinking while researching the coup, the students could be asked to make notes to prepare for the next lesson's discussion by using some or all of the following lenses: international law; justice; freedom of the press; justifications; Pinochet's fate; Allende's fate; negative consequences; morality; moral authority; and the families of those who died and disappeared. The provision of additional lenses such as these could help structure student thinking and in particular help them to explore additional layers and perspectives.

Additional fundamental questions related to knowledge, justice and equity that connect with the students' own classrooms, school, families and community that could be used to integrate meaningful content into language classes and encourage critical thinking are listed below. **They are a list of options. They are not a list of expectations.** These options can be researched and debated in language classes or used for developing a term project. The list of questions is followed by one example detailing how one question could be used to foster student learning of both content and language.

- In what forms, where and when does bullying take place in school life? What causes bullying? How can bullying be reduced?
- How does one protect oneself against identity theft?
- What are the sources of conflict among young people? What are the most effective ways of dealing with conflict among young people?
- Should junk food be sold in schools?
- How can we reduce the number of young people smoking?
- What are the signs of 'fake news'? Who uses it for what purposes? How can it be countered?
- How does extremism develop and how can it be addressed?
- Why do people migrate to our country and what challenges do they face when they seek to integrate into our society?
- Which agricultural/fishing/forestry practices are sustainable and which ones are not? Why?
- What leads people to a life of crime (e.g. literacy levels, mental health issues, lack of education, poverty, greed)? Which government actions could lead to a significant reduction in crime?
- What is modern-day slavery? What are its causes? How can individuals, organisations and governments fight against it?
- What are the dangers of social media and how can they be reduced?
- Should companies or government be allowed to discriminate based on a person's genetic make-up?
- How may artificial intelligence affect my future? What are the dangers of artificial intelligence (e.g. my 'smart home')?
- In which ways does our school respect the United Nations Declaration of the Rights of the Child? What should change in this school?

- Should future parents be able to genetically design their babies?
- What are the benefits and risks associated with the augmented reality provided by new information technologies?
- When and how has civil disobedience been used in a wise and effective manner to improve the world?
- What are the causes of homelessness and how can it be tackled?
- How can the digital footprint you are currently leaving behind affect your future? Please back up your conclusions with evidence.
- How can the rate of unwanted teenage pregnancies be dramatically reduced?
- Should governments finance stem cell research?
- Are genetically modified crops a blessing or a dangerous experiment?
- How should an energy resources-rich country prepare for a future where some of these resources are becoming depleted?
- What is the air quality of our community? What are the causes? How can they be addressed?

As discussed above, critical thinking involves exploring knowledge, information and experiences. Diverse points of view are taken into account. Students are asked to explore alternatives, make inferences and solve problems. They are also encouraged to reflect on their own thinking. If students are to think critically about these topics, and be able to use and learn the language they need to navigate the topic, learning tasks need to be well structured and scaffolded. An example of how to scaffold the answering of one of the above questions – *What are the causes of homelessness and how can it be tackled?* – follows.

Brinton and Masters (1997) suggest using a town meeting simulation to discuss the question. The implied intended content learning outcome is for students to be able to detail the causes of homelessness, and to propose and weigh potential solutions to the problem. The implied language outcome is for students to develop well-structured arguments and back up their arguments with evidence. The suggest activities are:

1. The students first work through some learning materials on homelessness. Alternatively, students could be guided to documentaries on homelessness to draw out causes, consequences and solutions. The research could be undertaken in the L1 and/or the L2.

2. The students are then divided into small groups. Each group is given a different card with a circa 100-word summary of a stakeholder perspective. These summaries provide students with additional content and language input. Stakeholders include: a city representative; a war veteran with post-traumatic stress disorder; a 50-year old farmer who lost his farm; a woman with three children who lost her job and whose husband has abandoned the family; a man with a mental health issue; a 19-year old homeless man who parents are abusive alcoholics. In order to build student comfort levels and to take into account unknown personal histories, Brinton and Masters (1997) suggest giving students some choice in the role they will assume. Alternatively, students could also suggest other stakeholders.

3. Brinton and Masters provide a three-column framework for students to propose solutions to homelessness. This guides students in weighing the advantages and disadvantages of each of their proposed solutions.

   Such a framework might also include a column for required investments related to each solution. A 'required investments' column might help students to reflect more deeply on the advantages and disadvantages of each proposed solution.

   It may also be appropriate to have students reflect on which stakeholders might react negatively to their proposed solutions and to prepare possible counterarguments. As a scaffold, students could be asked to review and analyse two lines of argument – one that is weak and another that is strong. This would help clarify the sort of quality of thought, argumentation and language that is expected. Additionally, students could be provided with some of the phraseology for developing an argument (e.g. There are three key points I would like to make ..., First, ..., The government has reported that ..., It is short-sighted to think that ...). Fellow students and/or the teacher could review a part of the preparatory notes by those students who are unsure of how to say something in the L2.

4. Brinton and Masters suggest that each group choses one member to represent their group in the town meeting simulation. In addition, they suggest numerous useful variations of the activity. In order to enhance student engagement, instead of having only one group partake in the meeting while others observe, they propose dividing the class into several small groups and conducting several meetings in parallel. They also suggest that some students could act as evaluators. This implies that the students and teacher would have agreed on how to evaluate the quality of participation in the

meeting. Time would need to be taken to discuss the assessments. They also suggest that the meeting could be video recorded and then viewed by the students so they can evaluate their own work. This would be a fine opportunity not just for students to analyse their own and their peers' work, but to improve it. The video can be stopped so specific segments of the meeting can be analysed with a view to enhancing arguments and language use. Based on feedback and self-reflection, students could then remake and test out their enhanced arguments.

ENQUIRY-BASED LEARNING

The questions proposed under the heading 'Critical Pedagogy' can align with an enquiry-based learning approach. Enquiry-based learning involves students undertaking an enquiry either to solve a small problem, to conduct a small-scale investigation or to undertake a more substantial research project. Enquiry-based learning can move from initially being a highly teacher-led process to one being led by the students, but supported by the teacher. Eventually students would seek to convert their research findings and analysis into useful knowledge.

Cammarata (2016) argues that an enquiry-driven approach provides an 'authentic language learning experience' as it motivates students to embark on a 'relentless search for answers to important questions that require deeper forms of thinking'. This point is reinforced by Hattie's (2012) meta-analysis that found that enquiry-based learning contributes substantially to the development of students' capacity to think critically (effect size of 1.02). By its very nature enquiry-based learning calls on students to think critically. That is to say that among other activities, they need to discriminate between useful and unhelpful information; distinguish fact from opinion; evaluate the validity and applicability of information; synthesise facts and evidence; analyse, summarise and organise their research findings; test their own thinking; build a line of argument; persuade others; pose solutions to problems; and weigh other people's feedback. The act of choosing their own object of enquiry and planning their own work can be considered as an exercise in building student agency.

Schleppegrell and de Oliveira (2006) discuss a content class where a simultaneous focus is maintained on content and language. In principle, the approach can be applied in a content-based language class. They report on a teacher who used World War II speeches – one by US President Truman and one by Japanese Prime Minister Suzuki during World War II – in order to have students investigate and reflect on the prejudices and biases of both sides. Schleppegrell and de Oliveira (2006) report the teacher stating that by analysing complex noun groups and 'words like *brute* and *arrogant* and *idiocy* … [students] were able to take apart those and figure out what Truman was trying to say, what the Japanese were trying to say, and understand the bias of both sides during WWII, the racism of both sides during WWII'. Cammarata (2016) considers this example as a 'cognitively stimulating' meaningful activity helping students to not only learn additional historical content, but understand 'the role of language in the shaping of reality and beliefs'. In principle it should also help students see how beliefs shape reality and how language can be used by politicians to manipulate the electorate.

Speeches provide a fine opportunity to integrate content-compatible material, critical thinking and an enquiry-based approach into language classes. For example, Elizabeth I's 'Speech to the Troops at Tilbury' (1588), Indira Ghandi's 'Martin Luther King' speech (1969), Martin Luther King Junior's 'I have a dream' speech (1963), Abraham Lincoln's 'Gettysburg Address' (1863), Emmeline Pankhurst's 'Freedom or Death' speech (1913), and Malala Yousafzai's Nobel lecture (2014). Speeches or parts of speeches can be used as an inspiration to recall and/or research historical or current context. They are also an opportunity for discussing purpose, audience and genre, analysing argumentation (e.g. structure, rhetorical devices, evidence, imagery) and language (tone, style, syntax, grammar, phraseology). They are a good point of departure for students to write their own speeches.

Hardwick and Davis (2009) describe a project in the American state of Oregon where language specialists worked with geographers to create content and language integrated units on Human and Physical Geography for high school Spanish language classes. In one of those units students seek answers to the following questions.

- Why do immigrants leave their homelands?
- How do they choose sites to start their lives anew?
- What impact does the immigration process have on immigrants and their host communities?

(MOSAIC, 2017)

The questions are relevant to the students as they connect directly with their community, and invite them to reflect deeply on emigration and immigration. The investigation is highly structured. (The Spanish-language materials, with English-language explanations, are all available online in the form of downloadable documents that teachers can adapt, at https://casls.uoregon.edu/mosaic/about_us.php). Tasks are structured to ensure that students have to think critically. Language processing is scaffolded primarily through the provision of glossaries and the breaking down of texts into small digestible chunks. For example, in one activity a timeline is cut into strips and students have to work through a series of very short texts about major events to determine the order of the timeline. In another activity, students work through a circa 700-word text on the political and economic conditions in Mexico from the 1980s until present day. They use a chart to compare and contrast what they have learnt from this text and compare that with what they had previously read about the 1940s and 1950s. The students analyse and plot settlement patterns and look at how these are related to economic activity. In the process, 'students describe physical and human characteristics of cities and geographic features of the different regions of the state' (ibid.). They explore the critical features of and create choropleth maps (a map using shading, colouring or symbols to indicate values in particular areas). Students also undertake language-focused activities in a context where they are expected to give advice using phrases that require the subjunctive. Finally, students summarise some of their learning in an imaginary letter sent home. As a scaffold, it is suggested that the letter address the following questions:

- Why did you decide to leave home?
- How did you learn about opportunities in the United States?
- Why did you choose Oregon over other locations in the United States?
- How did you travel from Europe to Oregon?
- What were the travel conditions like for you?
- What does your new home look like? Describe the physical geography of the area.
- What is the climate like in Oregon where you live?
- What type of work are you doing in Oregon? What other types of jobs are available?

- What plans do you have for the future? Do you plan to return to [your country of origin]? Why or why not?'

  (MOSAIC, 2017)

To ensure a high standard of learning, the lessons seek to meet the national standards set for both Geography and foreign language education. Rubrics are provided for assessment. The MOSAIC website also offers substantial background information that language teachers can use to improve their knowledge of the given aspect of Geography. The website is a work in progress so, for example, when it comes to the materials on Africa, teachers may wish to have students focus on additional investigations such as the reasons behind the fact that many African countries have some of the fastest growing economies in the world. The MOSAIC group appears to welcome feedback and input.

The next section will discuss how learning can be made more meaningful through the use of cross-curricular themes and projects. The cross-curricular projects mostly also focus on having students undertake enquiry learning. One of the cross-curricular projects is a student-led enquiry which constitutes a substantial research project.

CROSS-CURRICULAR PROJECTS AND ENQUIRY-BASED LEARNING

To help build a cross-curricular mindset and further reinforce cross-curricular learning, Portuguese school director Álvaro Almeida dos Santos encourages his CLIL and non-CLIL teachers to make all school excursions cross-curricular in nature. In addition, the school is now working toward turning excursions into projects by having students plan and make all the arrangements for the excursions.

Estonia requires that students in Grade 11 (ages 17–18), the penultimate year of upper secondary school, undertake a major enquiry-based project. This is a national graduation requirement. Below, Mihkel Kõrbe, who is the director of studies at the Kadriorg German Gymnasium in Tallinn, gives background information about his school and its CLIL programme, then describes how the enquiry-based learning projects, which are often cross-curricular, are organised.

VIEW FROM THE FIELD:

Talinn, Estonia

Mihkel Kõrbe, Director of Studies, Kadriorg German Gymnasium

The Kadriorg German Gymnasium is an Estonian-medium school that runs a German-language CLIL programme in primary school as well as in lower and upper secondary school. In primary school, in addition to two to three 45-minute language classes per week, students study two lessons of Music in German per week. Beginning in Grade 5 through to Grade 12, students have five 45-minute language lessons per week. In Grades 7 and 8, they study Geography and Country Studies in German. In order to graduate from Grade 9, students must complete a cross-curricular project.

In upper secondary school, in Grades 10–12 students undertake 35 lessons through German for each of the following subjects: Becoming a Tallinn Old Town guide; Translation and Interpretation; Cultural studies; and Debating through German. The focus is on developing practical skills. For example, in the course on becoming an Old Town guide each student must choose a different part of town to research. They then have to develop what would be part of the tour of the Old Town, research the buildings and the history of the town, and conduct a German-language guided tour of 'their' part of the town. Upon successful completion of the course, students obtain a certificate which allows them to work as a guide.

In upper secondary school, students can take Business Studies in German throughout the three years of upper secondary school. In Grade 10 students have a week of work-study in a German company in Estonia, and must report back on their learning in German. In Grade 11, each student spends a week working in Germany for a German company whilst being supported by our partner school in Germany. Students also take the German Federal State of Niedersachsen Business Studies exam and, if they pass the exam, they receive a certificate from our partner school in Germany.

My Grade 9 students can complete their cross-curricular enquiry-based project individually or in a group of two to three students. They need to integrate several subjects. For example, in Geography, students were studying tectonic plates and volcanoes. In Vocational Studies, students created a model of a volcano. Working under the guidance of the Chemistry teacher they learned how to make their model volcano erupt. In cooperation with the language teacher, the students created a German-language board game about volcanoes. Finally the work was presented to the class. In Country Studies, students created a model of the German Parliament (Reichstag). They worked with their History teacher to create a timeline related to the parliament. They created a quiz, and made a presentation of their work in German. Content teachers provided feedback on content and the language teacher did the same for language use.

In Grade 11, students can choose any topic for their research project. If students choose to do their enquiry-based project in German then their final report has to be about 12–15 pages in length as opposed to 25–30 pages for those students doing their project in their L1. The length is shortened due to the extra demand of producing a quality academic paper in German. To help prepare for the research project, Grade 10 students attend the Grade 11 students' presentations (a sort of viva or defence) before a jury of native and non-native German-speaking content and language teachers. The defence is discussed in Grade 10 classes to encourage students to begin to reflect on what they will do when the time comes for them to undertake their big research project. In Grade 11, several project reports from previous years are analysed by the students for both content and language. The analysis is focused on drawing out the characteristics of high-quality research papers versus average or below-average papers. For example, students draw out the structure of papers, how lines of argument have been developed, the validity of evidence, and the rich and poor use of academic language. Finally, students and teachers agree on the criteria for high-quality work both for the content (e.g. the paper has a clear statement of goals and actually achieves those goals; it uses multiple sources to ensure validity of key conclusions), and language (e.g. the paper avoids the use of social language, avoids unjustified repetition of language and uses key academic phrases from the class databank). All previous student projects are available in the school library. The filed projects do not include teacher comments or the final mark. Many projects take on a cross-curricular nature.

The students taking the CLIL Business Studies class must individually create their own business plan. At this stage they are expected to be autonomous learners and support each other in doing their work. That said, the language teachers help students to think through language use including how they are structuring the various parts of the plan. Content teachers support students when the students request help. Students must present and defend their business plan in German in front of a committee of teachers and business people. The committee includes native speakers of German and a language teacher. The project is a major motivator. It also teaches students to manage themselves.

THEME-BASED LEARNING

Two approaches are discussed. The first involves simply integrating one theme across many subjects. An example is given from Estonia. The second example, which is from Mexico, involves the integration of a meaningful theme into language classes.

Doing theme-based studies involves using a common theme such as the role of 'light' in a series of subjects: Literature (e.g. how authors use light as a symbol of mood or to reinforce a character's internal feelings), Sciences (e.g. the role of light in photosynthesis or in telescopes and microscopes, or in new communication technologies), Art (e.g. how light is used and depicted in paintings or architecture and to what effect), History (e.g. how the use of light has affected history), and Health (e.g. the role of sunlight in maintaining or damaging health, the use of light in medical equipment). Izabella Riitsaar (2012), the director of a primarily Russian-medium Pae Gymnasium in Estonia that has an Estonian-language CLIL programme, reported that, when she and her deputy worked hard with teachers for several years to do theme-based studies at the secondary level, student learning improved significantly. However, at one point they abandoned the practice. Student achievement dropped, so the school re-established a theme-based approach the following year. Theme-based learning is now a solid part of the work culture. Teachers and deputy head teachers propose themes. These are discussed and agreed upon for a term or full year. Teachers then simply teach their classes using the agreed upon themes. The school considers theme-based learning as part of its success story, feeling that it has led to a substantial rise in student achievement and improved teacher cooperation.

In Mexico, Wendy Díaz Pérez of the University of Guadalajara, David Marsh of the University of Jyväskylä Group, Finland, and Donna Lee Fields, of the International University of Valencia, Spain, have cooperated with teachers to develop a global citizenship programme. As the primary theme discussed in the Mexican example focuses on fairness, equality, rights and responsibilities, it can also be considered an example of critical pedagogy. Below, Díaz Pérez, Marsh and Fields describe the Guadalajara context and project.

VIEW FROM THE FIELD:
Guadalajara, Mexico

Wendy Díaz Pérez, David Marsh, Donna Lee Fields

Guadalajara is Mexico's second largest city, located in the state of Jalisco. The state has steadily lost economic influence in recent decades. One of the identified weaknesses is a lack of workforce foreign language competence, especially in English. Having experienced some 500 hours of English teaching, only 15% of high school graduates are at Level B1 (CEFR) when they enter higher education.[1]

Studies[2] have demonstrated that whilst curriculum, teaching competence, course content and methods play a role in explaining such poor outcomes, one key area of interest is the attitude of teachers and learners towards learning languages.

The University of Guadalajara operates 65% of all public schools and higher education (296,000 students) in Jalisco. In 2015, it launched a Language Policy alongside a strategic plan to improve the learning of languages.

One action was to explore ways to counter the negative attitudes of adolescents towards the learning of English, and towards themselves as foreign language learners.

A pilot (Global Citizenship) project was launched to test an across-the-curriculum English-language prototype. Fifteen participating schools invited volunteer teachers to launch projects in English. 90% of volunteers were content teachers, resulting in school-based teams of mixed but complementary subjects (e.g. Maths, Physics, Chemistry). The number of teachers in one school per project ranged from 2–6 persons. The students were in their first year of high school (aged 15 years).

The pilot had 3 objectives:

- raise the self-confidence and motivation of young people to learn and use English
- co-design a prototype of a learning environment within the curriculum that accelerates the learning of English
- raise teaching and learning standards by building teacher competences to use innovative methods.

1 Resultados ESLAT (2016). Universidad de Guadalajara: Guadalajara: FLIP.

2 Mugford, G. (2016). *La Enseñanza del inglés en la Universidad de Guadalajara.* Guadalajara: FLIP.

Themes were selected based on the interests of each school-based teaching team; the relationship to the concept of global citizenship; linkage to the curriculum; and phenomenon-based learning (learning about real-world phenomena relevant to the lives of the students).

Figure 1: *Range of Themes linking to High School Curriculum*

A 25-hour module was co-designed with the teachers in training sessions (30 hours). It blended project-based learning and the use of CLIL. Versatile content and language scaffolding resources were designed to enhance learner-centricity and autonomy, to support and guide the student's learning, and to accelerate their ability to learn through English.

Scaffolding was deployed according to the principle of timely support and minimal teacher intervention.

For example, one theme was Personal Health and Well-being with a special focus on unexpected pregnancy amongst adolescents entitled 'Passion or Pressure'?

Translanguaging between English and Spanish was used to enhance understanding of key concepts in both languages, and create opportunities for eliciting bilingual output through conversational routines when role-playing critical incidents. Academic language was deciphered as colloquial talk, and examined from the perspective of common usage and attitude in the different languages.

Students role-played parents, medics, social workers, career advisers, female and male students, economists, and religious and legal figures. This enhanced cooperative learning. Students depicted and assessed cases involving young people of different ages and relationships. This also involved modelling activities for students to teach and transfer knowledge about identifying fact, fiction, prejudice and feelings.

Written text (case notes, statistics and fact sheets) was verbalised, and dialogue written up as case notes. Reflective sessions were in the form of graphic organisers. Sentence structures and spoken language gambits were provided to ease communication in English, particularly with respect to politeness features when discussing emotive issues such as unexpected pregnancy.

Anchoring to prior and background knowledge was often in the form of visuals such as drawings, photographs, video and statistics. This included looking at family histories and regional pregnancy statistics. Critical discourse activities, especially through image and text, were used to enable students to compare, evaluate and describe how peer, social media, fashion and other pressures encourage sexual activities, alongside protective behaviour and contraception.

Role-plays were used to act out verbal and non-verbal communication in managing different types of situations, and to demonstrate the emotional and physical experience of a young woman as she goes through the stages of pregnancy.

Open-ended questions, often carrying new concepts, were used for situation appraisal and reflection on student's views on unexpected pregnancies, alongside assessment of prior knowledge about sexuality, behaviour, choice and peer pressure.

Students demonstrated their learning using a wide range of language-supported activities, games, predictive tests, role-plays, statistical analyses and interactive voting.

The project evaluation considered the learning outcomes with respect to: teacher and student motivation and self-image related to English use; student competences in problem solving; the capacity to undertake collaborative learning; and how students contribute to their own language learning using existing digital skills. As the project has proved successful, there is a plan to cascade the concept across state schools as an optional but recognised transversal curriculum option.

Common functions

All of the above ways of integrating new meaningful content into language classes call on students to use common functions. They are central to thinking critically in a wide range of subjects, and to demonstrating learning. Some common functions are listed below:

- extracting a line of argument, point of view or perspective from a text or other media
- synthesising, comparing or contrasting texts
- defining concepts and providing proof to back up descriptions
- creating coherent statements leading a reader or a listener to an adequate conclusion
- developing well-structured lines of reasoning that include evidence and examples
- discussing a topic from different stakeholder perspectives
- explaining causes and consequences
- separating opinions from facts.

By drawing student attention to these functions and the language required to undertake them, and by having students engage in meaningful tasks using these functions, language teachers can help students not only to learn generic academic language applicable to many subjects, but to develop their capacity to think critically. These common functions are discussed more thoroughly in **Chapter 4:** *Academic Language*. Becoming adept at using these common functions will also help learners 'to learn how to learn' by developing the learning skills required for studying various content subjects through the L2, as well as through the L1.

COOPERATION WITH CONTENT TEACHERS

> *CLIL cannot just rely on one content teacher who does his/her subject in English and that's it. The lone-wolf model has little impact. Our school's success with CLIL is based on English teachers and content teachers working together.*
>
> Teresa Rosa Socias Garriga, English teacher, Barcelona, Spain

Through co-operation, L2 and L1 language and subject teachers can build richer learning environments and reinforce the learning of both content and language, and encourage intellectual rigour. On a practical level that may mean that one L2 language teacher and one L2 content teacher regularly work in tandem or that several content and language teachers at one grade level regularly cooperate. In other cases such as with those teachers teaching through the L1 and those teaching through the L2, cooperation focuses on language issues or cross-linguistic and cross-curricular projects. These teachers may only meet twice a year, once to plan and once to evaluate the implementation of those plans. The foci of CLIL-related cooperation has been known to include the following actions:

Needs identification

- Based on curriculum intentions, jointly identifying academic language that needs to be understood in the L2 and what L2 language the students are expected to use in their output.
- Based on classroom discourse and student writing, having content teachers identify key newly apparent language learning needs (e.g. terminology, phraseology, grammar).
- Jointly deciding on the text types and genres students need to be able to navigate when it comes to both input and output.
- Having language teachers mention any major content learning gaps that become apparent when discussing content compatible materials with their students.
- Identifying students who may require enrichment or remediation and deciding on how that will be done (differentiation so that all make significant progress).
- Agreeing on how the learning of terminology and concepts taught through the CLIL language can also be used in activities and discussions in the L1 to ensure that students are comfortable using terminology in both their L1 and L2.

Planning

- Establishing a common intended language learning outcome for the week. This can help students experience more deeply the value of a given intended language learning outcome, and focus content and language teacher attention on supporting its achievement.

- Deciding on a core function that teachers in one grade will all work on during a given week (e.g. testing assumptions). This will help students better understand the core function and develop the language and thinking skills they need to successfully undertake it.
- Establishing a common learning skills outcome (generic or pertaining to language learning) for the week or for a longer period of time. Similarly to the above point, by having several teachers focus at the same time on one learning skills outcome, students will get more practice at using it and be more likely to appreciate its value.
- Sharing and discussing content compatible material for use in language classes. This can include discussing which related tasks students should be assigned. Content teachers could also suggest additional reading for language teachers in order to help them build background knowledge about a given content topic.
- Agreeing on a cross-curricular theme, and/or a cross-curricular and/or bilingual project. Planning for implementation would involve agreeing on intended learning outcomes, how to structure the project, and how to create several opportunities for students to self-assess their work and receive feedback on it before they hand in their final work, as well as agreeing on the assessment criteria and who will assess what.
- Deciding on how plans and learning materials will be shared (e.g. in a dedicated area of the school Intranet site).

Assessment and evaluation

- Agreeing on how student progress in learning language in content subject classes and content learning in language classes will be measured (what success looks like). This would in the ideal lead to a common policy for assessing language in content classes, and assessing content learning in language classes.
- Agreeing on a standard set of abbreviations for signalling language errors that students need to correct.
- Agreeing on some common means of seeking and processing student feedback (see the feedback sections in **Chapter 7:** *Assessment*).

Self-reflection and professional development

- Discussing the impact of teaching and learning strategies that have been agreed upon in meetings and that have then been implemented. This involves seeking out evidence of the impact of jointly planned interventions and planning new actions/ interventions based on this evidence.
- Sharing self-selected short video clips of parts of lessons and discussing them with a view to improving student learning.
- Reflecting annually on how to improve teacher cooperation.

Making visible and celebrating achievements

- Recognising student achievements and deciding how to celebrate success.
- Summarising the achievements that have resulted from the cooperation, and deciding whom and how to inform others about these.

To encourage cooperation it can be helpful to agree on some ground rules, such as always being constructive. In the ideal, the co-operation meetings are a place for risk-free, open, straightforward and honest discussions. In other words, ideas would be open to criticism, but not people. All professionals face problems and challenges, and need support. However, ultimately the major focus during co-operation meetings is best kept on **ways of helping students to learn.**

A SELF-REFLECTION TOOL FOR LANGUAGE TEACHERS on the integration of content and language [2]

This tool is intended for language teachers who are teaching students learning one or more subjects through their L2. It differs significantly from the self-reflection tool for content teachers discussed in the previous chapter. This tool suggests what language teachers can do to integrate the teaching of content into their classes, how they can cooperate with content teachers and which practices might be avoided.

Systematically supporting both content and language learning in language classes may require a major change in the way some language teachers teach. In order to adapt practices to a new context such as CLIL, it is

---

2 Inspired by the work of Stoddart et al., 2002.

often helpful to begin by reflecting on and declaring what one believes and where one currently stands on a particular issue. Once we shed light on our thinking, feelings and practices, we can move from the abstract to the concrete. This allows us: (1) to deepen our own analysis, (2) to discuss education and best CLIL practice with our colleagues, and (3) to hopefully improve our practice.

This self-reflection tool for language teachers is divided into four levels or stages from *CLIL novice* to *expert CLIL practitioner.* Level one describes the possible beliefs, understandings and practices of someone who has started doing CLIL by teaching some grammar points and/or stressing some common functions earlier than foreseen in the language curriculum so as to better prepare students for their CLIL class(es). In schools just starting the teaching of some subjects through the L2, many language teachers are likely operating at Level one. Level four describes the possible beliefs, understandings and practices of someone who systematically integrates the teaching of content and language. The statements within each category have been collected over the years from CLIL language teachers and their colleagues. We do not assume that all the comments in each category would apply to all teachers nor that the categories are completely discrete.

Each level is divided into three columns. The **first column** – *My beliefs and understandings* – describe where someone is in their thinking about CLIL. Decision-making is driven by beliefs and understandings. Without explicitly stating them, it is difficult to foster growth in beliefs, understandings and related practices. The **second column** – *What is visible to others* – describes practices reported by CLIL teachers and trainers. These are examples of tangible practices which either do or do not support best practice in CLIL. The **third column** – *What others can hear* – represents comments that have been heard from content and language teachers at each of the four levels or stages of their CLIL professional development. They are offered as reference points in order to support teachers in reflecting on their own practice.

It is important to note that this tool is intended for teacher self-reflection. It is not suitable for CLIL teacher evaluation.

Level 1: CLIL novice

Little or no integration: offering some support to the content teacher(s)		
My beliefs and understandings	What is visible to others	What colleagues can hear
I am only responsible for language teaching. In language lessons, content is used primarily to carry the language. I work on bringing in interesting content, but my focus is on language learning. I have little or no awareness of the intended content learning outcomes of those subjects being taught through the students' L2. At the request of the content teacher, I have agreed to teach some grammar points and/or stress some common functions earlier than planned so as to better prepare students for their CLIL class(es). I am not actively exploring how to integrate content into my lessons that is compatible with what students are learning in their content classes.	...me demonstrating some flexibility in supporting the content teacher. ... me working mostly with language colleagues, and very little with content teachers. ... me engaging in learning in general terms about the CLIL approach. ... me showing little active interest in trying to learn what the CLIL subject teachers are trying to accomplish in their lessons. ... me speaking mostly about teaching language as opposed to talking about some new content that the students engaged with. ... me giving feedback on language learning, but rarely on content learning. ... me giving feedback on critical thinking related to language, but not content.	Of course, I can teach this grammar point (e.g. if clauses and the first conditional) earlier than planned if this will help your students. I have to cover the language curriculum. I have to get students ready to take the language proficiency exam. I can't take much time away from that. I can't be taking time away from language teaching in order to work with topics and material that would be compatible with what students are learning in Geography, History, Maths or Physics. Language assignments and tests don't include marks for or feedback on content learning.

Level 2: CLIL beginner

First steps on the road to integration		
My beliefs and understandings	What is visible to others	What colleagues can hear
I recognise the importance of integrating content and language, but am unsure of how to do this. I accept the need for changing some of my practices to better take into account the CLIL approach. I wish to have more ideas for how to integrate content into language classes. Based on discussions with CLIL content teachers, I have a strong sense of what students need to be able to do in those classes and have a sense of how I might help the students learn the needed language.	... me occasionally experimenting/struggling with some content-subject compatible material in order to teach language. ... me mostly giving feedback to students about language use. ... me occasionally giving feedback about content learning. ... me occasionally fostering critical thinking by encouraging students to further explain their thinking. ... me occasionally enquiring about language problems students face in content subject classes taught through their L2. ... me learning more about CLIL. ... me occasionally asking students about their interests and trying to make connections to these in planning lessons.	*Does anyone have an idea for how to integrate content into language classes?* *What language are your students having trouble with?* (speaking with students) *Can you tell me what language you need help in learning?* *I know it is important that students learn new content, but I'm worried about taking time away from language teaching.* *Here is the language I have to teach this week. Can you suggest some interesting content materials that complement (are compatible with) what students are learning in your class? I could perhaps use these as a basis for also teaching language?* *What grabs students' attention in your subject?*

Level 3: Relatively proficient CLIL practitioner

Considerable integration is occurring		
My beliefs and understandings	What is visible to others	What colleagues can hear
I recognise the need for students to work with challenging and meaningful content as a motivator for language learning. I have developed curriculum awareness in particular in reference to one or two subjects taught through the L2. I believe it is important to occasionally create cross-curricular learning opportunities for students. I systematically try to find out what students find meaningful and useful in general, but also what they find meaningful and useful in classes taught through the L2. I want to learn more about integrating content into language classes. I believe it is sometimes useful for students to discuss in their L2 some material they have read in their L1.	...me exploring opportunities for the integration of content and language with colleagues, including with subject teachers. ... me enquiring about what is being taught in some content subject classes. ... me enquiring about problems students face in content subject classes taught through their L2. ... me often setting and discussing intended content learning outcomes with my students. ... me also giving feedback on content learning and quality of critical thinking about that content. ... me providing scaffolding of both language and content learning. ... me not yet feeling comfortable about assessing content learning. ... me teaching students the language they want to learn when they want to learn it. ... me seeking to learn more about CLIL. ... me regularly trying to find out students' interests.	(speaking to subject teacher) What are you teaching this week? Is there some way I could help you? Could we do a cross-curricular project together? Can you share content-compatible material and activities with me that I could use in my language class? Let's form a working group to tackle this issue. I don't really assess the content, just the language. How can I assess content learning? Here is how I have tried to integrate content into my language class. Any ideas how I can improve it? You are welcome to use these materials if you want. I do still worry that the content learning is taking too much time. Anybody have any ideas on how to make sure this does not happen? I asked my students to tell me what sort of help they need with language in order to be better prepared to study subjects through the L2. They told me that ...

Level 4: Expert CLIL practitioner

Expert: integration is the norm		
My beliefs and understandings	What is visible to others	What colleagues can hear
I believe it is not only possible, but essential that I teach content and language at the same time. I am well aware of the intended learning outcomes of some of the subjects taught through the L2. My students and I need to discuss progress made in achieving both content and language outcomes. They need feedback on both content and language learning. I think it is important to identify what constitutes general academic language common to several content subjects (e.g. functions such as explaining causes and consequences, hypothesising, inquiring collaboratively and synthesising), and teach this language. Where possible, I work with my content colleagues to see if we can develop an integrated curriculum (e.g. finding concepts, topics and materials that could be integrated into language lessons). I create cross-curricular learning opportunities for students. I believe that as students expand their repertoire of learning skills they become more effective learners of content and language.	... me partaking in professional development in CLIL. ... me cooperating weekly with one or more subject teacher(s) to plan for the integration of content and language, as well as the sequencing of language learning. ... me richly scaffolding both content and language input and output. ... me discussing intended language and content learning outcomes with students and measuring progress in achieving them. This includes drawing conclusions about how to move forward. ... my students and I also focusing on the content and the quality of thought related to that content. ... my students and I reflecting on and solving language problems as they arise. ... me drawing students' attention to the characteristics and component parts of academic language. ... me using exploratory talk and writing on an ongoing basis in order to help students clarify their thinking (develop lines of reasoning). ... me explicitly teaching and assessing the use of language learning skills.	My students speaking, reading and writing more, and generally being more active and doing 'more work' than me during the lesson. My students being required to learn the content, and be precise when they speak and write about it. My students explaining and defending their lines of reasoning in relation to the content. *Would you like to come and see what I am doing in my class, and give me feedback?* Let's build a joint inventory of language learning skills and agree on how we will teach these. Can we agree on some common language outcomes for the Year I students? When I had students first draft their essay in their L1 and then write it in their L2, I got much richer language and better developed lines of reasoning. I think I will continue having students sometimes translanguage. I regularly provide feedback on content learning. I do give some marks to content and critical thinking about it, but most of the marks go to language.

I explore and take into account student interests. I seek to build learner autonomy with a dual focus on content and language.	... me exploring and taking into account students' interests and needs. ... me systematically enquiring about what language support students need to cope with learning content through their L2. ... my students sometimes translanguage (e.g. writing a draft in their L1, but the final paper in their L2).	Sometimes students can get lost marks back if they show they have learned the content or can improve their lines of argument. (speaking to subject teacher) How could we co-operate this week? What generic functions are students having difficulty with (e.g. synthesising, building a line of enquiry, justifying, separating fact from opinion)?

CONCLUSION

This chapter has argued that language classes play a vital multifaceted role in CLIL. They too need to walk the talk when it comes to CLIL and integrate new meaningful content into their lessons. Whilst learning new content, students will be exposed to and supported in using a much wider and richer range of language than would be the case in a purely language-focused language class. This is believed to contribute substantially to language learning in particular if students are discussing content that they consider meaningful, and if they are being challenged and supported in thinking critically about that content. In addition to the benefit of learning new content, students in language classes will benefit from developing their capacity to think critically by learning to undertake generic functions such as developing well-structured lines of reasoning that include evidence and examples. Furthermore, as CLIL students in language classes wish and need to learn language that is of practical use in their content classes, there is a need to cooperate with one or more CLIL content teachers. This cooperation means that language curricula are to some extent aligned with helping students to meet the language needs they have when studying content subjects through their L2. As opposed to teaching this language in a decontextualized manner, language classes can integrate content-compatible material that a language teacher feels comfortable working with. Alternatively, students can undertake enquiry-based learning or be supported in exploring questions of social justice.

4

Academic language

Connections

How this chapter connects to other concepts in the book:

Affect

Academic language can overwhelm and thus frighten students. This can put them off (alienate them from) learning.

Objectives/outcomes

Intended language learning **outcomes** can make explicit and visible the elements of academic language that need to be learned.

Students and teachers can then plan how this academic language will be learned.

Learning skills

Language learning skills can help students to take more responsibility for the learning of academic language, and help them to learn substantially more language.

Assessment

By measuring progress in the learning of academic language students are more likely to value its use and concentrate of improving their command of it. Teachers need this data in order to plan for continue language development in their students.

Cognitive load

If heavy new content and academic language is being learned at the same time, it will overwhelm working memory, unless rich **scaffolding** is provided. The scaffolding includes breaking down learning content and language into a logical step-by-step progression, while still keeping students cognitively engaged.

Critical thinking

Critical thinking is improved through the precise use of academic language.

When students are supported in thinking critically about language as well as content, they are likely to improve their learning of both.

High expectations

If one assumes that a student who has a poor command of academic language is not capable of learning new language and substantial new content through the L2, this can become a self-fulfilling prophecy.

By contrast, high expectations regarding language use, critical thinking and content learning are likely to foster critical thinking and the learning of content and language.

Academic language is nobody's mother tongue.
(Bourdieu and Passeron, 1994)

A command of academic language underpins student achievement.
(Murphy, 2016)

Social language	**Academic language**
We got some strange results from the experiment so we decided to do it again to make sure we hadn't made any mistakes the first time.	Post-experiment data analysis revealed several unexpected results. Therefore, the experiment was carefully repeated to test its reliability.

INTRODUCTION AND CHAPTER NAVIGATOR

Academic language can leave students feeling as if their mother tongue has been turned into a foreign language. If students have difficulty understanding and using this 'foreign' language in a given subject, this can create a major barrier to learning. Not only can this impede learning in the short-term, but it can lead to long-term frustration and alienation from schooling.

We do not expect students to learn a foreign language on their own. Similarly, we should not expect students to learn academic language without **systematically supporting them in seeing it, understanding it (the input), and using it (the output) to speak and write about subject matter**. This is particularly the case when students are learning content through a second language.

This chapter explores what academic language is, and how it can be made explicit and visible to students so they know what language they are expected to use and learn. More specifically, this chapter answers the following questions:

- In broad terms, what is academic language?
- In broad terms, what drives the learning of academic language?
- Why is academic language important?
- How is academic language tied with literacy?
- What are the component parts of academic language and how can these be taught?

- How can teachers determine what academic language students need to learn?

Finally, key points in the chapter are summarised in the conclusion.

IN BROAD TERMS, WHAT IS ACADEMIC LANGUAGE?

Academic language is the language of schooling. It **is the language needed for learning**. That includes the language needed for understanding teachers and learning materials, for interacting with fellow students and teachers in order to co-construct meaning related to the curriculum, and for applying learning. More specifically, Zwiers (2008) defines academic language as 'the set of words, grammar, organizational strategies used to describe complex ideas, higher order thinking processes, and abstract concepts'. Academic language is also the special language or registers of language used by adults working in diverse professions. Academic language can be contrasted with social language used for social discourse (Cummins, 2001).

Good schools constantly help students to sort out and stretch their thinking. In order to improve their capacity to think, students are encouraged to operate at the outer limits of their current ability to reason – to process abstractions, facts, opinions, options, concepts and ideas, to think critically. This involves not only learning, manipulating and applying new content concepts, but also exploring, using and learning new academic language associated with those concepts. Content and language are inextricably tied together. Ultimately, schools expect students to express their thinking through academic language. Moreover, schools use academic language to assess students' learning. Thus, as academic language is the language of assessment, it can also be said to be imbued with power, and hold one of the keys to academic success.

IN BROAD TERMS, WHAT DRIVES THE LEARNING OF ACADEMIC LANGUAGE?

In order to learn academic language, students require **rich comprehensible language input**. This is particularly the case when working through a second language. More specifically, students need:

- to be helped to see the component parts of academic language
- to be exposed to the same academic language multiple times.

Multiple exposure to the same academic language is required before this new language can be stored in and retrieved from long-term memory.

Multiple exposure to the same academic language needs to be integrated with meaningful tasks. Meaningful tasks provide manifold opportunities to use academic language **(to produce rich output).** More specifically, students need to have:

- well-scaffolded, rich opportunities to use academic language for speaking, reading and writing for authentic/meaningful purposes.

Meaningful or authentic activities involve students participating in thinking critically, in making connections and in the planning of activities/tasks. More specifically, activities/tasks are particularly meaningful if students: (1) are supported in thinking critically and making connections between new learning and previous learning, (2) are guided in integrating knowledge from several school subjects, (3) are asked to explore connections between what is being learnt and their own lives, (4) negotiate decisions pertaining to the learning process for which they will be held accountable, (5) do their planned work undertaking the necessary research, (6) evaluate both the learning process and outcomes. Thus, meaningful tasks do not just foster learning, but also encourage **learner autonomy.**

Meaningful activities call for a move well beyond the word and sentence level to building a narrative about content concepts and ideas. From a content perspective, the consequence of not building narratives is that students' thinking and understanding will likely be shallow. School content class narratives also call for a rich and precise use of language. From the perspective of language development, the consequence of not building narratives is that students are not likely to be good at doing this. Building narratives creates opportunities for students to sort out their thinking in relation to a curriculum topic. This sorting-out process also helps students find, practise and learn the language they do not yet know. Narratives, be they short or long, also provide an opportunity for teachers to assess students' current understandings and to see what further content and language support students require.

Furthermore in CLIL, from a language perspective, students also require support in taking responsibility for their learning of academic language. More specifically, students need to be taught:

- to reflect systematically on the meaning of words, terms and phrases
- to reflect on the purpose of a text or other forms of communication they work with or create, and the sort of language that that communication requires

- the language needed to work with other students while doing group work tasks (e.g. the language for seeking out differences of opinion and for analysing data or opinions)
- to understand language learning outcomes and to assess progress in achieving those targets
- language learning skills (e.g. deconstructing words, reading a text several times for different purposes).

Next, the chapter discusses why academic language is important and then goes on to describe in greater detail the component parts of academic language.

WHAT ROLE DOES ACADEMIC LANGUAGE PLAY IN STUDENT ACHIEVEMENT?

There is a strong correlation between student achievement and having a good command of language, in particular academic language. Schools where subject teachers systematically support language learning (including their students' proficient use of the language of their subject – e.g. Mathematics or History) see higher levels of student motivation and learning (National Academies of Sciences, Engineering and Medicine, 2017).

The above implies that **content and language learning are deeply interdependent** (see Chapter 2). Both are central to improving thinking and learning. By using language to interact with others to discuss meaningful content, people improve their ability to think and that in turn can lead to an improvement in their ability to learn.

Academic language is also the language used to assess students. A core principle of summative assessment (assessment that leads to marks and decisions about further education) is that **one should not assess something that has not been taught**. If care is taken to teach the subject matter content to students then it is only right that the language used to assess students' content knowledge should also be explicitly taught. In particular this is the case in CLIL contexts where students are being taught content subjects through their L2.

Thus, **academic language needs to be proactively taught by the subject teacher** both in classes taught through the L1 and in those taught through the L2. The language teacher has an important supportive role to play in this. However, subject teachers carry the majority of the responsibility for helping students to learn and develop proficiency in using the academic language of their subject. Students require systematic, ongoing support throughout their schooling in seeing, using and learning L1, and in particular, L2, and L3 academic language. This support in learning academic language will help students understand, use and recall the subject matter content, be that in the Maths, Sciences, or History.

On a more abstract level, but with major consequences for students and society at large, **academic language is the language of power** (Cummins, 2000). Access to and success in higher education, high-paying jobs, and social mobility are all in part tied to possessing a command of academic language, to being 'highly literate' (OECD, 2013). Effective participation in many aspects of economic, political and social life are tied to a large extent to our ability to express ourselves.

HOW IS ACADEMIC LANGUAGE TIED TO ACADEMIC LITERACY?

Having a command of academic language is about much more than learning a series of words and phrases used in various school subjects. A command of academic language is demonstrated through literacy – the ability to read and write – in a register of language that is used by those working in a given area of study, be that Biology, History or Maths. Each subject places substantial expectations pertaining to language and work practices on students studying their subject area. For example, the following definition of scientific literacy is built on the PISA Consortium and the Pan-Canadian Assessment Program (O'Grady et al., 2016) definitions of scientific literacy:

Scientific literacy:

- involves a set of evolving competencies
- is focused on **understanding** the nature of science.

Understanding in science is achieved through:

- using science-related attitudes, skills and knowledge to conduct enquiries, to solve problems and to reason scientifically:
    - building logical, evidence-based arguments and explanations
    - addressing issues of relevance, reproducibility, validity, integrity and accuracy
    - recognising the tentative nature of knowledge claims and the need to be sceptical
    - establishing criteria and evaluating results against those criteria
- taking account of current, possibly emergent (dynamic) context

- exploring relationships between science, technology, society and the environment
- connecting to, and if necessary, adjusting existing knowledge
- communicating orally and in written forms clearly and succinctly in a manner that respects disciplinary norms and habits of mind. This includes the appropriate use of digital tools.

The **purpose of understanding** in science is:

- to make evidence-based decisions about science-related issues
- to advance existing knowledge and understanding
- to enrich/improve one's own life and the lives of others.

The complex nature of literacy reinforces the fact that students are expected to operate with a high level of abstraction while thinking critically at the outer limits of their current capacity to reason. That requires academic language that students rarely possess when first entering the classroom. This language needs to be taught when learning through an L1, but especially when teaching through the L2.

EXAMPLES OF THE COMPONENT PARTS OF ACADEMIC LANGUAGE

Once we can see and articulate the component parts of academic language, we are better placed to make this language explicit and visible to students. We can then pro-actively scaffold student understanding, learning and further use of academic language and related subject matter content. The table on the following page draws out key elements of academic language. These are discussed in greater detail below. Some teaching ideas are also provided for each proposed element.

Words and word families

Although academic language consists of words such as those in the table below, it is a considerably more complex concept.

Social *versus* academic language	Social *versus* academic language
make *vs* produce say *vs* state get *vs* obtain talk about *vs* discuss, explain	rain *vs* precipitation cattle-like *vs* bovine fattening *vs* calorifacient pill *vs* medication

Academic language

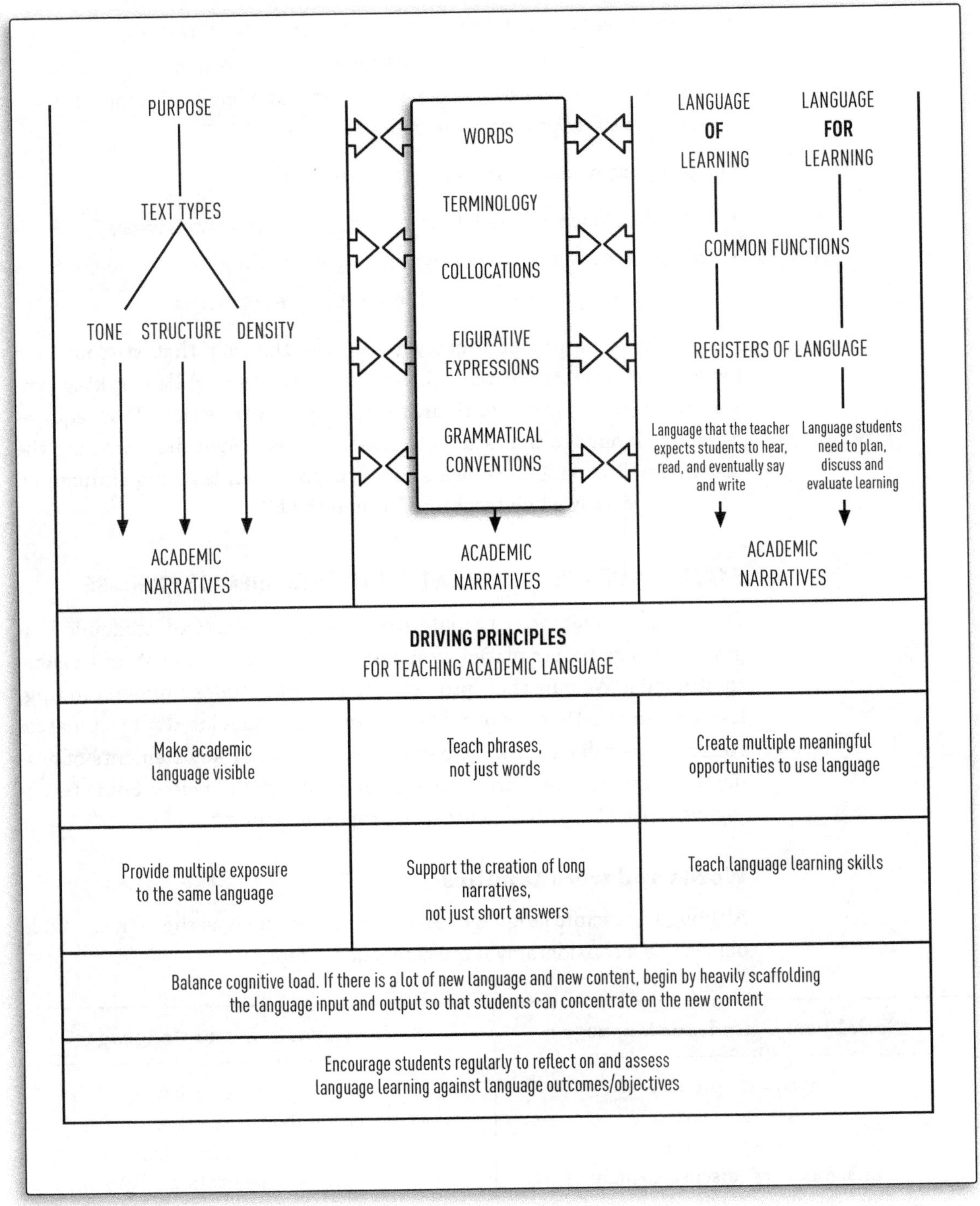

Nonetheless, the discussion begins at the word level and then moves to word families and in the next section to terminology. In contrast to academic language, social language uses a much smaller number of words. It is thought that 1000 words plus proper nouns (the names of people and places) make up 90% of all conversations in English (Cobb and Horst, 2004). So social language consists of a limited number of words that are heard frequently. By contrast, **academic language in English consists of 8000–9000 word families** (Schmitt, Schmitt and Mann, 2011; also see Hu and Nation, 2000). Word families share the same root (e.g. dispenser ⇨ to dispense, to dispense with, dispensability, dispensable, indispensable; eligible ⇨ ineligible, eligibility, ineligibility; skill ⇨ skilfully, skilled, unskilled). If a student knows the root of a word, that is no guarantee that they will understand the word. **Many students require teacher support in noticing the root of an unfamiliar word** and decoding the meaning of words belonging to the same family. To raise language awareness, students can be asked which other words they know in a language family. In addition they can be asked to experiment with the root of a word to see if it will take a suffix like '-tion' (e.g. operate ⇨ operation) or turn a verb into an adjective and/or a noun (to use ⇨ useful ⇨ usefulness).

A reader needs to know 98% of the words in an academic text to understand it (ibid.). In addition, students often need to know not just the definition (the denotative meaning) of a word, but also the associations that a word evokes (the connotative meaning). For example, Wall Street may be a street in the financial district of New York City, but it is also used in texts as a symbol of 'economic power' and 'wealth'. It personifies wealthy business people. An owl may be a symbol of wisdom in Ancient Greece, and in many contemporary English-speaking cultures, yet it was/is a symbol of fertility in Wales, and an omen of death for the Ojibwa.

Most 'academic' words are not frequently heard and used outside of school in social situations. This means that many 'academic' words will be unfamiliar to students particularly in the L2. Students need to be supported in noticing and learning these. The next section discusses terminology that can be formed of one or more words.

Terminology

In order to understand the meaning of some 'academic' words, a student requires knowledge of many other words. Terminology is a case in point. A term can take the form of:

- a word (e.g. genes)

- a compound word (e.g. photosynthesis), or
- a multi-word expression (e.g. black holes, an abandoned dirt road, an immune response, a low-fat diet or the somatosensory system).

Terminology can be particularly complex and dense in meaning. A term often embodies a concept. That concept may also be part of larger conceptual system. For example, the primary somatosensory cortex contains third-order neurons, second-order neurons and first-order neurons. In order to understand any new term being taught, a student may need to be aware of and understand several other terms or concepts. See the box below for a sample **deconstruction** of one scientific term – *hybridisation*.

The deconstruction of scientific language: one term

Cambridge Grade 11 Chemistry contains the term **hybridisation** (in organic compounds). Hybridisation is a process. The process of hybridisation consists of overlapping atomic orbitals to form a set of new orbitals suitable for bonding. As can be seen from this definition, this one term 'hybridisation' contains in it numerous concepts and is associated with several other terms (see below). This is the case with many scientific terms. Each of the terms associated with the primary term being learned (in this case hybridisation**)** requires definition and opportunities for students to use the concepts and terms in order to ensure comprehension, and correct future use.

Some of the concepts and other terms which require unpacking to understand hybridisation include:

- *hybrid*
- *atom*
- *carbon atom*
- *atomic orbital*
- *electron molecular orbital (or MO)*
- *molecule*
- *saturated organic compound*
- *covalent bonds*
- *double bonds*
- *triple bonds*
- *π-bonds*
- *probability*

In other words, giving students the translation of a term in the CLIL language may not be enough to ensure understanding. Students need to understand related terms and concepts. It can be helpful for students to distinguish simple words from terms and to place these in a conceptual system. The following graphic organiser identifies the concept of biodiversity and begins to flesh out the conceptual system by naming three related terms which represent types of biodiversity.

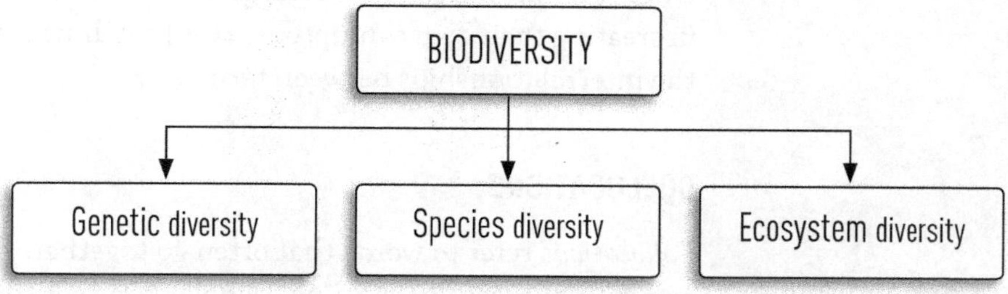

As an alternative, students can be asked to find the three types of biodiversity in a text or while watching a video on the topic, and to fill in the graphic organiser below. This not only helps them to learn the new terms, but to locate these in a conceptual system.

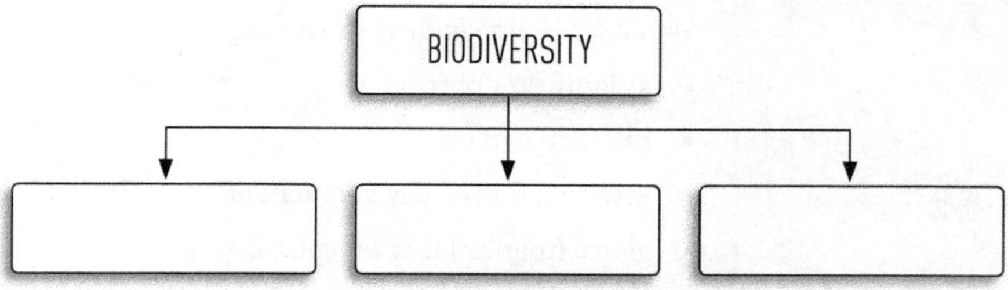

The complexity can be increased as necessary, allowing the students to draw out the key term and the larger conceptual system. By connecting terms to one another in a logical manner, it becomes easier to see the interrelationships, and recall them and the interrelated concepts. This helps students build a boarder narrative about the topic.

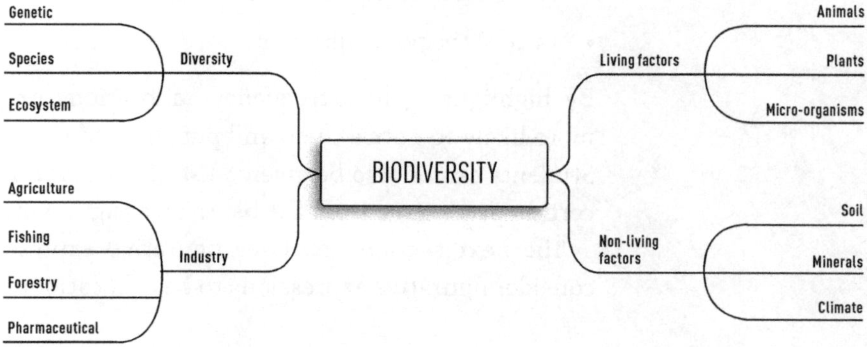

Once students have used several graphic organisers they can be supported in creating their own conceptual maps that draw out key terminology and the interrelationships between terms.

COLLOCATIONS

Collocations refer to words that often go together. They can be considered common phrases. By learning a whole phrase or collocation as one whole item, students are more likely to recall it than if they were to learn single words that they would later need to string together. Some examples of collocations would be:

- results are shown in Figure 1
- that accounts for
- low, average or high life expectancy
- a rise/decline in drug use among
- a significant portion of
- call for a ban on
- essential for the development of
- global financial market volatility
- strong export demand led by
- the majority of respondents
- the results obtained by/from/in/with
- the ceasefire came into effect at
- production came to a standstill
- concerns have been raised about
- is/are essential for the development of
- raise(s) the possibility that.

By highlighting high-frequency collocations or phrases, students are more likely to notice them and put them to use in their own narratives. Students can be also be given a list of collocations and be asked to use a certain percentage from the list in an assignment.

The next section discusses figurative expressions. Some academics consider figurative expressions to be collocations.

Figurative expressions

Figurative expressions are used in academic discourse to help listeners and readers imagine concepts or phenomena in numerous subjects including the Sciences. Three types of figurative expressions used in academic discourse are:

Analogies – a comparison of two things typically for the purpose of clarification but doing so without using a figure of speech – e.g. *Normally, tectonic plates move about as fast as fingernails grow; that is, 10–40 mm per year.*

Idioms – a group of words that has a particular meaning that is not immediately apparent from the meaning of the words on their own – e.g. *A blessing in disguise* meaning something that is only later recognised as useful.

Similes – a comparison of dissimilar or similar entities – e.g. *It burst like a bubble.*

Figurative expressions can be a real challenge for students to understand. A few out of the hundreds of commonly used figurative expressions are listed below, with domains of use indicated in parentheses:

- *Penny wise and pound foolish* (Economics, Geography, Political Science)
- *Teething problems* (Business Studies, Economics, Geography, History, Political Science)
- *The breadwinners* (Business Studies, Economics, Geography, History)
- *Tip of the iceberg* (Business Studies, Economics, Geography, History, Science)
- *To see light at the end of the tunnel* (Business Studies, Economics, Political Science)

To foster student comprehension, the first step is to be aware of figurative expressions oneself, and to make sure the expressions are explicitly noticed, and if need be, taught when they arise. However, students can also be encouraged to use imagery to support an argument or explanation. For example, a teacher can set the following language objective for students: to be able to use analogies in scientific descriptions, including explaining their limitations. Students would then need to present their analogies and to receive feedback on them.

Density

Academic English can be considered the art of *efficiency* and *efficacy* – a rich quantity of information in as few words as possible. In other words, academic texts tend to be dense in meaning. The density of an academic text can be calculated as the percentage of 'content' words 'packed into the grammatical structure' of a sentence (Halliday, 1993). Content words (nouns, adjectives, verbs, adverbs) are those that carry meaning related to the topic being explored in a content class such as Geography or Business Studies. For example, in the following sentence all the words carry significant meaning:

Unforeseen increases in costs could lead to negative net monthly cash flows.

Teachers can support students in decoding the sentence by first breaking it into three separate densely constructed sets of ideas and secondly by helping unpack the three sets of ideas:

- Unforeseen increases in costs
- could lead to
- negative net monthly cash flows.

This can be done by asking students to list what these 'unforeseen increases' might consist of or by inserting synonyms or an explanation into the text as was done in the *CUP AS and A Level Business Coursebook* – 'Unforeseen increases in costs – a breakdown of a delivery van that needs to be replaced, or a dip in predicted sales income, or a competitor lowering prices unexpectedly – could lead to negative net monthly cash flows' (Stimpson and Farquharson, 2015).

Grammatical conventions

Content teachers do not regularly explicitly and systematically teach grammar. That said, if students are stumbling in expressing themselves correctly and that stumbling block is a grammar point then content teachers may find it is worth taking the time to briefly teach the given point.

For example, if students are analysing causes and consequences and do not know the rules for using 'if' clauses, simply providing a few examples and asking students to follow the examples could save all concerned time and frustration. After teaching the point, if students continue to make errors with 'if' clauses, they can be prompted to self-correct using model sentences displayed on the board such as those shown below.

Causes and consequences: The use of 'if' clauses
Description of a current situation If this conflict is not resolved, people will continue to flee the conflict and migrate to neighbouring countries. **Description of a past situation** If the authorities had limited the construction of hotels along the coast, there would likely have been less destruction of coastal mangroves and therefore less flooding.

Another common grammar point that may require attention in content classes is the use of **active voice** over **passive voice**. Students' attention can be drawn to the difference between the two. Providing a few examples such as the ones below, and asking students to analyse these, will help them understand how to recognise and create passive and active voice sentences. Furthermore, by analysing the dangers and benefits of passive voice versus the dangers and benefits of active voice, the students are more likely to understand when to use each one for which effect.

Passive voice	Active voice	Analysis
Slavery was legally largely abolished in the USA in 1863 by executive order.	President Lincoln used an executive order to largely legally abolish slavery in the USA in 1863.	In the passive voice sentence, it is unclear who legally largely abolished slavery.
Asbestos used in the insulation of the pipes and walls of the building is currently being removed by the asbestos elimination team.	The Asbestos Inc. asbestos elimination team is removing the asbestos used in the insulation of the pipes and walls of the building.	In the active voice, the 'doer' of the action is the subject of the sentence. More information is provided. The active voice sentence may be easier to process as it follows the common pattern of many sentences. Passive voice is often used when the responsible party is unknown.
Research proves that bilingualism can delay the onset of dementia by 3.9 years.	Bialystock and her colleagues (2007) report that bilingualism can delay the onset of dementia by 3.9 years.	The passive voice sentence does not explain whose research is being discussed. In most disciplines, one study is often thought to be insufficient proof. Notice that in the active voice sentence the verb 'prove' has been changed to 'report'.

Some grammatical conventions used in content classes may be counter-intuitive. A case in point is the use of the past tense versus the historical present. In History, students may sometimes be expected to use the historical present as opposed to using various forms of the past tense. In that case, there is merit in drawing students' attention to when, how and why the historical present is used. On a practical level, that can involve asking students to compare and contrast two texts such as those below to help them understand the benefits of the historical present (e.g. the historical present may feel more dramatic; it is sometimes referred to as the *dramatic present*).

Past tense	**Historical present**
On 14 September 1822 the Russian army marched out of Moscow and Napoleon's army entered the city. On 15 September Napoleon arrived at the Kremlin. On the same day a massive fire took hold in Kitay-gorod, the cultural and historical centre of Moscow. The next day a firestorm threatened the Kremlin.	On 14 September 1822 the Russian army marches out of Moscow and Napoleon's army enters the city. On 15 September Napoleon arrives at the Kremlin. On the same day a massive fire takes hold in Kitay-gorod, the cultural and historical centre of Moscow. The next day a firestorm threatens the Kremlin.

Purpose

Academic language is driven by a purpose. That purpose is usually other than oneself. In other words, academic texts are usually not focused on the speaker or the writer but on analysis, concepts, context, concrete and/or abstract ideas, facts, evidence and relationships among various elements. Moreover, academic conversations, presentations or texts are directed at a specific audience. They aim to achieve a specific goal, and to reach well-grounded conclusions.

The purpose of a text will have an impact on the language used in it. Students will be better placed to reflect on purpose if they are asked to reflect on and articulate the purpose of any piece of writing they undertake. A short classroom discussion about how the purpose will influence the nature of the text can lead to improved student writing. For example, if the purpose of a text that students are writing is to offer a summary to fellow scientists, students could simply name the type of research conducted and only list key findings. Terminology would not need to be defined. The students can assume that the reader has significant background knowledge.

If the purpose of an academic discussion, presentation or text is to offer an *analysis* of an issue in Urban Geography for local government officials then students would be expected to define the problem or situation, and to draw out the component elements of a complex issue and explain how the elements relate to one another. It would likely have an unemotional and factual tone, avoiding words that could be considered vague such as *interesting* or *difficult*. It may avoid abstractions such as *culture, good, honesty* and *introspection*, or seek to define any abstractions that are used. The analysis might include compound sentences with connectives to signal a relationship between two elements. The analysis would likely finish with a conclusion.

If students are comparing and contrasting two products for company executives it will differ greatly from a text aimed at consumers. In writing for a business audience of insiders, the language would be much more business-like, using business terminology and turns of phrase common to business environments (e.g. *During the last quarter; the holiday quarter...; During Q4 ...; Our competitors have ...; This feature makes our app the most popular in the industry)*. A sample scaffold for comparing and contrasting two products for an internal company report is offered below.

Language required for comparing and contrasting

Introduction

This report provides an analysis of two products – our company's product A and company X's product B. The two products have been analysed from the following perspectives: consumer price, production costs, market share, aesthetics, features, efficacy, chemical composition, fragrance and size.

Body of text

The fundamental difference between the two products is ...

Products A and B also differ in regard to ...

Product A has 42% market share...

We need to be aware that Product B is increasing its market share by 10% per annum.

This difference has major implications for ...

Thus, product A can be classified as ...

Product B can be characterised by ...

The difficulty with such characterisation is that ...

While product A costs substantially more than product B, it has the advantage of ...

Our/their pricing policy ...

We/they have several new related apps in development.

The new apps should allow us to claw back market share.

Conclusion

In conclusion, the authors of the report suggest ...

By making the purpose of a writing assignment visible, and discussing how a given text is structured and the tone of the language that is to be used, and by drawing out some of the terminology and phraseology students are expected to use, students will be better placed to use academic language to achieve the intended learning outcomes.

Moreover, research tells us if students produce text for an audience other than the teacher, and the purpose of the text being produced is seen as meaningful, that will lead to a better and more explicit use of academic language (Bartolomé, 1998). **Purpose has power!**

Text types and structure

The purpose of a text is closely tied to text types and the structure of the text type. Various text types such as blogs, business letters, business plans, compositions, diaries, essays, film and video-clip scripts, guides, information bulletins, journal articles, laboratory reports, learning logs, magazine articles, newspaper articles, papers, PowerPoint presentations, public reports, podcasts, poems, portfolios, research reports, short stories, summaries, textbooks and Tweets have a particular purpose and to some extent a codified structure and tone. The structure of these text types varies greatly. If we expect students to use these text types and structures, they have a right to see exemplars that make visible the expected structure of these text types at two levels – at the level of an entire text type (e.g. see lab report structure below) and at the level of parts of each text type (e.g. see the structure of an essay introduction below). Only then is it possible to ask students to create their own versions.

For example, students can be told that in many English-speaking contexts a good introduction to an essay:

- has an introductory sentence that captures the reader's attention
- explains the purpose of the essay
- defines any complex terminology
- states the main ideas to be discussed and the order of that discussion.

However, in order to ensure deeper processing of this structure, students can be asked to analyse exemplars of three introductory paragraphs. First, students can be asked to classify these as a) excellent, b) good but needing improvement, or c) weak. Second, they can be asked to determine criteria for a developing a high-quality paragraph. Third, their analyses would be discussed in class and the criteria could be agreed upon.

An exemplar of such a task can be found in **Chapter 5**: *Scaffolding Content and Language Input and Output.*

Another example of a substructure that could sit within a larger structure is how a line of reasoning is often developed, be that in an essay, presentation or classroom discussion (see the figure below).

Scaffold for developing a line of reasoning

Introduction
Introduce the argument to the reader e.g. why it is a particularly relevant topic; why it is controversial.

↓

Reasons against the argument
State the position, evidence (available body of facts or information) and the reasons (causes, explanation or justification).

↓

Reasons in favour of the argument
State the position, the evidence and the reasons

↓

Conclusion
Summarise the two sides of the argument, state your own point of view and explain your reasoning

Students can also benefit from seeing examples of the structure of an entire text type. For example, the typical structure of laboratory reports includes the following sections:

- Title Page (the name of the experiment, name of authors and date)
- Abstract (aims, summary of purpose, methodology, major findings, significance)
- Introduction
- Methods and Materials (including equipment)
- Experimental Procedure
- Results

- Discussion
- Conclusion
- References
- Appendices

In order to turn the above example into a task encouraging students to think critically about structure, they can be asked to follow the example of the first two sections, which explain the structure of each section in parentheses, and detail the structure of the remaining sections.

As students create text for the various parts of a defined structure, they are likely to need support in tying together these various parts or in creating the bridges needed to move smoothly from one part to the next. Thus, it is likely that students need to also explicitly be taught the **language for sequencing**. This includes words and phrases such as: 'the process begins with/by ...'; 'first'; 'initially'; 'to begin with'; 'second'; 'third'; 'subsequently'; 'previously'; 'from thereon'; 'the above does not take into account'; 'another issue is a lack of ...'; 'based on ...'; 'a similar phenomena can be found in ...'; 'finally ...'; 'it is possible to conclude that ...'; 'in conclusion'. In addition, **connectives** for creating bridges between sentences and paragraphs likely need to be taught. These include: 'and', 'although', 'at the same time', 'however', 'in addition', 'furthermore', 'nevertheless', and 'thus'.

Although it is helpful for students to concentrate separately on structure and words and phrases for sequencing and connecting various bits of text, the purpose of why an entire text is being written also needs to be kept at the forefront of their minds. This helps students to avoid approaching writing simply as a mechanical exercise. For example, when it comes to laboratory reports students can be reminded that these are driven by a higher threefold purpose:

- to provide a record of the experiments and related data
- to provide sufficient information to reproduce the experiment or to build on the data set
- to analyse the data and to draw conclusions and make a proposal for further research.

Although students need to be introduced step-by-step to the various aspects of academic language, they eventually have to be able to maintain a focus on the multiple aspects of academic language. In other words, they need to focus on the correct and appropriate use of words, terminology, connectives and phrases. In addition, they need to maintain a focus on the audience and purpose of their communication, and the structure of their output.

The scaffold that follows synthesises several aspects of academic language. Having students write a newspaper article requires them to succinctly summarise their learning. This scaffold below describes for students the typical structure of a newspaper article. The scaffold also points out that many readers do not finish reading an article. This implies that the purpose of the article needs to be made immediately apparent to the reader. More specifically, the key point of an article needs to be presented right from the outset. Finally, some of the language associated with writing a newspaper is also shown. In this case, the students were working on an article on the consequences of the decline in three species – bees, corals and sharks.

Newspaper article structure (inverted pyramid)

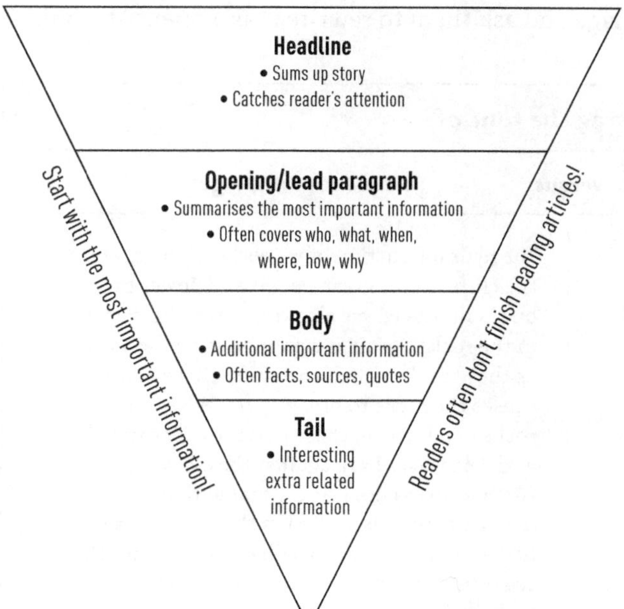

USEFUL LANGUAGE

Opening or lead paragraph

... play a very important role in ...
... considered by scientists to be a 'keystone' species ...
... their decline can lead to (is leading to) ...

Body (several paragraphs)

The primary cause ...
... important for human survival ...
Some xxx scientists believe that ...
Possible consequences include ...
The UN reports that ...
... had/have a positive impact ...
... had/have a negative impact ...
In the absence of ...

Tail

Where xxx are in decline, ...
Where xxx are eliminated, the ...
xxx have disappeared from ...

Finally, structure can be culturally dependent. A PowerPoint presentation in the United States of America might give the conclusions near the start of the presentation while in Germany the purpose and methodology of an investigation would likely be presented in detail before the conclusions (Meyer, 2014).

Tone and de-contextualisation

Academic texts usually have a particular **tone**. The purpose of a text and its structure may influence that tone. For example, an essay may use more emotive and colourful language than a government or laboratory report. Yet, many academic texts (e.g. articles, reports, textbooks) read by students may have a common tone (e.g. unemotional, highly precise, lacking in personal involvement, sparse use of synonyms, adjectives and adverbs).

Students will benefit from having their attention drawn to the tone of academic language. For example, this can be done by asking students to analyse the difference between two texts that describe the same topic as exemplified in the table below. Another option is to provide students with a text in social language and ask them to rewrite it as a scientist would.

Exploring the tone of	
Social language *versus*	**Academic language**
The sea is just swallowing up our coastline. It is just gobbling it up. Storms and big waves are the biggest culprits. The waves just crash against the cliffs and eat away at them. The cliffs keep breaking up and falling in the sea. It's like they are just melting away. Soon there is going to be nothing left of our community.	The hydraulic action of waves breaking against the cliffs brings great weight and power to bear on them. The waves also trap air in the cracks in the rock. The air is compressed by the waves as they break against the cliffs. This eventually causes the rocks to break apart. When the rocks break down, these particles are carried with the waves back against the cliffs causing further corrosion. It is estimated that unless sea defences are constructed in the near future, a fifth of our community will disappear into the sea over the next 10 years. (based on Cambers and Sibely, 2015)

In addition, most school subjects have what could be referred to as a low-context culture. This means that academic texts are often **decontextu-**

alized – they provide little background information. Therefore, meaning is often conveyed entirely by a limited number of linguistic clues, and it is assumed that the reader has considerable previous knowledge about a given topic. For example, in Mathematics a text may state that a given value has two significant figures but not explain what the term 'value' means or why there are only two significant figures. In other words, the language of Mathematics may be precise, but it may not give background information that the reader is thought to possess. The role of educators is to never assume that the students understand the terms, concepts and context, but instead to check for and scaffold understanding.

Language *of* learning versus language *for* learning

Teachers often concentrate on teaching the language used in texts and presentations. This is the language **of** learning (Coyle et al., 2010). However, the language **of** learning is insufficient for working with the content concepts being taught.

The language **for** learning is the language that students need to be able to use in order to discuss concepts being learnt (ibid.). The language **for** learning is the language of group work (e.g. asking for clarification, staying focused on the task, analysing, disagreeing, negotiating). The language **for** learning also includes the language needed to jointly solve problems, to conduct an experiment or to jointly interrogate a text, or to undertake collaborative enquiries. The table below illustrates some of this language.

Examples of language required for conducting group work	
Advising and persuading	**Clarifying/asking for more information**
✓ *What if we instead tried to ....* ✓ *The reason I suggest this is because...* ✓ *Can we weigh all three options, before we decide?* ✓ *That is a good point, but ...* ✓ *Maybe we need to gather more evidence before deciding. Let's look at ...*	✓ *I would find an example useful.* ✓ *Are you saying that ...* ✓ *Could you be more specific about ...* ✓ *What did you mean when you said ...* ✓ *Could you expand on what you said about ...* ✓ *What do you feel/think about this?*

(Continued over page)

Managing the discussion
✓ *Let's start by looking at ....* ✓ *So, I think we have agreed that ....* ✓ *Is this our joint decision?* ✓ *Does anyone disagree with this?* ✓ *Rashid, we haven't heard from you. What do you think about ... ?* ✓ *We are going off track.* ✓ *Can we come back to the objectives again?* ✓ *We only have 15 minutes left.* ✓ *The next thing we should do is ...* ✓ *Let's check our work against the evaluation criteria.* ✓ *Let's summarise what we have achieved so far.*

Students can benefit from having this language **for** learning made available to them electronically or on paper in order to facilitate peer collaborative work. Without having this language made visible to them, students are likely to do much of their classroom discussion through their L1.

Common functions

Each subject discipline expects students to undertake certain common functions. Some of these are common to many subject areas and some are common to a limited number of disciplines or just to one discipline. For example, in most if not all subjects students need to develop a line of reasoning, whereas they would be expected to mathematize a problem in a smaller number of subjects. Only Computer Science might expect students to analyse computer coding.

Some functions common to many subjects include:

- analysing (separating key elements and showing interrelationships)
- arguing for or against a standpoint in a calm manner
- categorising or grouping in a variety of ways
- comparing similar and dissimilar objects

- creating coherent statements that lead a reader or a listener to an adequate conclusion
- critically examining and evaluating information
- deciding on a hierarchy of causes
- defining concepts in the students' own words and providing proof to back up descriptions
- describing context, objects, situations and events
- developing a line of reasoning
- discussing a topic from different perspectives
- enquiring collaboratively
- evaluating results based on previously agreed-upon criteria
- explaining causes and consequences
- exploring issues from different perspectives
- extracting a line of argument, point of view, or perspective from a text or other media
- hypothesising
- identifying and explaining the structure of a text
- identifying, analysing and describing patterns
- interrogating a text to look for hidden meanings
- prioritising
- justifying conclusions and opinions
- reformulating another person's argument

Connection to critical thinking

Some of these functions require the verbalisation of a student's knowledge of the facts (surface level thinking). Knowledge of facts helps underpin critical thinking. However, **most of these functions require deeper order thinking** *(critical thinking). All of these functions require students to sort out their thinking and to express it in mini-narratives.*

- separating facts from opinions
- situating objects, events, people and phenomena in time and space
- summarising findings, concepts, interrelationships, processes, results and/or texts
- synthesising, comparing or contrasting texts
- testing assumptions
- weighing evidence
- verbalising data from diagrams, figures, formulae, maps, photographs and tables.

To successfully undertake these functions students need to: 1) identify the function, and 2) be shown the phrases associated with each function, and then be supported in using and learning them. Each function is evidenced by students being able to create a mini-narrative.

One example of some language associated with one of these functions (comparing and contrasting) follows in the table below.

Examples of language required for comparing and contrasting
X and Y are both similar and different in a number of ways.
Both X and Y are similar in that they ...
However, X and Y also differ in that they .../ in several ways.
X is comparable in size to Y, but their weight ...
X differs from Y in a number of respects. First, ...
By contrast, Y ...
X is more colourful/larger/robust/complex than
Mosquitos are more/less likely to .... than
Finally, almost four times as many ... than
In conclusion, it can be said that ...

Another example would be the language related to developing a line of reasoning. Part of this language can involve criticising another person's point of view. A sample of this language follows in the table opposite.

<table>
<tr><td colspan="3">Could you explain further what you mean by ...</td></tr>
<tr><td colspan="3">Would you please expand on that point / the point you made about ...</td></tr>
<tr><td rowspan="2">This
These views
The statement ... X ...</td><td>is/are</td><td>highly debatable.
highly speculative.
incorrect.
not always the case.
not necessarily true.
open to doubt.
opinion(s) not fact(s).
unlikely to be true.</td></tr>
<tr><td colspan="2">is /are not grounded in evidence.
is/are simply personal opinion.
is/are an exaggeration of the current situation.</td></tr>
<tr><td>I disagree with X when he</td><td>argues
claims
proposes
states
suggests
writes</td><td>that ...</td></tr>
</table>

Furthermore, many of the above-listed functions are interrelated. For instance, analysing, describing, evaluating and summarising may involve among other functions assessing, comparing and contrasting, characterising, locating and quantifying. These functions require students to use a wide range of language. A lack of this language can act as a barrier to discussion and learning. This is particularly the case in CLIL where students are operating through their L2. Thus, it is helpful to make explicit and visible the functions and the language needed to undertake these functions.

Simply making visible the language you expect students to use through charts/tables like the ones above and then giving students tasks that require them to use this language will make it easier for them to learn it.

This is the case whether one is trying to help students learn the *language **of** learning* or the *language **for** learning.*

Registers of language specific to a given school subject

Each subject domain such as Mathematics, History or Chemistry can be said to have its own specific academic language. The academic language of each subject area contains subject-specific terminology. The diagram below shows the diverse uses of the term 'mass' in several subjects.

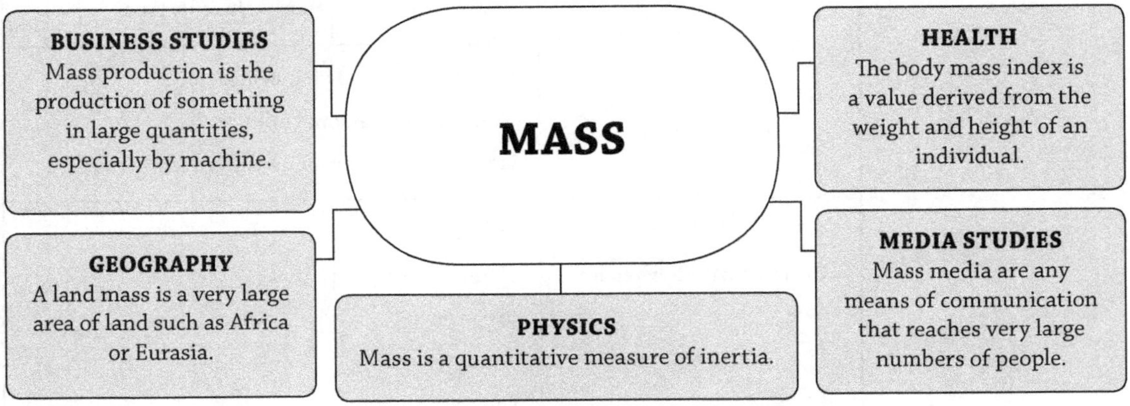

There are also subject-specific grammatical conventions. For example in Biology, Latin names of animals and plants are italicised. In addition, the first word (the genus) of Latin names of animals and plants is capitalised and the second word (the species) is in lower case – *Homo sapiens*. In History, the historical present is often used to describe events that took place in the past (see the previous section entitled 'Grammatical conventions' for an example of the historical past).

A very limited sampling of the language of Geography, History and Science follows in the table below. Some characteristics, terminology and phraseology will be common to several subjects.

Language of Geography	Language of History	Language of Science
Characteristics uses graphs, maps, photographs, tables and text contains many prepositions (e.g. in Asia, on Cuba) uses many colocations (e.g. methods of data collection) uses many acronyms such as MDC, EMDC, LEDC, NIC	**Characteristics** uses abstractions such as the 'underground economy' (both words are abstractions) summarises events and activities in a single term (e.g. industrial revolution) can use the present tense to discuss past events	**Characteristics** concrete, exact, seeks to allow only one possible interpretation unemotional and factual (uses adjectives frugally) information presented hierarchically in a logical and sequential manner
Subject-specific terms anemometer, drumlins, exfoliation, nucleated settlements, population pyramid, striations	**Subject-specific terms** absolute monarch; Intifada; Politburo; prohibition; serf; Sputnik, suffragette, WASP, Wehrmacht, yurt, xenophobia	**Subject-specific terms** acidity; amphibian; *bona fide*; carbohydrate; *in vitro*; mineral (inorganic); omnivore; probability; thorax;
Phraseology low/high pressure systems are usually associated with ...; the pattern of rural settlement is characterised by ...; the current level of economic develop-ment is indicated by ...; their distribution is dependent on ...	**Phraseology** X demonstrates bias by...; this can be considered a primary source because ...; one of the underlying causes was ...; X acted as a deterrent to ...; the evidence is questionable because ...	**Phraseology** based on the first example, it is possible to conclude ...; this is likely caused by ...; in comparison with a spider, an insect has ...; trial and error ...; by substituting the value of X in equation ...; the evidence suggests that ...

A much more extensive breakdown of the academic language of Geography, History, Mathematics and Science can be found in Appendices 1, 2, 3 and 4 (available online at www.cambridge.org/9781108400848).

Students need their attention drawn to the academic language of a given subject to ensure that they have noticed and understood it. They also need guided practice in using this language. See **Chapter 5**: *Scaffolding Content and Language Input and Output* and **Chapter 8**: *Learning Progressions* for more teaching strategies that support students in learning academic language.

HOW CAN TEACHERS DECIDE WHAT ACADEMIC LANGUAGE STUDENTS NEED TO LEARN?

In any content class, a **first step** in deciding what language students need to learn is to ask oneself **what the students must be able to understand, say and write** in order to demonstrate that they have achieved the learning outcomes. The lesson's or unit's intended content learning outcomes will give a strong indication of what students must be able to do. For example, perhaps the students needs to be able to:

- describe the structure of the heart (its anatomy)
- describe how the heart pumps and oxygenates the blood (its physiology).

In such a case, by the end of the unit on the heart the students may be expected to be able to say and write the following:

> *The heart is comprised of four chambers. The* ***upper chambers*** *are called* ***atria****. The singular of atria is atrium. The* ***lower chambers*** *are called* ***ventricles****. The atria are smaller than the ventricles.*
>
> *Anatomically, the heart is an example of* ***left-right symmetry****. The left and right sides of the heart are approximately mirror images of one another. The right side of the heart is separated from the left by the* ***two septa****. Septa are walls of tissue.* ***One septum*** *separates the left and right atria of the heart. This is called the inter-atrial septum. The other septum is called the inter-ventricular septum. The inter-ventricular septum separates the left and right ventricles of the heart. The two septa ensure that the* ***deoxygenated blood*** *never mixes with* ***oxygenated blood****.*
>
> *Deoxygenated blood enters the right side of the heart and is pumped to the lungs where it is oxygenated. The oxygenated blood, which returns from the lungs, enters the left side of the heart where it then returns to the body.* ***One-way valves*** *throughout the* ***circulatory system*** *ensure that blood flows in only one direction.*

If you have trouble finding this language it is possible to **first formulate the questions students should be able to answer by the end of a unit and then write the answers to those questions**. It is important that the answers to the questions form a narrative that reflects the achievement of the intended learning outcomes. This narrative would represent a summary of the content and academic language a teacher wishes his or her students to use. Once it is clear what language students need to learn an intended language learning outcome can be created to support planning for the learning of this language.

Once this language has been found then thought can be given to how student attention can be drawn to some of the categories of academic language discussed in the previous sections of this chapter. For example, word families (e.g. oxygen, oxygenated, deoxygenated); terminology (e.g. circulatory system, oxygenated blood); tone (e.g. precise, avoids pronouns and instead repeats nouns); language specific to heart anatomy (e.g. *septa* as opposed to walls); common functions (e.g. compare and contrast); purpose (e.g. explaining to other students and their families the structure of the heart and the relationship between the human circulatory and respiratory systems as part of a flyer on heart health); and the structure of the text (e.g. starts from major elements, then explains related minor elements, then explains the concepts of deoxygenation and oxygenation, then explains the movement of deoxygenated and oxygenated blood). A review of these categories can also help make visible the elements of academic language that students have not mastered and that they need to learn so they can also achieve the content learning outcomes. (See **Chapter 8:** *Learning Progressions,* for a series of activities on how this can be done.)

It is also important to **share average and high-quality student work** from previous years so students can get a strong sense of the academic language in all its richness (e.g. appropriate tone, density, phraseology and required structure), richness of language and required structure) that you expect them to use.

Another option is to collect key phrases, terms and other words students are expected to learn and use during a module or a course into one document. The students are given the document in hard copy or preferably in electronic form at the start of the course. Queta Valdez in Guadalajara, Mexico, has her students mark off each week what language they have had to use and learn that week. Students know that, as they are exposed to this language in class and in their readings, they must use it in texts, presentations and essays. Queta Valdez returns to this language with her students at the end of each course to have them notice and recall the language they have learnt.

Further ideas for scaffolding student understanding, use and learning of academic language can be found in **Chapter 5:** *Scaffolding Content and Language Input and Output* and **Chapter 8:** *Learning Progressions.*

CONCLUSION

Academic language is the language of schooling and importantly the language used to assess learning. Therefore, a command of academic language can help students unlock academic success, and access further education and jobs. Yet academic language is like a foreign language, and to learn it most students need systematic ongoing support in noticing and using it. In CLIL, where students are learning content through their L2 or L3, it is doubly important to make visible to students the academic language they are expected to use and learn. As a first important step, teachers can identify for themselves what it is they want their students to be able to say and write. Within that discourse, educators can identify the generic academic language and the academic language specific to their discipline that they want their students to learn. This academic language includes, among others: words; word families; terminology; phraseology; common functions; and the purpose and structure of academic texts. Students need help in seeing and using this language. It needs to be explicitly taught. Finally, its learning needs to be assessed even if it is not for a mark (see **Chapter 7:** *Assessment).*

5

Scaffolding content and language input and output

Connections

How this chapter connects to other concepts in the book:

Academic language

Academic language is the medium of instruction and learning. In particular, when working through an additional language students require systematic support to see, understand, use and learn academic language. That requires rich scaffolding (Gibbons, 2009).

Assessment

Even exemplary teachers tend to depend on the responses of a small number of key students as indicators of how learning is progressing (Nuthall, 2005). To make effective decisions about scaffolding, teachers need all students to consistently provide them with feedback about whether additional/different steps or scaffolds are required to keep all students on the intended learning path.

Critical thinking

Although scaffolding is meant to facilitate learning, it is also intended to encourage students to think deeply about both content and language, and the learning process. Critical thinking is key to student engagement.

Learning skills

Learning strategies are tools (scaffolds) that students can use to help them to progress along their learning path. Both generic and language-specific learning strategies are tools for increasing self-efficacy. Teaching learning strategies can help students to become more skilled learners and to take greater responsibility for their own learning.

High expectations

In the long-term, students tend to exert just enough effort to meet their teachers' expectations (Hattie, 2012). As a counterweight Hattie suggests high expectations.

Having high but realistic expectations of a student, and being confident in each student's capacity to succeed scaffolds a student's belief in him or herself.

Teachers can reinforce this belief by scaffolding step-by-step learning that allows a student to experience intellectual and affective engagement, and success in learning.

Examples of scaffolding	
Content and critical thinking (input & output)	**Language and critical thinking (output)**
• providing students with an advance organiser that diagrammatically depicts a key concept that will be learned, or alternatively, asking students to fill in a graphic organiser which summarises previous learning.	• providing students speaking frames with some potentially useful phrases and core elements of the structure of a debate such as opening statements, arguments for and against a stance and the presentation of evidence.
Content, self-efficacy and critical thinking (output)	**Learning skills, self-efficacy and critical thinking (output)**
• providing students with one to three sample business plans that they analyse for structure, tone, phraseology, and alignment of goals, product development, budget and marketing. Their analysis is discussed in class. Students then use their analysis as a basis to develop their own business plans.	• co-constructing with students a template to help them plan their essay writing. This could include steps such as: gathering information; deciding on a structure for the essay; and how self-and peer-assessment will take place so the draft versions of the essay can be improved.

INTRODUCTION AND CHAPTER NAVIGATOR

Scaffolding is a powerful tool for learning. In the challenging context of CLIL, **scaffolding** is not simply a powerful learning tool, it **is indispensable**. Scaffolding is the primary vehicle for helping students cope with the challenge of learning content through an additional language, and learning new related language. This is the input students need to learn. In addition, **scaffolding is the primary tool for fostering critical thinking** about both content and language. It can also foster rich student output. Ultimately, scaffolding helps students in CLIL programmes to engage with learning and meet curriculum expectations.

This chapter defines scaffolding and related concepts and offers practical tips for using scaffolding in order to improve student engagement and learning. More specifically the chapter:

- defines scaffolding whilst providing some short examples
- explains why scaffolding is indispensible in CLIL through two interrelated lenses – (1) the affective side of learning and (2) cognitive load
- describes the primary purpose of scaffolding and 14 different types of scaffolding
- provides a repertoire of content and language scaffolds which are organised under one or more of the 14 types of scaffolding.

WHAT IS SCAFFOLDING?

Effective scaffolding consists of a variety of temporary measures and mechanisms that foster critical thinking as well as learner engagement and autonomy. Scaffolding helps students reach beyond what they could do on their own. The helping and inspiring hand of scaffolding can be offered to students by teachers or other adults, by more knowledgeable and experienced students, and/or by learning materials. Ultimately, scaffolding aims to support students in progressively moving towards not only improving their knowledge and skills base, but also becoming more independent learners.

Although scaffolding eases learning, it is not meant to make learning so easy that it requires little intellectual effort or that it undermines learner engagement or autonomy. Instead, scaffolding is used to help construct cognitively and linguistically challenging learning environments that support students in engaging with and completing meaningful

Research perspective

Up to 90% of classroom activities can be completed by students using only surface-level skills (Hattie, 2012). Instead, increasing the use of activities that require deep-level thinking and deep learning is likely to lead to substantially improved learning overall (Fisher et al., 2016).

tasks. Challenging and effective learning environments cannot be constructed without providing students with scaffolding. Consequently, learning cannot be maximised without scaffolding.

Good schools constantly help students to stretch their thinking, to operate at the outer limits of their current ability to reason, to reach beyond what they could do on their own. In other words, good schools seek to place students in a space or zone where they are constantly intellectually challenged, while also being supported in going further in their thinking than they could on their own. This space is called the Zone of Proximal Development (ZPD) (see Figure 1).[1] Rich scaffolding of both content and language learning can maximise the size of the ZPD and what a student can accomplish (see Figure 2).

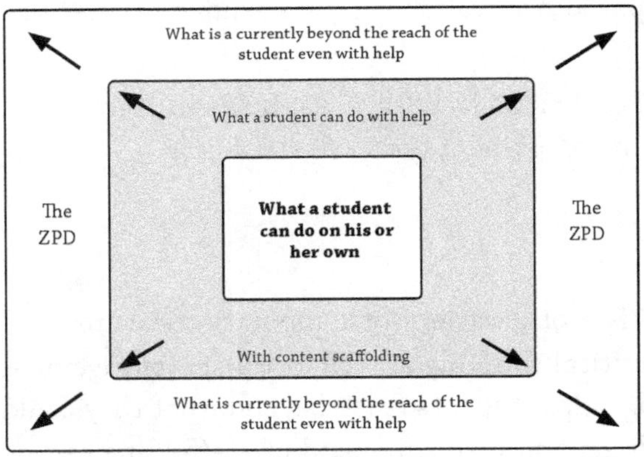

Figure 1: *The ZPD (Zone of Proximal Development) with content scaffolding*

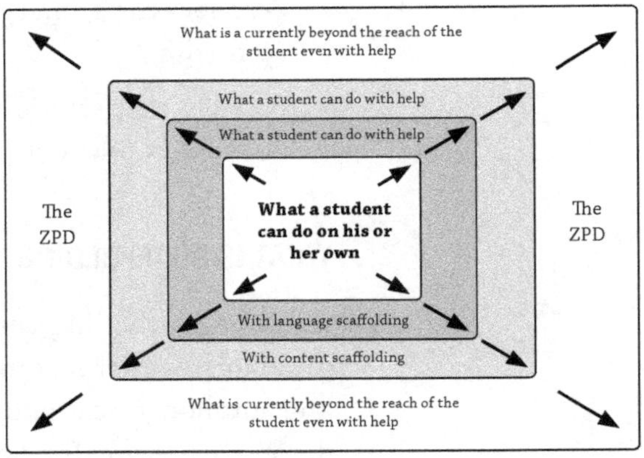

Figure 2: *The ZPD (Zone of Proximal Development) with content and language scaffolding*

In CLIL content lessons, if language input and output are not scaffolded, the maximum potential of the ZPD cannot be realised. Less content will

1 Lev Vygotsky coined the term 'ZPD' and wrote extensively about a socio-constructivist view of education where community and cooperation play important roles in meaning-making. The term 'scaffolding' was coined by Jerome Bruner.

be learned, and the learning may be shallower. Instead, rich scaffolds can support students in understanding content and language (the input), in testing and organising their thinking, in building narratives about content and in applying their learning (the output), and in learning how to learn while also building a desire to learn more. Equally importantly, in language classes, content scaffolds (e.g. for learning substantive new content, for critical thinking) need to be offered concurrently with the language scaffolds to make language learning more meaningful and hence more durable. In addition, students also need scaffolds to help them become autonomous language learners.

Therefore in CLIL, **as a practice, scaffolding of content and language needs to be omnipresent**. This can involve creating activities that include the use of support mechanisms/structures that help students understand and engage with new content and language and work with peers. As required, individual pieces of scaffolding are provided quickly on a temporary basis to move student thinking forward. When one piece of scaffolding appears no longer necessary, it is slowly withdrawn. The no-longer-needed piece of scaffolding is replaced with new scaffolds in order to move learning forward and maintain the learning progression. As indicated by the arrows in Figures 1 and 2, normally, a student's current knowledge and skills base is always expanding. This also means that a student's ZPD is always dynamic and shifting. It changes in substance as well, while new knowledge and skills are explored and eventually acquired.

Classroom catchphrases:

If I am not making mistakes and trying to fix them with support from people or materials, I cannot be learning very much. My learning is not likely to be very deep.

Suggestion: Have the students distil the above sentences into one short sentence.

Although scaffolding can support students in undertaking discrete tasks, it is above all meant to support students in achieving short- and long-term learning objectives/ outcomes. This means that scaffolding is focused on helping students **develop narratives** about the concepts, ideas and facts they are learning in various subjects such as History or Science, and how these may be connected to one another and how learning could be applied in their lives. In addition, scaffolding aims to support the development of underlying:

- **broad-based competences** (e.g. social and civic competence, entrepreneurship, digital competence)

- **skills** (e.g. undertaking historical enquiry, developing and undertaking a research project, language learning), and
- **habits of mind** (e.g. regularly pursuing active enquiry and research demonstrating rigour, thoroughness, scepticism and care; regularly demonstrating humility with respect to one's opinions combined with the courage and skill to defend them; constructively weighing diverse opinions; reflecting on content and language learning; developing a growth mindset interested in and capable of independently learning more).

In order to provide a quick overview of scaffolding some concrete examples are provided below. Later in the chapter, substantially more detailed examples of scaffolding are provided.

Content scaffolds

- breaking challenging information or tasks into chunks so students can better process these
- adapting a text by removing extraneous information that is not absolutely necessary to meet the intended learning outcomes/objectives
- providing students with a well-structured research task such as investigating the interests, arguments and actions of the following stakeholders who contributed to and/or undermined the abolition of slavery in the USA: abolitionist societies, former slaves, national, state and local level legislators, slaves, slave owners, religious activists and writers. Unless they are adept at stakeholder analysis, students may need further scaffolding suggesting they first investigate each stakeholder group's sources of income, social status and long-term interests.

Critical thinking scaffolds

- providing a list of common errors in logic with examples and asking students to analyse their own line of reasoning against common errors (e.g. *the red herring* – an observation that seeks to draw attention away from the key part of an argument, or *the slippery slope* – falsely claiming that one change will inevitably lead to another)
- providing a 10-step framework for working on a project (e.g. (1) review task and success criteria; (2) establish your goals; (3) plan your work; (4) gather information; (5) analyse information; (6) act on information to

create your product; (7) seek feedback from fellow students; (8) improve your product; (9) conduct a final self-evaluation against success criteria; (10) separately do a final polish of content and language).

Language scaffolds

- once students have some knowledge of a topic, first brainstorming language that students think they may need to discuss the main topic of the lesson (to achieve the day's objectives/outcomes) before working with the learning materials (e.g. having all of the objects to be used in an experiment on display and asking students to brainstorm the language they think will be used during the lesson; this language is then recorded and displayed)
- highlighting terms and underlining phrases in a text that students are expected to remember and use
- during group work, providing each student with a handout containing some of the language they need to complete a task related to new content
- having students read a short text in social language that acts as a bridge to a more challenging text written in academic language on the same topic (more detailed examples of how this can be done are provided later in the chapter)

Simultaneous content, critical thinking, language and learning skills scaffold

- providing exemplars of an excellent, average and poor piece of writing or presentation. These are analysed to determine criteria for creating a high quality product.

A scaffold for managing feelings and the development of learning skills

- instead of saying *'well done'*, saying that *'that is a good result that meets the agreed upon criteria. Please tell the class how you achieved that result.'*

Scaffolds for engaging interest and making learning meaningful

- asking students to explain how they think they will be able to use what is being learned in class later in their lives

- directing students to explore and explain how new material being studied connects with previous learning.

A cautionary note, although scaffolding is meant to maintain students in their ZPD, there are times when students may also need a rest from being constantly challenged so they can consolidate learning and celebrate their achievements.

Before drawing out scaffolds in greater detail, a more **detailed rationale** is given to back up the bold statement in the introduction to this chapter that *in CLIL, **scaffolding** is not simply a powerful learning tool; it **is indispensable.*** The indispensability of scaffolding is first explored through an affective lens and then through a discussion about cognitive load.

WHY IS SCAFFOLDING INDISPENSIBLE IN CLIL – THE AFFECTIVE SIDE OF LEARNING?

'The aspects of cognition that are recruited most heavily in education, including learning, attention, memory, decision-making, motivation and social functioning, are both profoundly affected by emotion and in fact subsumed within the processes of emotion' (Immordino-Yang and Damasio, 2007). Scaffolding helps students to be emotionally better disposed to learning. Scaffolding can be used to build students' confidence in their ability to learn, and motivate them to achieve more. It can also help lower student anxiety levels as it helps them to manage cognitive load, self-regulate, work with others, and experience success. In short, learning is not just a mechanical process; it is often driven or hampered by beliefs and emotions.

According to a meta-analysis by Durlak et al. (2011), students who are taught social and emotional skills not only become more socio-emotionally competent, but also see on average an 11 percent increase in their achievement on high-stakes tests. In addition, Carol Dweck (2010) from Stanford University has shown that the affective climate of a class has a major influence on student achievement. Perhaps surprisingly, teachers' mindsets can lead to an increase or a decrease in the amount of scaffolding offered in a classroom. Dweck (2007, referring to Rheinberg et al., 2000) reports that if teachers believe that their low-achieving students are destined to remain low achievers – a fixed mindset view – those students generally speaking remain low achievers. Dweck (citing Good et al., 2003), argues that these fixed mindset teachers are more likely to offer comfort to low-performing students but are less likely to offer constructive suggestions about (scaffolds for) how they could improve. By contrast, teachers who believe that current low achievers can improve their capacity to think and learn – a growth mindset view – are more likely to provide constructive feedback about (scaffolds for) how to improve. Low-achieving students who have growth mindset teachers are themselves likely to develop growth mindsets and become at least moderate achievers if not high achievers.

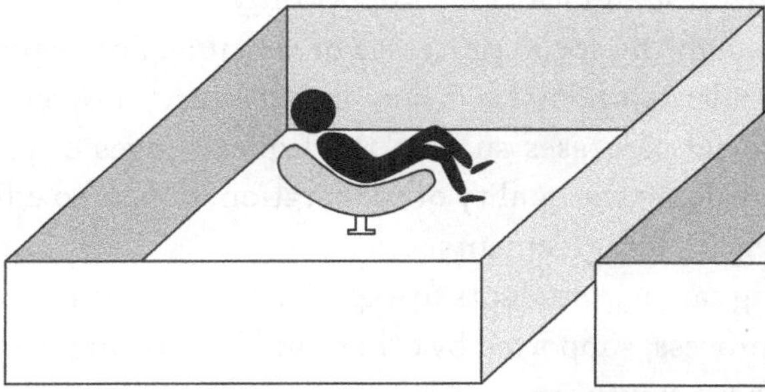

Figure 3: *Fixed mindset*

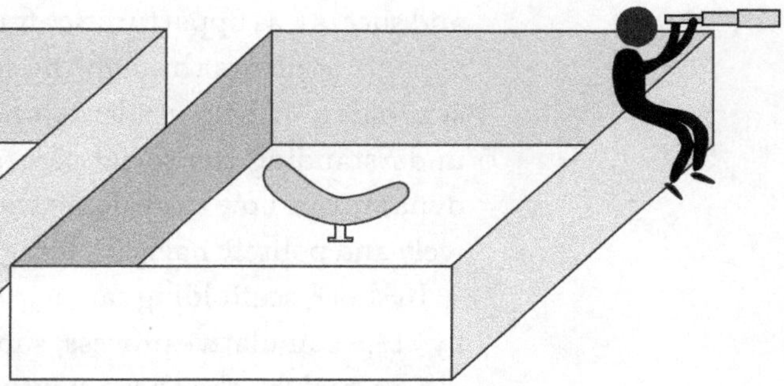

Figure 4: *Growth mindset*

The value of growth mindsets is complemented by the importance placed on teacher expectations in both CLIL and non-CLIL environments. In Finland, the widespread societal expectation that all children can keep up with the Grade 1–9 comprehensive school curriculum is considered to be one of the success factors of Finland's high-performing education system (Crehan, 2016). Across numerous diverse nations and regions, there is a strong correlation between high levels of student achievement and:

- teachers having high expectations of all of their students regarding both content and language learning
- students having high expectations of themselves regarding both content and language learning (Baker, 2006; Black, 2008; Cloud et al., 2000; Nuthall, 2005; Willms, 2006).

We extrapolate that in CLIL contexts, the **most important scaffold** that both content and language teachers can provide students is the **unconditional belief that all students can succeed in learning through an additional language**. This will help students to construct a mindset focused on high achievement and on the measures they need to take in order to succeed in learning both content and language. This belief in students will also help teachers to stay focused on systematically offering rich scaffolding of both content and language in order to make student success more likely.

Scaffolding is the primary vehicle for ensuring that students can meet their teachers' high expectations. Scaffolding can support students in developing a growth mindset, helping them to step out of their comfort zone, and build the competences, skills and habits of mind needed to actively use feedback, and their own and other people's setbacks, mistakes and success, as opportunities for learning. Importantly, scaffolds can also support students through the social processes of learning. For example, scaffolds can help students understand how to work with others (e.g. understanding the social processes such as the typical stages of group dynamics or how to evaluate the quality of cooperation, or how to effectively and politely navigate disagreements).

In short, scaffolding can help students to experience learning as a step-by-step, cumulative process, supported by others and by learning materials, over which they have significant control.

WHY IS SCAFFOLDING INDISPENSIBLE IN CLIL – COGNITIVE LOAD?

CLIL students are faced with the two-fold challenge of simultaneously learning new language and using that new language to learn new subject content. Learning Business, Geography, Maths or Science content through an L1 is in principle already challenging. Learning through an additional language places an added weight on thinking processes including working memory. More specifically, the use of a second language by a non-fluent speaker is thought to slow down the processing of new content information, thereby reducing the capacity of working memory to process that new content (Harrington and Sawyer, 1992).

Working memory is central to the learning of both content and language. It has been called the **gateway to all learning**. It is the mental workspace where we seek to understand, sort out and use those words, facts, ideas and concepts that are new to us. Working memory is not a purely rational workspace; as discussed in the previous section, having a growth mindset can foster learning.

In order for a student to move new content and language input into long-term memory, and ensure that that input can be retrieved and applied, students need first to: a) believe in their capacity to learn, b) employ their working memory to use that new input in a meaningful way, and c) connect new input with something they already know. Novel input that is not perceived as meaningful is quickly dismissed. CLIL is potentially well disposed to making language meaningful as students need to seek to understand new language in order to work with and understand new content. At the same time, **unless CLIL teachers provide new content and language input in digestible chunks, in a well-sequenced manner, and help connect that new input with previous learning, there is a risk that it can overwhelm their students' working memory**.

Working memory can be divided into **short-term** working memory (short-term storage of new visual and verbal information), and **active** working memory (structures and processes used for manipulating new information). In other words, people need to hold not just new input in their working memory, but simultaneously decide if and how they will structure and otherwise process that new input. Furthermore, the active part of working memory seeks to connect new incoming content and language with content and/or language that are/is already stored in long-term memory. If the working memory cannot connect new content and language with already stored content and/or language, the novel input is likely deemed as irrelevant and immediately lost. (See Baddeley et al., 2015 and Bailey and Pransky, 2014, for more on memory. We draw on these sources throughout this section.)

Figure 5: *Working memory*

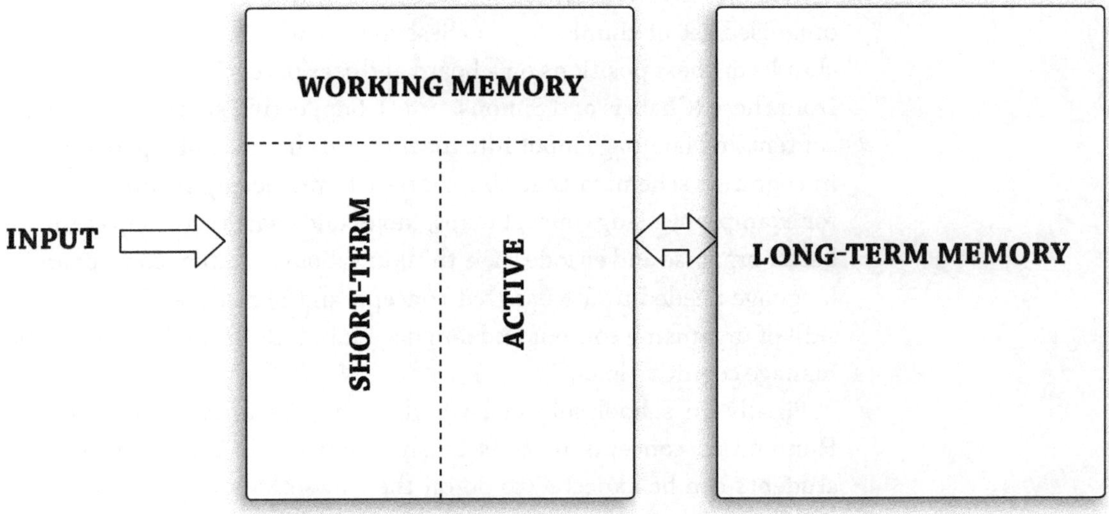

Working memory is highly limited in capacity and duration. If learners are intently listening to a teacher's explanation rich in new content and language, students may still be processing the first sentence by the time the teacher has uttered his/her third sentence. It is thought that, generally speaking, a person can retain some seven digits, six letters, five words or four chunks of new information or up to three new concepts for about 20 seconds unless that information is actively refreshed. This is usually done by repeating or otherwise using the new information. **Scaffolding can act as the 'refresh' button for working memory.** Scaffolding helps keep new content and language input visible/audible and offers tools for working with new input to accomplish meaningful tasks. Keeping tasks meaningful is central to helping students move new content and language input into their long-term memory. When input is deemed as not meaningful, it is quickly dismissed as people seek to process new incoming data.

Short-term memory and long-term memory can be considered part of one system of memory. The better-encoded newly learnt content and language are in long-term memory, the easier they are to retrieve and use. Well-encoded learning equates with deep learning that includes a thorough understanding of underlying concepts. Well-encoded, easily retrieved content and language put little strain on working memory while the opposite is true when recalling weakly encoded learning.

Well-encoded content input is not stored randomly in long-term memory. People who become experts in a field have organised information and knowledge as one complex element (e.g. dehydration as a chemical reaction that involves the loss of water molecules) or as one complex and organised set of chunks (e.g. a chess master who recognises meaningful chunks of chess positions on a board and sees potential moves that derive from these (Chabris and Simons, 2011). Supporting students in grouping content and language input into meaningful chunks and organising these in cognitive schemata that also connect to previously acquired learning, for example by using concept maps, tables and charts, can help them: a) to better organise and encode their thinking about a content concept and the language needed to discuss that concept, and b) to develop the learning skill of organising content and language input. Both can help students to manage cognitive load.

Finally, in school subjects, whether they be in the Sciences or the Humanities, concepts are consciously constructed. This is not something students can be expected to do on their own. Moreover, one concept is always tied to others. Furthermore, the relationship between concepts in any given field is often hierarchical, and has been agreed on by those working in that field. Relationships or connections between concepts help us to understand them. Learning and using related language also helps bind new language to new and previously learnt concepts. Once we understand new concepts and related language, and how they relate to previous concepts and language we have learned, it is possible to better encode that new learning in long-term memory. Ultimately, well-encoded learning is more likely to be recalled when needed, be that to work with concepts or to answer questions on a test.

The previous two sections have explained the value of scaffolding. The next section explains in broad brushstrokes what can be scaffolded, and how.

WHAT TYPES OF SCAFFOLDING EXIST?

The concept of scaffolding can be organised under two major headings:

1. **What** (the focus/primary purpose of scaffolding)
2. **How** (types of scaffolding actions)

Broadly speaking, the **primary purpose of scaffolding** is to support students in actively engaging with **the entire learning process.** The learning process involves having students: explore their beliefs and understandings; build knowledge of facts, concepts and ideas in context (building a conceptual framework); seek out and resolve internal inconsistencies; organise knowledge in ways that allows for retrieval and application; restructure their own (mis)conceptions; work effectively and efficiently with others; take the time and make the effort to practice; seek out ways to use newly acquired content and language knowledge and skills; and develop plans and define goals whilst also reflecting on the learning process by analysing/evaluating work processes and progress in the achievement of intended content and language outcomes/objectives (drawing on Bransford, Brown and Cocking, 2000; Vosniadou, 2001). In addition, scaffolding can focus on supporting students in building broad-based competences, skills and habits of mind that encourage a sustainable desire to learn. In other words, an ultimate aim of scaffolding and schooling is to help students build a growth mindset and the capacity to learn autonomously.

Various **types of scaffolding actions** can be undertaken by teachers and/or students, and/or initiated through the use of learning materials in order to support the learning process. These can be planned for or created on the spot as needed during the teaching and learning process. For example, planned for scaffolds can encourage students to see and reflect on **learning strategies** that they use or do not use to learn content and language. This would involve helping students to reflect on the utility of various learning strategies and the potential negative consequences (lost opportunity costs) of not using given learning strategies. At other times, when students are facing an obstacle, a learning strategy can be offered on the spot in order to maintain student engagement.

The various types of scaffolding detailed below are not entirely discrete. To some extent they overlap with one another. For example, the scaffolding actions of engaging with prompts and asking questions are a case in point. Prompting students to think of a way of solving a challenging problem can consist of a well-formulated question. Building on Gibbons (2002, 2009) and Walqui (2006), we offer somewhat overlapping scaffolding actions to emphasise major types of scaffolds that we feel can be used to drive the learning of both content and language. With several of the scaffolding types, we have chosen not to simply emphasise the type of scaffolding being offered to students – e.g. *modelling* – but to stress the need for students to engage with the scaffold – e.g. *having students engage with models*. We do this to stress the need to move beyond using scaffolding for facilitation of comprehension in order to support deep-order engagement and critical thinking.

- **having students engage with models** (e.g. providing examples for analysis and imitation; providing and analysing non-examples so students know what not to do)
- **having students engage with schema building** (e.g. viewing and/or creating thinking frameworks such as charts, graphic organisers or advance organisers; drawing out the structure of a text)
- **bridging** (e.g. using social language to access academic language; moving from the concrete to the abstract; building on previous knowledge and understandings; making connections between concepts and with what is being learned in other subjects)
- **highlighting language** (e.g. listing key words and phrases; underlining new language; brainstorming language needed for a writing assignment)

- **creating digestible chunks** of information and knowledge (e.g. breaking down both tasks and information/knowledge to avoid cognitive overload and maintain learner engagement)
- **sequencing** activities and the learning of information and knowledge in a logical order (e.g. first learning about the concept of a polynomial and related language before speaking about and applying the concept to sketch and discuss a range of curves)
- **contextualising** (e.g. exploring context to help students situate the content and academic language)
- **re-presenting and having students re-use content** (e.g. using a new genre to present the same content; having students use the same content in new ways; having students explain in academic language what was learnt using social language)
- **providing prompts** (e.g. providing clues that help students answer a question or correct an error)
- **asking questions** (e.g. questions can focus on literal comprehension; involve reorganisation or reinterpretation – combining, reordering or reinterpreting information; can ask students to deduce/infer or evaluate; can invite a personal opinion; ask for the analysis of language and style)
- **having students engage with planning** (e.g. providing and analysing planning frameworks, defining intended learning outcomes/objectives; using success indicators to decide where to invest the most thought and time)
- **having students engage with self-, peer- and learning process assessment** (e.g. negotiating evaluation criteria; providing, analysing and using rubrics; reflecting on learning and the learning process and drawing conclusions for implementation)
- **having students engage with others** (e.g. offering rubrics, frameworks and guidelines for conducting effective group work)
- **having students engage with learning strategies** (e.g. guiding students in using self-generated cues to make connections that will help them recall learning).

The remainder of the chapter will discuss each type of scaffolding suggested above and provide examples.

EXAMPLES OF SCAFFOLDING

This section offers and discusses a series of examples of different types of scaffolds including for content and language learning. In some cases, standalone scaffolds are presented. These are intended to exemplify a given discrete step in a series of tasks and scaffolds. In other cases, to reinforce the importance of the ongoing use of scaffolding, two or more related scaffolds are offered in order to show how they might fit into a learning progression or support differentiation. Engaging with self-, peer- and learning process assessment, although touched upon below, will be discussed in more detail in **Chapter 7:** *Assessment.*

BRIDGING, HIGHLIGHTING LANGUAGE AND RE-USING CONTENT

Social language can act as a bridge to academic language. For example, students can compare two sentences and discuss how they differ. In this case, the academic text avoids the use of the second person. It is also more precise. Lemon juice does not stop the oxidation process, but it slows it down. It is the oxygen that causes the discolouring process, not air in general, which is composed of water, nitrogen, oxygen, carbon dioxide, argon and other gases, as well as water.

Social language	Academic language
The apple slices will turn brown if you leave them out in the open air. If you don't want them to turn brown, you can put lemon juice on them because it stops the oxidation process.	When slices of apple are exposed to oxygen they turn brown. Lemon juice, which is rich in citric acid, can be used to slow down oxidation and the discolouring process.

It would be important to also work with longer texts. In the example below, taken from a CLIL textbook for Italian learners, students are asked to read through two texts – one written in social language one in academic language. This task is part of a learning progression, en route to developing an understanding of the Chemistry concept of *electronegativity*. Previously these students had been made aware of how the size of atoms in the periodic table change systematically, following a periodic pattern.

The students are told that the two texts are a result of a fellow student typing the following question into an Internet forum: 'Why does the atomic radius *increase* when you go down the Group but *decrease* when you go across a Period?" The students' task is to identify the highlighted words and to find how the ideas are expressed in the opposite text. To facilitate reading the students were also provided with a Glossary (see below).

Social language	Academic language
It's like this: as you go down a Group, you add more and more new "levels" or "shells" to the atom and this makes it bigger. Also, the electrons at higher energy levels are farther away from the nucleus and are **shielded** by electrons in shells that are closer to the nucleus. Because of these two reasons, the nucleus cannot attract far-away electrons very strongly and that is the reason why atoms with more energy shells are bigger. As you go across a Period, atomic radius decreases because you are **no longer** adding "shells," just adding electrons to the shells that are already there. Since you are also adding more and more protons into the nucleus when you move across a period, the positive attractive force in the nucleus pulls more strongly on the electrons, and, since they are **pulled closer** to the nucleus, the atom is smaller. Hope this helps! *Fran Ken*	Descending within a Group, the number of energy levels and thus shells increases. Since consecutive shells are increasingly more distant from the nucleus, atoms become progressively bigger. In addition, since outer shell electrons are shielded by those occupying more internal shells, electrons at higher energy levels experience weaker proton-electron attractive force from the nucleus: atoms with electrons occupying higher energy levels are thus (*quindi*) bigger. Across a Period, from left to right, electrons are added to the same energy level. At the same time, increasingly more protons are also being added to the nucleus. A greater number of protons in the nucleus correlates to a "higher effective nuclear charge." In other words, the nucleus exerts a stronger attractive force on the electrons which, being drawn **closer to** the nucleus, results in a smaller atomic radius. Best wishes with your studies *Prof. Stein*

HANDS-ON GLOSSARY

Shielded:
Schermati

Far away:
Distante

No longer:
Non più

Pulled/drawn closer:
Attirati più vicinu

(Ting et al., 2015)

In the above task, social language provides a scaffold into the academic language. The task requires students to read, interpret, and compare and hopefully contrast both the social and academic registers of language several times. At the very least, the task exposes students twice to the same subject matter content and to two different registers of language. It is also possible that the academic language and content may act as a scaffold for learning social language. For example, for speakers of Romance languages, since academic language in English often has roots in Latin, academic language may at times be easier to understand than social language. Social English often uses phrasal verbs and idioms that cannot be easily deciphered one word at a time.

It is possible to further support students in learning the distinctions between the social and academic language text by working through a more detailed analysis of each sentence. Below, we have compared and contrasted the first few sentences of the above text on the periodic table to show some of the differences that can be discussed.

Social Language	Academic Language
It's like this: as you go down a Group in the Periodic Table, there are more and more new levels or shells added to the atom and this makes it bigger.	Descending within a Group of the Periodic Table, the number of energy levels or shells of the atom increases.

How does the above social and academic language differ?

- *'Going down' is social language. The academic language equivalent is 'descending'.*
- *'You' is avoided in academic language. In social language, 'you' can be understood in two ways as either a personal 'you' or as a generic or unspecified 'you', which in this case describes what one ought to see when looking down the periodic Table. Learning this social language is also essential for second language learners as it is high-frequency language. By contrast, in academic language, one would either say as 'one descends within a Group' or simply avoid any reference to a person.*
- *Add 'more and more' in academic language is 'increase'.*

Social Language	Academic Language
Also, the electrons at higher energy levels are farther away from the nucleus and are shielded by electrons in shells that are closer to the nucleus.	Since consecutive shells are increasingly distant from the nucleus, atoms become progressively bigger.

How does the above social and academic language differ?

- *'Also' is used to start the sentence in social language, but it is an unnecessary bridge between the previous sentence and this one. The academic language version simply provides additional information in a logical progression.*
- *The use of 'farther away from the nucleus' in the social language version is conceptually correct but the academic language equivalent is 'increasingly more distant from the nucleus'.*
- *The academic text is assuming the reader understands that energy levels = shells.*

A few rules of thumb for scaffolding both the learning of social language and academic language and thereby making content information more transparent are in the initial stages: (1) to use non-idiomatic language, (2) to provide synonyms in parentheses, or (3) to provide a glossary, and (4) to make certain the new language is returned to several times over the next few days and weeks so students see the utility of the language. This increases the likelihood that they will recall it. The use of social language is simply one step along the learning progression, as students eventually need to be able to use authentic academic texts without scaffolding.

BRIDGING, CONTEXTUALISING, HIGHLIGHTING LANGUAGE, SEQUENCING, RE-PRESENTING AND RE-USING CONTENT, AND ENGAGING WITH LEARNING STRATEGIES, PLANNING AND SELF-ASSESSMENT

The following four tasks seek to scaffold students' understanding of potential and kinetic energy in a step-by-step manner. On an affective level, the first three tasks (which could have been one task) break the processing of challenging language and content into digestible chunks or pieces. The four tasks also require that students use and re-use academic language and increasingly higher order thinking skills. They also use concrete examples as a bridge to foster the understanding of abstract concepts.

The four tasks are built on a free online video regarding potential and kinetic energy developed for children but used with adolescent students in a Physics lesson. The exercise starts with the video, which the students may replay in part or in whole, to make certain they have understood the contents. Once the tasks have all been completed, students can re-use the video to assess their work or other students' work.

You will find the information you need to complete the following four tasks in a video. The link is below, but first let's explore how you could obtain (get) the most out of the video.

Try using the following sequence – **foresee, play, stop, fill in, check**:

- before starting the video, ***foresee*** what you need to do by skimming the text and noticing the blanks
- then ***play*** the video and ***stop*** it at the indicated time
- then ***fill in*** the missing words
- when you have complete each task, replay the video so you can ***check*** your work.

Foresee, play, stop, fill in, check

Here is the link: https://youtu.be/IqV5L66EP2E

Task A:

This video is about ________ and ____________ Energy (time: 0.59) and the Law of ___ ____________ ________ (1.06) which states that ____________ be ______ (1.12) and ______________ be ________ (1.16): It can only be CONVERTED ____________ one ____________ to ____________ (1.19). The first example of 'the conversion of energy' is demonstrated by the boy's hat that has a fan that cools down the boy on a hot day. Here, ____________ Energy is accumulated in a battery and this battery provides the ____________ energy necessary to move the fan through ____________ Energy. This is an example of 'The ______________ of Solar Energy into ______________________________' as summarised below

(1.23-1.28) Solar Energy

⇨ (solar panel on hat) ⇨ ___________ Energy

⇨ ______________ Energy to move the blades of the fan.

*Again, **foresee, play, stop, fill in, check***

Task B:

Starting at 1.39, the video discusses __________ Energy which is defined as '_________ to __________' (1.44). At the beginning, the boy was at the bottom of the hill. Since he had a good breakfast, he had enough **physical energy** to *move* the pedals of his bike and *move* himself to the top of the hill. So physical energy was used to change the boy's _______________ from the bottom of the hill to the ________ of the hill. When the boy is sitting at the _____________ of the hill, he is in a position of 'high-energy' that can be used to 'do something' ... we can hypothesise that he will use this ________ Energy to roll down the hill without pedalling! We can summarise the situation as:

________________ Energy (thanks to the **chemical energy** in his breakfast)

⇨ ______________ Energy which is the *movement* of the pedals

⇨ ______________ Energy because he is in a higher-energy position.

Foresee, play, stop, fill in, check

Task C:

Since energy cannot be created or ____________ but only ________, as the boy rolls down the hill he is **not** 'not using energy'... he is *converting* _____________ energy into ______________ energy which is defined as 'Energy due to _________' (1.51).

The unit of energy is called _________ (1.56)

To summarise, we can say that, up to this point, the video demonstrated the following:

Energy from food = _______________ energy ⇨ _______________ energy to move the pedals and boy up the hill = ______________ energy; at the top of the hill = ______________ energy

⇨ energy to roll down the hill.

Task D:

Now watch the video from minute 2.00 to 2.56. You will see a tyre-swing that swings back and forth to demonstrate the relationship between **potential energy** and **kinetic energy**. Decide which summary is most suitable for answering an exam question to show you understand the relationship between kinetic and potential energy.

- When the tyre is not moving there is no kinetic energy. But when the boy uses energy to hold the tyre to one side, the tyre has gained potential energy. When the tyre is released, potential energy starts getting converted to kinetic energy. At the bottom of the swing, kinetic energy is at its maximum. As the tyre swings back and forth, energy is converted back and forth between kinetic energy and potential energy.
- When the tyre is stationary, there is only potential energy but no kinetic energy. When kinetic energy is used to position the tyre farther away from the centre, it gains potential energy so that, when the tyre is released, potential energy is converted to kinetic energy, which is maximum at the bottom of the swing. A tyre, which is swinging back and forth, demonstrates how potential energy and kinetic energy are interconverted.

Prior to actually doing the tasks or watching the video, students are directed to skim the text. Regularly familiarising oneself with a text prior to having to work with it and a video and/or a broadcast/podcast can be considered an effective learning strategy/habit that is being modelled here. The task also invites students to assess and improve their own work. This too can be considered a useful strategy/habit.

The above sequence of tasks illustrates how learning followed a gradual and tightly scaffolded progression. For example, Task A is an introduction to the topic. It requires students to simply watch and listen to the video and to fill in the missing text. Students will find it easier to complete the task if they have familiarised themselves with the text prior to watching the video. Task B introduces the concept that chemical energy in food provides the physical energy necessary to move the pedals. This is a form of kinetic energy that is converted to potential energy when the boy's position is changed. Task C is not a simple listening exercise. It brings together all the notions from the task B text and requires higher order thinking to complete. Finally, in Task D both summaries are correct but the second is the more academic answer. For example, the first answer contains more colloquial language, such as 'not moving' instead of 'stationary', and 'converted back and forth' rather than 'interconverted'. As the students need to read both texts, this is a meaningful opportunity for the students to re-use language and content. In addition, the social language in the first example may also act as a bridge to the denser academic language in the second example.

ENGAGING WITH MODELS AND OTHERS, AND SELF- AND PEER ASSESSMENT

Exemplars of excellent, average and poor writing can serve as powerful tools for students to improve their writing and thinking skills. They help show students the language of successful writers, and how successful student writers have organised and/or systematised their explanations and thinking about subject matter content.

In addition to helping students understand what constitutes quality work, the analysis of exemplars can support students in becoming autonomous learners through the development of:

- their capacity to assess work and to articulate what constitutes high-quality, medium-quality and poor-quality writing
- the habit of undertaking in a systematic manner self- and peer assessment with a view to taking greater responsibility or offering support for improving the quality of their work.

Exemplars can consist of complete essays or reports, or of their constituent parts. Exemplars of introductions can be particularly valuable as they usually make visible both an essay's or report's aims and organisation. In order to help students to improve their introductions, the following tasks and scaffolds could be offered:

- give students three introductions (see sample below) and have them decide, on their own, which one is excellent, which one is acceptable but still needs improvement, and which one is poor
- have the students then work in pairs to agree on the quality level of each introduction and why each introduction falls into the category of (A) excellent, (B) acceptable but needs improvement, or (C) poor
- discuss the students' findings as a class and agree on criteria for writing introductions (e.g. states the main aim; explains how the composition, essay or report will be organised; captures the reader's attention; is short and concise)
- practice writing and improving introductions
- conclude why introductions are so important (e.g. it reveals immediately how well-organised the author's thinking is; the better organised the thinking, the easier the whole text will be to read; first impressions are lasting).

Figure 6: *The writing of introductory paragraphs*

Scaffolding the writing of introductory paragraphs for an essay/paper/report: excellent; acceptable, but needs improvement; poor.

Please note: It is advisable to take actual examples of student work. The following is just a model.

An excellent introductory paragraph

Global bee populations are in major decline, and this can lead to a decline in biodiversity and threaten global food supplies. This paper explores the three major causes of the decline in bee populations, and the consequences for plants, animals and people. Finally solutions for addressing the problem are discussed.

The first half of the first sentence tells the reader what the problem is, and the second half explains two major consequences. This grabs the reader's attention.

The introduction is short. It is not wordy. There are no extraneous words. The author does not start to discuss the topic.

The second sentence explains the aim of the paper and how it will be organised – 3 causes and 3 consequences for 3 species.

An acceptable introductory paragraph, but one that needs improvement

Global bee populations are declining in great numbers and this is worrying for several reasons. This means less pollination of plants is taking place. Less pollination of plants means that farmers will be able to harvest fewer crops, and people will be able to buy less food. This essay will answer three questions: why bees are in decline; what is causing their decline; how the decline can be stopped or slowed down. In particular, I explore the impact the decline in bee populations will have on people, plants and animals and will propose solutions.

The first sentence tells the reader part of the problem, which does grab the reader's attention. The second part of the first sentence informs the reader that this is worrying. Telling the reader this is worrying is not necessary as we have been informed that it is a problem.

It is easy to follow the planned structure of the paper. Three questions will be answered. Although as one reads on, it seems there are actually four questions that will be answered.

The second and third sentence explain part of the problem. These sentences are clear but they could be removed. In the excellent version, the problem is explained in broad terms. Here the explanation is more detailed than necessary. In addition, only part of the issue is presented. No mention is made of the bigger concept of biodiversity.

'In particular' is the wrong word or bridge to the last sentence. 'In addition' would be more appropriate as the impact is something in addition to the previous three questions. Also, normally one would explain the impact or consequences before explaining the solutions 'how the decline can be stopped or slowed down'.

A poor introductory paragraph

In this essay I will write about bees. Bee populations are in decline. Something needs to be done about this. First we need to understand the problem. Therefore, I will explore the causes. For example, one of the causes is the use of pesticides. Global warming is another reason more bees are dying early. Parasites are also killing bees. There are less meadows with flowers because we are building on meadows. Next I will explain what will happen if bees keep disappearing. Bees pollinate plants. That means there will be less plants. If there are less plants, people and animals will have less food. That means some animals could disappear from the planet. More people might starve to death. I will discuss all those things in my report

The first sentence is unnecessary. The second sentence would make a good first sentence, because it explains the key problem and grabs the reader's attention.

The use of language is not precise enough. Bees are not simply disappearing (vanishing from sight); their populations are in decline because they are being killed by pesticides and mites or because they cannot find sufficient food to survive.

The word 'less' is generally used for things that cannot be counted and 'fewer' when something can be counted.

The author uses the word 'I' a great deal. This leaves the impression that he or she is talking about himself/herself as much as about the bees.

The author begins to first discuss in detail the causes of the decline in bee populations and the consequences of that decline. This is not done in an introduction. Detailed discussion should take place in the body of a paper.

The last sentence is unnecessary. There is no new information here. The author has already told us what he or she will discuss in his/her report.

The full stop is missing from the end of the sentence.

Finally, **anonymous exemplars of student work** can be used to analyse entire essays, compositions or reports to determine success criteria. To highlight how to develop a high-quality explanation of content subject concepts, it is possible to ask students to analyse the structure of explanations, their clarity and precision, and the suitability of given examples and/or evidence. It would be important to have students discuss language use. This should help them avoid language errors as well as notice valuable terminology and phraseology that they might wish to use in their work.

HIGHLIGHTING LANGUAGE AND SCHEMA BUILDING

Key words and phrases that are the focus of an upcoming unit can be listed on the board at the start of a unit. This is a way of drawing student attention both to key concepts and to the language that will be learned.

Three examples follow below. The first scaffold focuses on *key words* from a Chemistry unit on chemical solutions, while the second and third make visible in a more integrated manner *key words, phrases* and *concepts* from the same unit.

Example 1:

Key words: *saturation, solvent, polar, soluble, solution*

Writing key words on the board (*Example 1*) can act as a scaffold in many ways. It informs students of the focus of the lesson. Even if they do not immediately understand the words, the scaffold signals that these are important words and/or concepts. Students can be told that by the end of the unit they will need to be able to understand and use these words. It is also possible to use such lists to draw out existing knowledge or what meaning students might currently assign a term such as *polar.*

However, the key words in *Example 1* are not presented in a well-ordered manner. No cognitive schema is provided to aid retention of the words. The list mixes a concept, which constitutes a process (saturation) with the simple nouns (solvent, solution), which are constituent elements of the concept of saturation. There are also two adjectives (polar, soluble) in the list.

Examples 2 and 3 present the key language in a more meaningful manner. *Example 3* is simply more detailed. It names the topic and provides a definition. Both options organise the language according to concepts. In addition to words, each also provides some key phraseology.

Example 2:

Solute + Solvent = Solution		
Solubility soluble insoluble	***Nature of solvent*** polar nonpolar	***Saturation*** saturated unsaturated super-saturated
is soluble in	only dissolves in	a saturation point depends on

Example 3:

Topic: Chemical solutions **Essential knowledge: Solute + Solvent = Solution**		
Solubility soluble low solubility insoluble	***Nature of solvent*** polar nonpolar	***Saturation*** saturated unsaturated super-saturated
is soluble in	only dissolves in	a saturation point depends on
Concentration is the ratio of the mass or volume of a solute to the mass or volume of the solution or solvent.		

Again, the teacher can tell the students that by the end of the unit these are concepts and language that they will be able to use when discussing chemical solutions. Either table (*Examples* 2 and 3) can be on the board or taped onto each student's desk as a crib sheet. Crib sheets are very effective as they are often in the students' field of vision, and are thus more likely to be used than vocabulary on a wall or a board.

Once the various tasks related to chemical solutions have been completed, if students cannot find the words to explain something, and if those words are in the table, the students can be referred to the table to search for them. The table can be used at the end of the lesson as a review.

Students can explain the key concepts and how solutes and solvents lead to the creation of solutions.

Frameworks can make visible useful language and help students to structure their thinking and work. Broadly speaking, the following framework seeks to support students in developing their skills in critiquing paintings. More specifically, the scaffold aims to support students in critiquing paintings by:

- noticing useful words and phrases
- noticing key elements worthy of critique such as line and colour
- offering a structure for undertaking the critique, and
- encouraging them to think more deeply about the painting than would be the case without the framework.

When using the framework students can be asked to mention each of the eight categories below and to use at least one word or phrase from each box.

Critiquing contrast or lack thereof	**Critiquing colour**
dramatic strong subtle uniform	bold earthy naturalistic pale subtle vibrant
Critiquing line	**Critiquing movement or lack thereof**
The artist uses ... lines. This creates a sense of ... in the viewer. bold delicate flowing simple thick thin	*... movements dominate the painting leaving the viewer feeling ...* dramatic dynamic flowing static swirling

Critiquing scale	**Critiquing shape**
The scale of the painting is/can be considered ... because/as... intimate large miniature monumental small	*The painting is predominantly .... This creates in the viewer ...* angular curvaceous elongated geometric organic
Critiquing texture	**Critiquing tone**
coarse fine rough smooth uneven	contrasting dramatic muted subtle

Additional language for speaking about paintings
asymmetry/asymmetrical – containing elements that are unequal in proportion *(e.g. The painting is far from being symmetrical. The figure in the centre is [looms] larger than life. Its facial features are exaggerated.)* **broken colour** – dabs or small amounts of colour **depth** – the illusion of space **distorted** – a shape that is changed and no longer looks proportioned **flat tones** – little or no difference in tone of colours, no tonal effect **focal point** – the spot/point that stands out in the artwork **geometric** – refers to the shapes such as circles, triangles, squares, etc. *(e.g. Geometric shapes, in particular rectangles and squares, dominate the painting.)* **negative space** – the area around the primary object in the painting **organic** – free-flowing or rounded **symmetry/symmetrical** – meaning it is equal on both sides **saturation** – refers to amount of bright colour (often intense and unshaded)

After students have arrived at conclusions about a topic they have researched, they can be encouraged to take their thinking a step further. The following framework encourages students to reflect on each other's lines of reasoning, and to help each other to think critically about their work. As with all the examples, this would need to be adapted to the given context.

Testing your ideas		
Questions	***Written responses***	***Group discussion***
How did you arrive at that conclusion/ hypothesis/ answer? *Where is your evidence?* *Can you back that up?* *How do you define that term?*	Based on data from the Department of Statistics, it is possible to conclude ... The United Nations Development Programme report states that ... In this paper, term X is defined as ...	*I looked at government statistics ...* *My neighbour whose mom works at X says ...* *X magazine wrote about this and they found ...* *I consulted/checked out X websites.* *Let's define our terms.*
Does anyone have a counter argument? *Who has a different opinion?* *How will the other group try to counter this argument?* *What will they object to the most?*	X argues the opposite. He states that ... It is also important to consider ... The logic is faulty in that ... An alternative would be to say ...	*I think we also need to look at ...* *We seem to be forgetting ...* *There are some inconsistencies in what we are saying.* *They are probably going to say ...* *That counter-argument is faulty (doesn't hold water) because ...*
How would X influence Y?	X is likely to also influence Y because ... There may be some unintended consequences. It is possible that ...	*That might solve one problem, but just cause another one.* *That is going to make the situation worse because ...* *Let's weigh up the evidence.*
Is that relevant to your argument? *Are there any inconsistencies in this line of argument?*	There are inconsistencies in the argument made by ... This is an example of ...	*That is beside the point. You're digressing.* *That's not relevant because ...* *We need to refocus.* *It seems to me X undermines your argument.*
Are those figures recent enough? *Is the data up-to-date?*	Newer/more recent figures suggest ... In 2017, the OECD reported that ...	*5% of all ...* *Those are old numbers/figures.* *Let's look for fresher data.*
Can we trust that source? *Is that a reliable source?* *Is that a respected expert?*	The same results have been replicated by ... X is considered a leading expert in her field.	*I am not sure we can believe what is written on this website. No sources are quoted.* *This author seems to be making a false assumption.*

When students' verbal or written output is not as rich as required, they can be provided with key phraseology they are expected to use. The following framework offers some of the academic language used to discuss substantive concepts and second-order concepts in History, as well as specific functions such as explaining causes and consequences.

Time
During the early nineteenth century, ... In the mid 1800s, ... In the late nineteenth century, ... In the last decade of the nineteenth century, ... At the end of X period and at the beginning of Y period ... Each of these dates marks a ... ... until the beginning of the ...
Location
The first historical mention of a settlement in X was in ... (year) ... X developed around the Caspian Sea On the north shore of the Caspian ... ... in the mountains ... X is/was at the crossroads of ... X spread across ... X established a state in what is now...
Change in circumstances and/or rulers
... to fall under the rule of / fell under the rule of ... ... declined in importance and was progressively replaced by ... ... take over power in / took over power in ... ... people were subjected to the ... The territory was annexed / conquered / occupied by ... ... take an entirely new course / took an entirely new course ... ... was born ... ... ceased to exist.

Making and breaking alliances
X allied itself with ...
The allies attacked at dawn
X and Y signed a secret pact / made a secret pact
X betrayed Y ...
X sided with Y in ...
Making an argument
The following evidence points to ...
X is important / significant due to ...
... the counter-arguments include ...
This would be the equivalent of someone today ...
... the validity of the counter-argument is questionable because ...
Most historians are of the opinion that ...

As an alternative option, students can be asked to analyse an academic text in order to identify and write out phrases that they think they will be able to use in the future. Students could be given categories such as those suggested in the above framework to structure their work. This language can then serve as a scaffold for students' future writing assignments.

Some additional language scaffolds that can support students in using generic academic language or undertaking some common functions follow. In order to make sure students engage with the scaffolds, they can be asked to use a certain number of the given suggestions in their writing.

Language for writing up research on a variety of topics
Introducing your topic
This report seeks to answer the question ...
To answer the question 'xxxx', I ...
First, I report on ...
Second, I explain ...
Finally, I suggest ...

Drawing out your key points, or writing lists
First(ly), ...; Second(ly), ...; Third(ly), ...; Finally, ... *In the first stage; in the second stage* *In addition, ...; next; then*
Reporting on what someone else has said
X argues that ...; Y asserts that ...; *X concludes that ...; Y contends that ...;* *X proposes that ...; Y maintains that ...;* *X suggests that ...*
Introducing an alternative viewpoint
Alternatively, ...; Although; *An alternative viewpoint is offered by ...;* *By contrast, ...; Conversely, ...; In comparison, ...;* *On the one hand, ... ; On the other hand, ...*
Introducing examples
An example of this is ...; For example, ...; For instance, ...; *including; in other words, ...; namely;* *chiefly; in particular; mainly; mostly; notably*
Restating your point in a different manner
In other words, ...; As stated above, ...; This would be equivalent to ...
Drawing conclusions from a discussion or evidence
In conclusion, ...; To conclude, ...; In short, ...; To sum up ... *Accordingly, ...; as a result of ...; Overall, ...; Therefore, ...;* *It can be argued that ...; The evidence suggests that ...* *As a consequence, ...; Thus, ...; Hence, ...; For this reason, ...*

Language scaffold for giving reasons

It is	essential helpful important necessary revealing telling	to	bear in mind consider point out that remember analyse speak to take into account	...

Language scaffold for criticising another point of view

<table>
<tr><td rowspan="2">This
These views
The statement ... X ...</td><td>is/are</td><td>highly debatable.
highly speculative.
incorrect.
not always the case.
not necessarily true.
open to doubt.
opinion(s) not fact(s).
unlikely to be true.</td></tr>
<tr><td colspan="2">is /are not grounded in evidence.
is/are simply personal opinion.
is/are an exaggeration of the current situation.</td></tr>
<tr><td>I disagree with X when he</td><td>argues
claims
proposes
states
suggests
writes</td><td>that ...</td></tr>
</table>

ENGAGING WITH SCHEMA BUILDING AND RE-USING CONTENT AND LANGUAGE

Creating and using **concept maps** tends to have a high positive impact on student achievement (Hattie, 2012). Concepts maps usually take a key concept and then show how the key concept can be broken down into its constituent elements. It is also possible to show how the concept under discussion relates to other concepts. This helps students to see how various pieces of knowledge relate to one another. It helps structure their thinking. Furthermore, classroom activities with concept maps and discussions of them help make transparent what students know and or do not know, and therefore what they still need to learn. Eventually students should be able to create their own concept maps. An example of a concept map about the consequences of deforestation follows.

Figure 7: *Consequences of deforestation with two cross-curricular links*

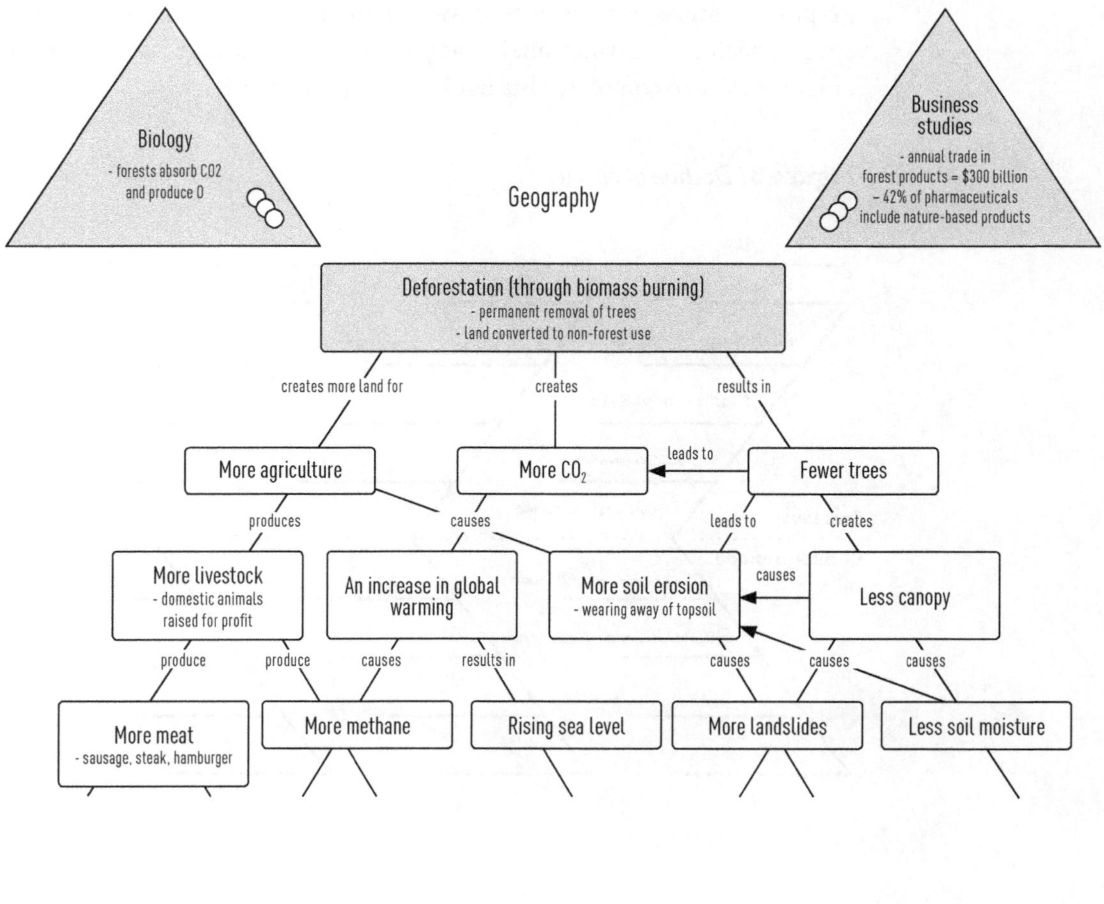

The concept map defines deforestation, draws out information about deforestation, provides some of the key language and related concepts such as soil erosion. It aims to organise the information (facts, key concepts and some of the related language) in a manner that fosters its long-term storage and later recall. Once students have seen a used a concept map for an activity about one topic, they can be supported in:

- filling in a partly filled in concept map, and
- creating their own concept maps for another topic. This would require that students have access to the facts and knowledge needed to create the concept map.

As making connections between school subjects can help make learning more meaningful, the above graphic organiser also shows how the topic of deforestation is tied to Biology and Business Studies. This aims to underline for the students the utility of what is being learned.

Some examples of other graphic organisers used by students to summarise their learning about biodiversity are shown below. The first graphic organiser was used to draw out the causes and consequences of species decline or extinction. It was partly filled in so as to serve as an example of how to complete this fishbone graphic organiser.

Figure 8: *Decline of species*

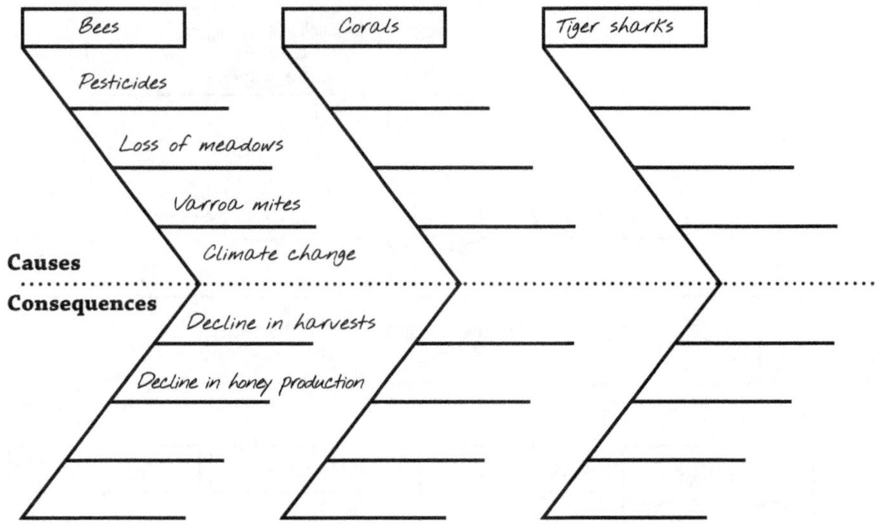

The next graphic organiser can act as a framework for critical thinking. It supports students in determining facts, making inferences/deductions, determining what they still need to know, and in formulating questions.

Figure 9: *Building a need to know*

THE FACTS	DEDUCTION	MISSING INFORMATION	REMAINING QUESTIONS
What does this source tell me for certain / for sure?	What can I infer (deduce, conclude) from this source?	What does the source NOT tell me?	What questions would I like answered?

The next graphic organiser can help students to draw out the core information about a topic and to visualise it. In this case the objective is to draw out the core content information and language about the topic of biodiversity. However, as it is filled in it can serve as a model for a future topic.

Figure 10: *Fleshing out a concept*

CONCEPT
Biodiversity

RELATED WORDS AND PHRASES	DEFINITION	CURRENT SITUATION	POTENTIAL CONSEQUENCES	KEY CONCLUSION
• *levels of diversity* • *species* • *genes* • *variations in the gene pool*	*Biodiversity represents the degree of diversity among and within plant and animal species in an ecosystem*	• *numerous species threatened* • *Key species that play a major role in the food chain such as bees and coral are critically threatened* • *awareness of danger growing*	• *less food security (loss of bees could have a catastrophic effect)* • *loss of revenue* • *more unpredictable weather* • *diseases could spread more easilty*	*We need to move quickly to protect biodiversity or risk major negative consequences for the planet and its inhabitants*

For a review of the key concepts of a topic and their importance students could be asked to fill in the chart below. The chart can be partly filled in to model expectations or it could be left empty. Students would need to fill it in without looking at their textbooks or notes. This would allow them to assess their learning and identify any gaps. Finally, once the students have checked their own or a partner's work and are satisfied with their responses, the teacher and the class as a whole could work to construct an ideal response to each question. Ultimately, the chart and the just-described activities are aimed at helping students to reflect on and articulate the core essence of the topic in a structured manner which should in turn lead to the better encoding of the learning. Alternatively, in order to conduct a review of a topic, students can be asked to develop test questions and work in groups to answer them.

Levels of Biodiversity		
Genetic diversity	***Species diversity***	***Ecosystems diversity***
What is it? (10–25 words) *Genetic diversity reflects the ________ present at the level of ________*	What is it? (10–25 words) *Species diversity includes both:* *a) species richness (the number of different species in a given community)* *b) species ____________* *(____)*	What is it? (10–25 words)
Why is it important? (10–25 words)	Why is it important? (10–25 words)	Why is it important? (10–25 words)

In addition to using graphic organisers to help students process their content learning and re-use new language, teachers can help students to process content learning by breaking up their own explanations and having students reprocess what they have been taught. This can also help build listening, concentration and co-operative skills. Before, during or after a teacher speaks for 5–15 minutes, students can be asked to undertake the following activities:

- Students work in pairs. One person takes notes on the content and the other writes down as many words and phrases that could be considered 'academic language' as he or she can. After the teacher has finished speaking, they then try to reconstruct the key points from the talk, and present them to another pair of students.
- Interrupting note-taking: just before the teacher begins to talk about an important point, students are asked to stop taking notes or close their notebooks or laptops for the next few minutes (up to 3 minutes). The students are asked to listen carefully for the next 3 minutes and see what they retain. Three minutes later the teacher asks students to work alone and write down the most important information/message from the previous 3 minutes. The students then work in pairs, share what they have written and improve each other's notes. Then two pairs form a group and create a joint improved product. One or two groups present their summaries. Other groups give feedback, and the teacher adds in any information that has been left out or corrects any errors in thinking.
- After the teacher's talk, the teacher hands out (or projects on the screen) a very brief summary of the talk with some missing information represented by blank spaces. Groups of students work together to fill in the missing information.
- Students condense the information from a teacher talk into a series of Tweets.
- Before the teacher speaks, students are given a series of sentences from the talk they are about to hear. Working in pairs or groups of three, students must rewrite these in social language. A few are reviewed and then the teacher gives his/her lecture.

BRIDGING, CONTEXTUALISING, CREATING, DIGESTIBLE CHUNKS OF INFORMATION IN A LOGICAL ORDER AND HIGHLIGHTING LANGUAGE

Two texts about cinema for use in an integrated Music and Art class follow. They were produced during a drafting process as the Nazarbayev Intellectual Schools of Kazakhstan were writing an L3 integrated music and art textbook. **Scaffolds in the first text (**in the left-hand column) include the provision of some synonyms in parentheses. They were considered insufficient. **Scaffolds in the enhanced text (**in the right-hand column) are much more numerous. They support students in the following ways:

- The text is given a title and two subtitles. This aims to immediately help students orient in the text. The title explains the focus of the text and the two subtitles draw out the two types of film that will be discussed.
- The original one-paragraph text is broken into four.
- Information is contextualised, and rendered more precise. Watching a silent movie was not actually a totally silent experience. Students are informed that piano players played music during the screenings in order to draw out the emotions expressed in the films.
- Additional synonyms or explanations are provided in parentheses, which should facilitate comprehension.
- Several nouns have been repeated instead of using pronouns (e.g. reel, film score, film music) in order to increase exposure to the new vocabulary.
- The 1927 date is now in a more logical place and only one pattern is used for presenting dates.
- A sentence containing two clauses has been made into two sentences and one relative clause has been placed in parentheses.
- Key academic language has been drawn out (terms in bold, collocations or phrasal verbs underlined with a dotted line).

Minor scaffolding	Major scaffolding
The first films in the 1890s were silent movies because they were only moving images without recorded sound (no soundtrack). Sound films coupling moving images with a soundtrack appeared later and were called talkies or talking pictures. These quickly replaced silent movies. The first talking picture was the *Jazz Singer*, which was produced by the American film company Warner Brothers in 1927. The movie starred Al Jolson who sings six songs in the film. There is also some synchronised dialogue although the film and soundtrack were on separate reels which had to be played at exactly the same time. Despite the early technical difficulties, talkies (talking pictures) were a major development for cinema. Nowadays, sound is an integral part of the film. Music written for films is called film music and it is part of the soundtrack. Usually it is written by one or more composers under the guidance of the film director and/or the film producer.	**Music in films** *The silent era* Cinema in the 1890s had no recorded sound (no **sound track**). These early films were **silent movies** (silent films). However in the cinemas (movie theatres), piano players played music *to draw out* emotions expressed in the films. *Talking pictures* In 1927, the first sound film was created. A sound film (movie) has a **soundtrack** coupled with the moving images. Viewers in the cinema could hear the sounds that they saw people make as they made them. These films became known as **talkies** (**talking pictures**). They quickly replaced silent movies. The first talking picture (film) was the *Jazz Singer*. This was **produced** by the American film company, Warner Brothers. The movie star and singer Al Jolson performs six songs. There is also some **synchronised** dialogue (although the film and **soundtrack** were on separate **reels)**. The film reel and the soundtrack reel had to be played at exactly the same time, which was difficult to achieve. Despite the early technical difficulties, **talkies** (talking pictures) were a major development for cinema. Nowadays, films often have **background music** (a **film score** or film music). A film score is usually original music written specifically to accompany a film. Film music is part of the **soundtrack**. Generally (usually), it is written by one or more composers under the guidance of the **film director** and/or the **film producer**.

To build a progression to lead into reading the above adapted text, it is possible to first further scaffold reading of the text by breaking it into even smaller chunks. For example, nine short sentences can be taken from the text or be created based on the text. Each sentence is written on a separate piece of paper. Students can be asked to work in pairs to place the sentences shown below in a logical order. This activity scaffolds the reading of the full text because: (1) it requires less reading but helps students to become familiar with key messages in the text, (2) there are fewer words to process and likely fewer new words to look up in a dictionary or to discuss, (3) the strips of text require critical thinking to understand the logical order of what is written, and (4) the activity is done in pairs and students can support each other.

Students can also be asked why some words are in bold. They can be guided in reviewing words in bold and underlined phrases. Similarly, students can be asked about the two different types of underlining (e.g. Why is your attention being drawn to these words or phrases?). The students can be asked to suggest ways in which they could use these phrases in other contexts.

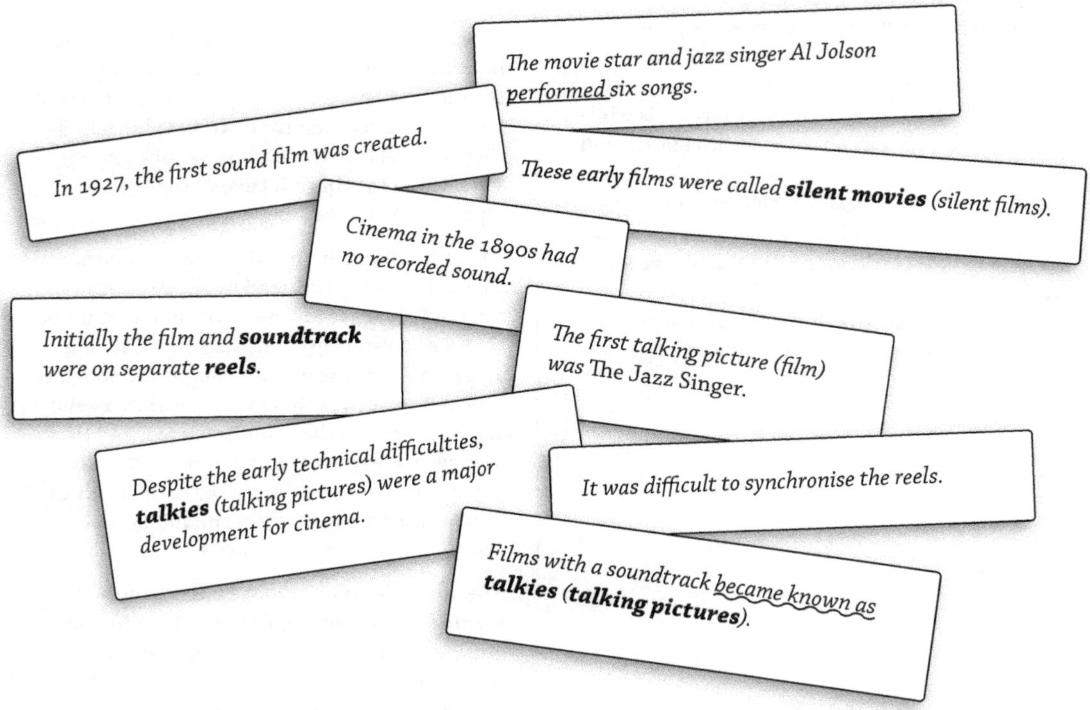

One of the purposes of scaffolding is to **capture students' attention** and build interest in what will be learned. Prior to working with the strips of paper or the entire text, students can be shown the following picture,[2] and asked to state what they know for certain and what they can infer from the picture and why. A picture of this nature can pique students' curiosity and thereby increase involvement. The picture is rich with information. If necessary, to further structure the students' thinking, they can be directed to explain what event is being depicted and why they think that is the case, the importance of the event, which country this is taking place in, who the central figure is, what race he is, why an actor today would be very unlikely to apply makeup to appear black, and what era it is.

SEQUENCING ACTIVITIES IN DIGESTIBLE CHUNKS IN A LOGICAL ORDER, ENGAGING WITH SELF- AND PEER-ASSESSMENT, ASKING QUESTIONS, CONTEXTUALISING AND PLANNING

The scaffold below is intended for use in both Art and History. In the art class the focus is on Estonian painting from the 1920s and 1930s. The topic in the History class is the lead-up to WWII. The lesson targets students operating at a B1 or B2 level in their L2. But the ideas can be adapted for students with lower levels of L2 proficiency.

---

2 Premiere of *The Jazz Singer*, 1927. Wolf Tracer Archive.

1

2

3

4

5

6

7

8

Above: Andrus Johani, *Elderry Woman with a Rooster*, courtesy Estonian Art Museum, KUMU

Students are shown the above images one at a time. With each image students are asked first to identify what they know for certain, and to justify their answer. Other students are asked to challenge their classmates' thinking. For example, if a student looking at the first image is certain that there is an old oil painting in the frame and says as a justification that s/he has seen frames like this in the museum, this can be challenged. The frame could just as well include a mirror or be part of a contemporary sculpture or mixed media artwork. Typically, when students are shown the hand (image 2) they state it is a man's hand and justify their response by saying it is large and rough. They can then be challenged to explain what visual evidence might prove the gender of a hand. In this image there is no such evidence.

By deconstructing the painting into smaller chunks, students' interest in the painting is maintained and their analysis of the paintings' various constituent elements is encouraged. Each and every step of making an evidence-based judgement or inference is an opportunity to assess one's thinking. Central to maintaining momentum is asking students challenging questions or having students question each other's logic. To encourage analysis and questioning, students can be provided a language scaffold such as the table below. In addition, new language that arises in the discussion about the painting can be written on the board.

Justifying	Inferring	Questioning
What I can see for certain is ... We do not necessarily know if ... We can be quite certain that ... because ... To my mind ...	We can infer that ... because ... Normally/typically, ... The colour could represent the following: ...	Is that proof positive? I am not convinced, can you provide more evidence? Aren't you inferring? Aren't you just making an inference?

This painting was created in 1939 by Andrus Johani. In 1939 Estonia was an independent country under threat of Soviet and Nazi occupation. In this light, the central figure in this painting can be seen as the 'salt of the earth', a symbol of resolve, in part because the blue, black and white colours, which are so prominent in the painting, are also the colours of the Estonian flag. The red on the white cloth or shawl can be seen as blood. The rooster with its red comb can be considered a symbol of the Soviet Union and the women's firm grip on the rooster's claws seen as a determination to manage the danger. At the very least the sharp claws can be seen as a source of danger and the woman's grip as resistance to that danger. The above interpretation can be triangulated with key facts from the artist's personal life to see if there might be additional interpretations.

The final image, which includes lines drawn onto the painting to divide it into sectors, also structures student thinking as it directs attention to the focal point of the painting and four additional sections of the work. In order to facilitate a written analysis of the painting, students can be provided with a scaffold (see example below) that offers: (1) the structure of the writing analysis, (2) some of the needed phraseology, and (3) some useful vocabulary that can be organised according to semantic (interrelated) categories.

The title of this picture is ... This picture is called / is entitled ... It was painted by ... in ...
This is an important year in Estonian history because ...

Upper left-hand corner/quadrant

The colour ... dominates the ...

This helps ... stand out

Other predominant colours include ...

The colour black contributes to ...

Upper right-hand corner/quadrant

Above all, this quadrant includes ...

The elderly woman appears ...

She is looking (away from/toward) ...

This creates a sense of ...

The colours ... and ... evoke the main colours in ...

The centre / focal point

At the centre (heart) of the picture ...

The predominant colour is ....

This colour often symbolises ...

The elderly woman's hand is ...

Lower left-hand corner/quadrant

In the ... the artist painted a ...

Superimposed on the black background, there is/are ...

This colour symbolises ... /
This echoes the same ...

The woman's lower hand is /appears ...

This colour ... / These colours relate to / evoke ...

Lower right-hand corner /quadrant

Here the artist places ...

In the lower right hand ...

The rooster's claws are ...

Around the claws ... This has the effect ...

The shawl is ... This could mean ...

In conclusion ...

Vocabulary

Blood	*To bleed*	*Bloody*
Claws	*To claw*	*To scratch*
Sharp claws		

Vocabulary

Abstract *Realistic*

Shawl draped on the arm

Head scarf

Another option for scaffolding both structure and language is to use noun, verb or phrase chains. The following noun chain was provided to students who were studying acid rain. The students were asked to carry out research and write a report on the causes and consequences of acid rain. They were also asked to propose solutions to the problem.

Noun chain **ACID RAIN**

- Industrial revolution
- Emissions
- Sulphur dioxide
- Nitrogen oxides
- Atmosphere
- Growth in population
- More industry
- Increased emissions
- Precipitation (wet disposition)
- Dry deposition
- Dead lakes
- Loss of marine life
- Soil damage
- Less crops (drop in agricultural production)
- Damaged vegetation
- Poorer crops
- Human health
- Solutions

The noun chain, using limited language, tells the story of how acid rain has developed, and some of the resulting consequences. This means that these words, which are key to discussing acid rain, are presented in a meaningful context. The language is thus more likely to be retained and put to later use. In particular, the noun chain provides some of the links between the causes and consequences of acid rain. Links create meaning and foster critical thinking. More structure can be offered by providing subheadings in a given chain (e.g. Introduction, Historical Context and Causes, Current Reality and Consequences, Potential Solutions, Conclusion). To encourage further reflection, students can be asked to find at least two more causes that are not listed in the chain.

Before beginning the writing assignment, students can be asked to identify cause-and-consequence pairs from the noun chain (e.g. 'soil damage' leads to 'a drop in agricultural production'). In order to first plan the writing of an essay, students can create their own noun, verb or phrase chains. In addition, students can create their own noun, verb or phrase chains to describe any given process. This could be very helpful as a review exercise to see how well students have understood a process under study.

As the above tasks all require students to sequence their narratives then it may be helpful to offer the students an additional language scaffold to support sequencing.

Also, Additionally First, First of all, Second, Third, In addition, Furthermore, Subsequently,	it is important it could be useful it is essential	to determine to consider to evaluate to examine to weigh

Finally, the following description of a History lesson comes from Belgium. The students were 14 years old and in the third year of doing 20% of their programme through English. Martens and Van de Craen (2017) describe a lesson about the fall of the Berlin Wall. The Berlin Wall symbolised the divide between Eastern and Western Europe and the Cold War. The day in 1989 when East Germans first broke through the wall and streamed into West Berlin is hugely symbolic in marking the end of the Cold War. In order to build context about the event and to engage students, the teacher showed a short BBC news clip about that remarkable day. To increase engagement with the video, the students were given two tasks or goals. They were asked to take notes about facts they could pull out from the video, and to make note of the emotions being experienced by all involved. The language about emotions was mostly easily accessible to the students (e.g. celebration, excitement, joy, party mood, night of euphoria). Therefore, the teacher began the discussion by asking students about the emotions as opposed to the facts. This scaffolded the later discussion about facts as it helped get the discussion going. Next, the students worked through discussion to reconstruct the narrative from the news report (the facts). This task models how students can work together to recall and process learning. One student statement can jog the memory of other students. Once a 'fact' is drawn out, the description can be improved. Finally, the students were encouraged to think more deeply by moving from 'what' questions to 'why' questions. Martens and Van de Craen (2017) stress that the History and Language teachers reported meeting on a weekly basis to coordinate the planning of their lessons.

ASKING QUESTIONS AND PROVIDING PROMPTS

Asking questions of students is one of the primary ways teachers scaffold student learning. The following advice about forming questions on texts or about what has been taught in a class are based on the work of Nuttall (1996):

- The questions should determine whether the student has understood the key concepts or points being made, not just check for factual information. Ultimately, the questions should help students to understand the key concepts or points being made in a text.
- The language used in questions about a text should not be more difficult than the language in the text (e.g. does not introduce new difficult words or phrases in the questions).
- The answers to the questions should not require students to use language that they have not yet been taught. If new language is required in the answers, its use must be scaffolded (e.g. the needed new language is visible on the board and students' attention is drawn to it).
- Questions must be clear (e.g. cannot be interpreted in several ways).
- It should be impossible to answer the questions without reading the text.
- There should be at least one question for every paragraph or every 5–6 lines of text.
- It is best to begin with general questions and move to more detailed questions.
- Questions should focus on important rather than unimportant details.

Key fact:
Students are more likely to recall details from a cognitively challenging question than an easy question.
(Baddeley, 2004)

Nuttall (1996) has categorised the types of questions that can be asked of students. They are offered as a tool for reflecting on the types of questions that teachers can ask their students:

- Questions for literal comprehension – the information found in the text (e.g. What are the key criteria that banks use to decide whether to lend money to new businesses?)
- Questions involving reorganisation or reinterpretation – combining, reordering or reinterpreting information (e.g. What are the similarities and differences between insects and spiders?)
- Questions of inference – deducing what is implied, but not stated in the text (e.g. What hypothesis do these research results confirm?)
- Questions of evaluation – making a judgment about something in a text and explaining why (e.g. The evidence given by the author is not really evidence. S/he is confusing fact and opinion.)
- Questions of personal response – using the text as a point of departure, but expressing a personal opinion (How might you have behaved differently in this context?)
- Questions about language and style (e.g. How would a scientist say the same thing?)

A word of caution: as discussed in Chapter 2, the **overuse** of an **initiation-response-feedback (IRF) pattern** – asking a question, listening to a response and providing some form of feedback/evaluation – will undermine learning. **Students often find it difficult to remain engaged when the IRF pattern dominates classroom discourse.** Questions need to be used to build a dialogue – a narrative leading to a common understanding of what needs to be learned. Affording students rich opportunities for dialogue and writing helps students to rearrange their thoughts and to search for and use language to express those rearranged thoughts (see pages 13–16 for a discussion of dialogic learning). Students' dialogue and writing also reveal the gaps in their current knowledge base, thinking and language proficiency. Once revealed, a teacher can help students address these gaps.

Ultimately, questions need to keep students in their Zone of Proximal Development, that is to say moving further on in their thinking than they could on their own. Interestingly, Baddeley (2004) argues that students are more likely to recall details from a cognitively challenging problem than an easy one. Yet some teachers may believe that cognitively challenging work may be too difficult for students. Lindholm-Leary (2001), however, found in her research into dual-language education that 'students were no more likely to incorrectly answer a high-order question than a lower-order one'. It is important to be aware that several studies have found that most of the questions asked by teachers do not encourage critical thinking (Brown and Wragg, 1993; Gibbs, 1995). To overcome this widespread tendency, time and thought are needed to formulate questions and tasks that foster critical thinking.

In addition to many of the questions suggested on the previous page, the following prompts, questions or tasks can act as a scaffold to foster critical thinking:

Content

- not asking whether carbon is a metal, but instead asking why carbon is a metal (Wiliam, 2011)
- not asking what a prime number is, but instead asking why 17 is a prime number and 15 not a prime number (Wiliam, 2011)
- on occasion giving students a problem to solve that cannot be solved
- asking students to reinterpret information from different stakeholder perspectives
- asking students to analyse the validity of a claim
- asking students how they would defend, justify or validate a stance
- asking students to devise an experiment to test a hypothesis
- asking students to offer another interpretation of the data
- asking students how an opponent might argue against the point they have just made
- asking students to evaluate the quality and/or impartiality of the counter-argument
- asking students to explain the logical consequences of their analysis
- asking students to provide evidence to back up or challenge a point of view
- asking students to persuade someone to adopt a different view of a situation.

Language

- asking students to analyse the language being used in a text and how that might influence the reader (e.g. unemotional, provocative, factual)
- asking students to use richer language or scientifically more precise language
- directing student attention to a language error such as a wrong use of a verb tense or a preposition and asking them to correct it
- asking students to restate a point written in academic language in social language
- asking students to restate what they have just said using the language of a scientist, historian or geographer
- directing students to undertake self-talk in order to organise thoughts and identify gaps in language knowledge before they are asked to explain their own beliefs or understandings. They can be allowed to use dictionaries and then to ask for peer support for a short period of time.

In CLIL it is also helpful if instructions are provided orally and in writing so students can concentrate on the task as opposed to using working memory to recall the details of the task. Finally, when asking questions, students can be provided some categories to jog their memory and/or structure their answers – 'What do you know about the civil rights movement in the USA? – origins, leaders, key events, setbacks, accomplishments.

For more ideas on using prompts see **Chapter 7:** *Assessment*.

ENGAGING WITH PLANNING

In order to help students to experience learning as an incremental process over which they have significant control, they can be supported in planning their work. For example, if students are assigned a group project, they can be asked first to develop a plan for how they will implement it. Many would be challenged to see all the stages of the planning process. In reflecting on the planning process students could be asked: to decide on the tasks; how they will divide responsibilities; when and how often they will review the success criteria; to decide on sources of information; and, to agree on and plan for building in a review process (e.g. showing a draft to friends, rereading the work several times to ensure (1) all criteria have been met, (2) editing several times for different purposes such as checking the accuracy of the content, and checking spelling, punctuation, word choice and bridging between paragraphs).

In a similar way students can be encouraged to develop a plan for studying. This can be scaffolded by offering categories for students to reflect on such as: what (content and language) needs to be learned, what mark they are seeking, when they will study, where they will study, their top five strategies, whether they will work alone or with others, timelines, risks, and when and how they will evaluate whether the plan was a success. Central to developing skills in and getting into the habit of planning is taking the time to evaluate the plan (e.g. once an assignment has been turned in and again when the students have received their mark. Conclusions would need to be drawn about how to improve the plan the next time the students plan similar work).

ENGAGING WITH LANGUAGE LEARNING STRATEGIES AND SKILLS

A more practiced eye.
A more receptive ear.
A more fluent tongue.
A more involved heart.
A more responsive mind.

Rebecca Oxford (1990) began her seminal book on language learning strategies with the above lines, saying that teachers want to stimulate in students the listed characteristics 'in order to enable them to become more proficient language learners'. Proficient learners are also largely autonomous language learners.

In CLIL, the L2 is one of the gatekeepers to content knowledge. Students need to learn the language in order to access the content. There is much language to learn and ultimately it is the student who must do the learning. Highly competent language leaners have internalised learning strategies that allow them to self-scaffold future learning. This section will focus on language learning strategies that students can use to improve language learning and thereby also content learning.

This section will include:

- a definition of language learning skills
- an explanation of why language learning skills are important

- some references to research on learning skills
- ways of supporting students in acquiring language learning skills
- lists of language learning strategies and skills that students can use to become more effective language learners
- affective language learning strategies
- cognitive language learning strategies
- social language learning strategies
- meta-cognitive language learning strategies
- suggestions for teaching language learning strategies.

What are language learning skills? Language learning skills are manifested in strategies that students can use to enhance their language learning. Skilled language learners use strategies to work with unfamiliar language, to recall it and put it to use.

Why are language learning skills important? Language learning skills can help students to gain greater control over their own learning. As students actively **take charge of their own learning**, this should help increase their pace of learning and the enjoyment derived from learning.

Importantly, language learning skills and learner autonomy also help students to meet intended language learning outcomes/objectives. As content and language learning are deeply interdependent, improved language learning should also lead to improved content learning. This is because the precise use of language is helpful in explaining, working with and understanding in detail content concepts. Equally importantly, a precise as well as an imprecise use of language can reveal misconceptions related to students' understanding of content concepts under study. Misunderstandings can then be addressed.

Primordial point

Language learning skills are best learned while working on a content subject assignment. This helps students to experience immediately how language learning skills can help them learn content subject matter, and improve their performance in the content subject.

What does the research say? Students who are taught, and use, learning skills can substantially **improve their learning and achievement**. When a group of people with an average IQ score who have good learning skills are compared with a group of people with high IQ scores but who have weak learning skills, the group with the good learning skills tends to outperform the group with weak learning skills when given difficult problems to solve (Veenman, Prins and Elshout, 2002).

Equally importantly, students who are performing below average tend also to be less likely to use written texts independently. This places them at a disadvantage when compared to higher performing students.

There is general consensus among researchers in the area of language learning that proficient and successful language learners use language learning skills (see the work of Legenhausen, 2009; Knouzi et al., 2010).

How can students be helped to acquire language learning skills? A teacher can:

- first, explain why language learning skills can help students to learn, and then have students identify the language learning skills they are currently using
- identify and explicitly teach language learning strategies in the context of learning new content matter
- afford students well-structured opportunities to practice using language learning strategies, and do this whilst doing content or language lesson assignments
- support the simultaneous use of language learning strategies along with general learning skills
- show students which language learning strategies they could harness to better achieve which learning objectives, and provide them with an opportunity to experience how the given language learning strategy can improve learning
- support students in reflecting on how language learning skills have helped to support their learning of content matter or how the lack thereof have hindered learning.

More concrete examples will be offered at the end of this chapter.

What are the language learning strategies students can use to become more skilled language learners? Below you will find a list of L2 language learning strategies. Once students develop the habit of using these strategies, the strategies become a part of their language learning skills repertoire that they can draw on to improve learning. To facilitate their processing, the strategies have been divided into the following categories:

- affective strategies
- cognitive strategies

- social strategies
- meta-cognitive strategies.

The following categories and subcategories are drawn from Oxford (1990) and some of the exercises that follow on are based on her work.

AFFECTIVE STRATEGIES

(regulating one's own attitudes, one's emotions such as fear and anxiety, one's motivation to learn)

⇨ to reward oneself for success in communicating with others in the L2 or L3 *(e.g. being more focused and pleased with successful communication than concerned about making a few grammar errors that can be corrected in future conversations)*

⇨ to not be afraid to take risks with language when one does not have all the words or grammar knowledge needed to perfectly express a point

⇨ to be aware of fatigue related to working through the L2 or L3, and to take breaks as need be

⇨ to increase awareness of feelings related to language learning so as to reduce or eliminate self-handicapping and self-discounting *(e.g. avoiding effort in order to have an excuse for explaining possible future failures, and saying 'I am poor at languages')*

⇨ to minimise negative self-talk (e.g. *not being highly self-critical and beating oneself up about mistakes)*

⇨ to increase positive self-talk *(e.g. saying 'I have done a good job as the other person understood me')*

⇨ to self-motivate *(e.g. to recognise and reward accomplishments and to set new short-term and long-term goals)*

⇨ to seek pleasure from learning

⇨ to explore one's beliefs about language learning *(e.g. identifying a belief such as some grammar point being too difficult to master and then seeing if that belief can be challenged)*

⇨ to write down feelings and think about what has caused them and how they can be managed

⇨ to calm oneself down when one is anxious about working through the L2 or L3 *(e.g. deep breathing, doing exercise, being mindful of tensions in the body, avoiding stimulants such as energy drinks)*

- ⇨ to have the patience to return to something (a task or goal) one has not initially succeeded in completing/achieving, and use a step-by-step process to eventually complete that task or achieve that goal
- ⇨ to supress the impulse to give up.

COGNITIVE STRATEGIES

(e.g. generic strategies, retrieval strategies, rehearsal strategies, compensation strategies)

Generic cognitive strategies:

- ⇨ to guess meaning from context
- ⇨ to build dictionary skills including dictionary use, and the creation and use of student-generated dictionaries/glossaries
- ⇨ to first skim texts for words one does not know and look them up
- ⇨ to analyse words for clues such as prefixes, roots and suffixes
- ⇨ to skim texts for key ideas
- ⇨ to do other forms of self-talk in order to organise thoughts and identify gaps in language knowledge *(e.g. explaining personal beliefs, identify and formulating unanswered questions about the topic under study, summarising orally and in writing a content concept)*
- ⇨ to read a text several times for different purposes
- ⇨ to make inferences from context
- ⇨ to make connections between new pieces of knowledge not just connecting to previous knowledge
- ⇨ to first brainstorm language that might be needed for a task before actually beginning the task
- ⇨ to look out for words that have a different meaning in different languages
- ⇨ to develop the habit of comparing languages
- ⇨ to develop the habit of reading for pleasure in a second/third language
- ⇨ to develop the habit of exploring websites in one's second or third language
- ⇨ to stop and start recordings to try to catch unfamiliar words or phrases

- ⇨ to learn to use a monolingual dictionary in the L2 or L3
- ⇨ to look up words one does not understand
- ⇨ to put quotation marks around a phrase and do an Internet search to see if that exact phrase exists in the Internet and the frequency of its use
- ⇨ to do part of the research for L1 school projects in the L2.

Retrieval strategies:

- ⇨ to listen and read selectively *(e.g. listening for the three key facts or for information about a character's past)*
- ⇨ to visualise words and concepts
- ⇨ to group words or concepts into categories
- ⇨ to seek out associations between hard to remember words and familiar words
- ⇨ to link one L2 item or concept with another
- ⇨ to use mnemonics *(e.g. Please excuse my dear Aunt Sally. This helps recall the order of maths operations – parentheses, exponents, multiplication, division, addition, subtraction)*
- ⇨ to use rhyme
- ⇨ to use flash cards or hiding L2 answers to test one's knowledge
- ⇨ to jot down in a phrase book interesting turns of phrase one comes across in a second or third language
- ⇨ to reuse information and language in different ways (e.g. creating a graphic organiser to explain key points).

Rehearsal strategies:

- ⇨ to role-play in one's imagination a possible dialogue with a person one is about to meet
- ⇨ to build up a repertoire of things to say to someone before meeting them
- ⇨ to analyse texts others have written on a similar topic looking for phraseology one might be able to use
- ⇨ to mimic the movements that can be associated with a concept or words being learned whilst one is also learning the language *(e.g. total physical response)*

- ⇨ to use the L2 or L3 to explore the Internet
- ⇨ to dedicate a fixed number of hours per week to using the L2 or L3 for media consumption *(e.g. watching TV, listening to music, watching videos, reading newspapers)*
- ⇨ to try to state in the L2 or L3 something you have just learned through the L1
- ⇨ to explain a concept to oneself aloud
- ⇨ to practice a speech in the environment it will be presented in, as environmental clues will help one to remember the ideas and language practiced in that environment.

Compensatory strategies:

- ⇨ to paraphrase *(e.g. saying the same thing in a different way)*
- ⇨ to use gesture in addition to language in order to help get across a point
- ⇨ to use a dictionary or a translation tool during a conversation.

SOCIAL STRATEGIES

(getting support from and speaking/working with other students, the teacher or other speakers of the language)

- ⇨ to ask people to slow down and to do this several times if need be
- ⇨ to ask questions for clarification of meaning as opposed to requesting translation
- ⇨ to ask lots of questions and make the most of opportunities to speak and publically organise one's thoughts
- ⇨ to seek support from others or materials until one has tested how one might have a future conversation about a given topic
- ⇨ if someone else is having difficulty finding words, help them to find the needed word or phrase; this models the sort of behaviour expected from others
- ⇨ to ask group members to set group norms about language use *(e.g. Let's try to do at least 50% of our group work through the L3)*
- ⇨ to ask more proficient speakers of the language to correct your language errors and to thank them when they do that

- to seek out opportunities outside of class to practice communicating in the L2 or L3.

META-COGNITIVE STRATEGIES

(e.g. being able to plan, monitor, evaluate, improve performance in the L1, L2 and L3, being able to think about one's thinking)

- to set personal language goals/objectives/outcomes, to plan for their achievement and to measure progress being made in achieving these
- to evaluate task success
- to monitor language comprehension and production
- to record a presentation or a discussion and to analyse the recording
- to identify language learning strategies, to practise them and self-evaluate their use
- to self-record and then evaluate that recording whilst seeking to improve self-expression or accuracy in language use
- to identify one's own learning style preferences (e.g. using that style to one's benefit but trying to expand one's range of learning styles)
- to reflect on one's own learning needs
- to seek out learning materials and to organise these
- to arrange a study space
- to develop a study schedule that includes clear targets and measuring progress in meeting those
- to self-question in order to increase the accurate and precise use of language
- to plan for when and how to use newly acquired words
- to look for patterns in language
- to be aware of the most common errors made when listening to others and assessing if one makes those mistakes *(e.g. thinking more about your answer than listening carefully to what the person is saying, interrupting the speaker, jumping to conclusions, finishing someone's sentence for them, changing the subject to something that interests you more, expressing anger when you don't like a point being made).*

TEACHING SUGGESTIONS ABOUT HOW LANGUAGE LEARNING STRATEGIES CAN BE TAUGHT: (inspired by Oxford, 1990)

Using scenarios to determine language learning strategies:

Have students look at the following scenarios:

1. You are nervous about speaking in the classroom in the L2.
2. You are having trouble following what the teacher is saying.
3. You always make a lot of spelling and grammar mistakes when writing texts.
4. You have to give a speech or make a presentation in front of the class.
5. Someone has repeated what they said twice, but you still don't understand what they are saying.
6. You have difficulty understanding people with accents.
7. You find it difficult to read texts in the L2.
8. The teacher keeps saying you need to do group work in the L2. Some people in your group don't even try to do this.
9. You have been told you need to use academic language when writing your paper, but are unsure of what that means.

Ask the students to suggest language learning strategies for coping with those situations. As they arise in the discussion, students can help list them on the board, or key them into an electronic device for projection. Next, either give students a handout or project 30+ language learning strategies on the screen. Students should scan these to see if there are any additional language learning strategies they could apply to the above situations. Those strategies can be selected from the above lists of affective, cognitive and social strategies. Finally, students could develop a guide to language learning, which can be placed on the class website. This could become a living document that is improved from year to year.

ACTIVE LISTENING AND QUESTIONING

It has been estimated that of all the four language skills used in communication, people spend much more of their time listening than speaking, reading or writing. Listening is an important skill needed for success in our work and personal lives. For example, the capacity for people to listen is one of the primary criteria used in choosing friends.

For this exercise, students work in pairs. Student A has a diagram depicting the causes and consequences of a war, or energy consumption patterns, or a chemical process, or a business or other work process, or possibly a famous painting. Option 1: Student A describes the diagram or painting and Student B tries to recreate it based on active listening and questioning. Option 2: Student B asks a series of questions about the diagram or painting and tries to recreate it using Student A's answers.

As a scaffold, a series of questions or question stems could be displayed on the board. Some of these might include:

- How many square centimetres is ... ?
- Can you be more precise?
- How far is it from the left hand margin?
- How wide is the line?
- What colour is it?
- What else has to fit on the page?
- What does the diagram depict?
- What else ... ?

It is also possible for students to use the following two rubrics to evaluate their own listening skills. They self-assess their own listening practices. The total self awarded points in Table B are deducted from the total self-awarded points in Table A.

Table A:

While listening to others:	often +3 points	sometimes +2 points	rarely or never +0 points
I look at the speaker and maintain at least intermittent eye contact			
I restate the key messages I heard			
I ask follow-up questions			
I observe body language and try to take this into account			

Table B:

While listening to others:	often - 3 points	sometimes - 2 points	rarely or never +0 points
I interrupt			
My mind wanders			
I don't ask for clarification as needed			
I don't respond to what is said			

Any score of 9–12 indicates excellent listening skills whilst a score below zero indicates that much work remains to be done.

Reviewing a topic

To review a unit of work in pairs students are each given a topic they have to summarise. Student A presents his/her summary to student B. Students B restates key points to affirm his/her understanding. Student B can also ask for further clarification. Student B can also makes suggestions. If suggestions are forthcoming, student A restates his/her point and student B mirrors back what he/she understood. Student A confirms that the understanding is correct or not. Before doing the exercise, two people would model the process for the class.

Filling in a questionnaire

By simply listing 30 language learning strategies on a questionnaire and having students fill it out, the students will not only reflect on their own practices but be exposed to additional language learning strategies.

It would be important to provide students with an overview of results of the questionnaire, and to discuss these with them. This will help them to see where they stand in relation to other students in using language learning strategies. There are electronic Internet application for conducting surveys that provide instant results.

When creating a questionnaire, listing language learning strategies in groups of five helps to scaffold the reading of the questionnaire. The questionnaire statements can be drawn up based on the learning strategies listed above. Normally this type of questionnaire would be written in the students' first language. A few examples of questionnaire statements are provided below.

Language learning skills questionnaire

Instructions: Please read each statement. Mark the box that most closely represents whether or to what extent you use the given strategy.

Strategies for managing emotions

1. When I get nervous about speaking in the second language I take a moment to calm myself down before continuing.

   ❑ **never** ❑ **almost never** ❑ **sometimes** ❑ **often**

2. I take risks with language when I do not know the words or have the grammar knowledge needed to perfectly express a point.

   ❑ **never** ❑ **almost never** ❑ **sometimes** ❑ **often**

3. I am aware of when I get tired working through the L2, and take breaks when possible.

   ❑ **never** ❑ **almost never** ❑ **sometimes** ❑ **often**

4. I can suppress the impulse to give up.

   ❑ **never** ❑ **almost never** ❑ **sometimes** ❑ **often**

Social strategies

1. I ask people to slow down and to do this several times if they are speaking too quickly.

   ❑ **never** ❑ **almost never** ❑ **sometimes** ❑ **often**

2. I ask questions for clarification if I have not understood what was said.

   ❑ **never** ❑ **almost never** ❑ **sometimes** ❑ **often**

3. I ask people who speak my L2 or L3 better than me to correct my mistakes.

   ❑ **never** ❑ **almost never** ❑ **sometimes** ❑ **often**

4. I seek out opportunities to practice using my L2.

   ❑ **never** ❑ **almost never** ❑ **sometimes** ❑ **often**

5. If I have to make a presentation or a speech, I practice it in front of friends.

   ❑ **never** ❑ **almost never** ❑ **sometimes** ❑ **often**

Rehearsal strategies

1. I imagine what I will say in the L2 and role-play it in my mind before speaking.

   ❑ **never** ❑ **almost never** ❑ **sometimes** ❑ **often**

2. I analyse texts others have written on a similar topic looking for phraseology that I might be able to use in the future.

   ❑ **never** ❑ **almost never** ❑ **sometimes** ❑ **often**

3. I allocate a fixed number of hours per week to using the L2 for media consumption (e.g. surfing the Internet, watching TV, listening to music, watching videos, reading newspapers).

   ❑ **never** ❑ **almost never** ❑ **sometimes** ❑ **often**

4. I try to explain to myself aloud in the L2 things I have learned in my L1 and then look up words I do not know in the dictionary.

   ❑ **never** ❑ **almost never** ❑ **sometimes** ❑ **often**

Retrieval strategies

1. I try to visualise words and concepts.

   ❑ **never** ❑ **almost never** ❑ **sometimes** ❑ **often**

2. I group words or concepts into categories.

   ❑ **never** ❑ **almost never** ❑ **sometimes** ❑ **often**

3. I look for links between hard to remember words and familiar words.

   ❑ **never** ❑ **almost never** ❑ **sometimes** ❑ **often**

4. I listen and read selectively (e.g. listening for the three key facts or for information about a character's past).

   ❑ **never** ❑ **almost never** ❑ **sometimes** ❑ **often**

5. I jot down in a phrase book interesting turns of phrase I come across in my second language.

   ❑ **never** ❑ **almost never** ❑ **sometimes** ❑ **often**

A learning skills research project

Students can be asked to research content and language learning skills being used by their fellow students as well as what experts recommend. Their research findings can be summarised in a student handbook for their Grade (Year). All classes in one Grade could collaborate to create this handbook. This can help: (1) to raise student awareness about learning skills, (2) to build the students' repertoire of learning skills, (3) to build learner autonomy, and (4) to provide a meaningful learning opportunity by creating a useful product.

CONCLUSION

Ongoing scaffolding of content, language and critical thinking are indispensable in CLIL. They help reduce the affective filter and increase student engagement and achievement. Scaffolding helps students build a growth mindset in regard to the learning of content and language, and critical thinking. Scaffolding can support students in meeting the increased demands of working through an L2. In particular, it can help avoid cognitive overload. In other words, it avoids placing excessive demands on working memory, the gateway through which all learning must pass. By concurrently scaffolding both content and language the Zone of Proximal Development - what students can do with the help of others or materials – increases. Importantly, students can use both general and language learning skills to take greater charge of their own learning. The ultimate goal of scaffolding is to help students develop the knowledge skills and attitudes they need to self-scaffold and to become more autonomous learners.

VIEW FROM THE FIELD:
South Korea

Kyungsuk Chang is a researcher at the Korean Institute for Curriculum and Evaluation. From 2013 to 2015, she was in charge of government-financed projects supporting CLIL implementation.

In 2009, South Korea adopted a new curriculum that focused on creativity and character building. This includes an emphasis on non-cognitive skills for the twenty-first century (e.g. social, emotional, practical and character-building skills). The national curriculum involves major changes. These include subject and grade clustering, reduction of the number of subjects listed as intensive courses, introduction of creative hands-on activities, and reinforcement of career education. In addition, under the revised curriculum, CLIL became an emerging practice at both the primary and secondary levels. It has had a substantial impact on English language teaching.

Before the introduction of the new curriculum, CLIL was widely perceived as a privilege of the upper-middle classes or the wealthy. CLIL was criticised for potentially contributing to an increased gap in English skills among different social classes. CLIL seemed to have no place in the national curriculum.

The revised curriculum gave momentum to the introduction of CLIL in some schools. This occurred mainly in secondary schools in metropolitan areas. CLIL was integrated into the school curriculum to develop students' creative thinking and the non-cognitive skills emphasised as a requisite for the twenty-first century. The approach to teaching CLIL is based on the following pedagogical principles:

- establishing routines to enable students to feel comfortable and confident in learning content through English
- encouraging students to consolidate their learning by referring to supplementary materials
- facilitating pair and small group work so students can support each other
- offering individualised attention and differentiated learning
- using a variety of learning activities such as project-based learning, storyboarding, dramatisation, visual thinking, graphic organiser creation and flipped learning
- valuing kinaesthetic activities, including games.

The factors that have contributed to a satisfactory implementation of CLIL at the secondary school level include the:

- adaptation of the national curriculum to accommodate individual school and student needs
- availability of qualified teachers with the required content knowledge, knowledge of the CLIL approach and the appropriate level of competence in English
- willingness of subject teachers to teach English through a subject area
- scaffolding to ensure students can understand the key concepts and English language terminology and phraseology
- classroom learning resources required to implement a CLIL programme.

Challenges that secondary schools face in implementing CLIL are being addressed through:

- dissemination of successful cases to schools, in particular in rural areas
- putting teachers at the centre of the change process, fostering collaboration and offering professional development opportunities
- research on and practices regarding how to assess CLIL classes in a context where traditional paper-and-pencil tests have dominated.

6 Culture and intercultural competence

Connections

How this chapter connects to other concepts in the book:

CLIL

'If [...] culture determines the way we interpret the world, and [if] we use language to express this interpretation, then CLIL opens an intercultural door, where learners can have experiences which they could not have had in a monolingual setting – meaning, for example, that it provides a rich catalyst for 'living' intercultural experiences which are fundamental to a deeper understanding of global citizenship' (Coyle et al., 2010).

Attitudes and affect

Everyone holds some preconceived ideas or beliefs about their own and other cultures. These become apparent in attitudes.

Attitudes represent a psychological tendency 'to react favourably or unfavourably to a class of objects' be those people, ideologies or events (Sarnoff, 1970). Attitude can act as a strong filter for or an obstacle to the acquisition of knowledge and skills.

Knowledge and skills

Culture is at times a highly emotive topic. In such circumstances, teachers may consider reversing the Knowledge, Skills, Attitude (KSA) paradigm and switch instead to ASK. An ASK approach involves first concentrating on supporting students in developing the attitudes and then the skills. This may help students be better disposed to and effective at acquiring and integrating 'new' knowledge (OECD, 2016 referring to Proctor, 2016).

Critical pedagogy

In order to build intercultural competence, one must be able to identify and investigate one's own prejudices, and those prevalent in society. This invites teachers and students to explore 'fundamental questions about knowledge, justice, equity in their own classroom, school, family and community' (Wink, 2000). The aim of such discussions is to build understanding about how to reduce inequalities and injustices which is the essence of critical pedagogy.

A man grew up in humble circumstances in an industrial town. He was religious. He went to synagogue services. He took seriously the needs of others and helped out at the local soup kitchen.

The man eventually started a business. Over the years he became more and more successful, at each step buying a new bigger house further away from the neighbourhood where he grew up.

Each time he moved, he also went to synagogue less frequently. He stopped helping out at the soup kitchen.

Finally, in his fifties he bought a mansion on the hill overlooking the town. There, he lived alone.

One day, the rabbi came to visit. In the drawing room he took the man to the picture window overlooking the town. 'What do you see?' asked the rabbi. The man talked about the town: the people that he knew, the business that he owned and the good works that he used to do.

Then the rabbi took the man to the mantle-piece. Above it hung a large gilded and ornate mirror. 'Now what do you see?' he asked. 'Myself' answered the man. 'Mmm' said the rabbi. 'That's the problem – just yourself.'

All religions have times of fasting and giving to charity. At these times people see less of themselves and more of the needs of the world around them.

The above story (and commentary) was told (given) by a Jewish rabbi, speaking in 2016 at a British mosque to Muslims, Buddhists, Christians, Hindus, Jews, and Sikhs attending an Iftar, a meal eaten by Muslims after sunset during the holy month of Ramadan. The audience nodded and applauded warmly. It is an **intercultural competence** to be able to offer a narrative that speaks to the values of people from several cultures. This account also underlines that **culture** is not simply defined by what divides different groups, but also by what unites them.

INTRODUCTION AND CHAPTER NAVIGATOR

Language is considered inextricably intertwined with culture. That can be said about content subject knowledge as well. However, there is no agreed upon definition of culture, because as Seelye (1993) points out it is 'a very broad concept embracing all aspects of human life'. That poses a problem for CLIL, as culture is considered a cornerstone of CLIL, despite the fact that it does not often receive the attention it deserves (Coyle et al., 2010). Hence, if in CLIL one is going to explicitly teach culture, it is important to define the construct for oneself, and to draw out its component parts. Furthermore, as proficiency in speaking and writing an additional language implies being able to successfully partake in inter- or cross-cultural action and communication, it is helpful to define the intercultural competences that allow one to cross the intercultural divide.

This chapter examines the constructs of culture and intercultural competence. More specifically, it:

- fleshes out the link between language and culture
- explores definitions of culture and offers a considerable list of cultural elements worthy of study
- draws out inter- or cross-cultural competences
- suggests some ways of teaching culture and fostering the development of intercultural competence.

THE BOND BETWEEN LANGUAGE AND CULTURE

> *The acquisition of a second language, except for specialized, instrumental acquisition ... is also the acquisition of a second culture.* (Brown, 2007)

There is a general consensus among academics that language and culture are inextricably tied. A person who speaks several languages is defined as having the ability 'to use languages for the purposes of communication and to take part in intercultural action' and that person is also 'viewed as a social agent, [that] has proficiency, of varying degrees, in several languages and experience of several cultures' (Council of Europe, 2007). The definition stresses the ability and the responsibility of the plurilingual individual to bridge the multilingual social order. A plurilingual individual is not only defined in linguistic terms, but is considered capable of crossing both a linguistic and cultural divide, having linguistic and cultural competences that are evidenced by intercultural communication and enrichment.

In other words, language 'is bound up with culture in multiple and complex ways', representing shared beliefs and attitudes and a common stock of knowledge (Kramsch, 1998). Sometimes culture is reflected in our language, and at other times culture has a strong impact on our language. In other cases the language itself appears to affect our culture.

For example, Chinese culture's respect for family is embedded in Putonguhoa (Manadarin Chinese). When speaking about one's uncle the speaker must also identify whether or not the uncle is from his or her mom's or dad's side, whether this is an uncle by marriage or birth, and if this was the father's brother whether he is older or younger than the speaker's father (Chen, 2012). Several cultures may have the same word for a notion, but accord it a different symbolic meaning. The colour blue represents sadness in English-speaking countries, but happiness and peace in Cameroon and Nigeria, and indicates that one has had too much to drink in Germany (Finkbeiner and Koplin, 2002).

Kuuk Thaayorre speakers from Australia refer to someone's brother standing to the southwest of them and the salt on the table being to the north of them instead of using more relative terms such as to the left or in front of (Boroditsky and Gaby, 2010). In other words, these aboriginal Australians orient themselves in geographical terms – north south, east, west. 'This is done at all scales, which means [they] have to say things like "There's an ant on your southeast leg" or "Move the cup to the north northwest a little bit"'(ibid.). This means these people need to always stay oriented according to their given geographic location. Their context may well have demanded it and had an impact on their language. 'The result is a profound difference in navigational ability and spatial knowledge between speakers of languages that rely primarily on absolute reference frames (like Kuuk Thaayorre) and languages that rely on relative reference frames (like English)' (ibid.).

It also appears that language itself may have a very significant impact on culture, including on people's saving patterns and sexual behaviours. Chen (2013) investigated if people behave differently based on whether the language they speak has strong or weak forms for expressing the future. Estonian has no future tense *per se*. One uses the same form of the verb to say 'It is raining' (*Vihma* ***sajab***) versus 'Tomorrow, it will rain' (*Homme* ***sajab*** *vihma*). The future is indicated by context, in this case by 'tomorrow' (*homme*). Finnish, Chinese and Yoruba are examples of languages that do not have a strong future tense. English, French, Hausa and Turkish are languages with a strong future tense. Chen studied nine countries with large populations where one group speaks a language with a strong future tense and another group speaks a language which uses a 'weak form' of the future. No matter how many times he revisited the data, he found that speakers of 'futureless' languages are:

- 30% more likely to put aside savings in a given year (having 25% more savings at retirement)
- 20–24% less likely to be smoking
- 13–17% less likely to be obese
- 21% more likely to have used a condom in their last sexual encounter.

Chen speculates that speakers of 'futured' languages perceive the future as further away than speakers of 'futureless' languages, who may have a more acute sense that the future is close and that it cannot be ignored.

Finally, if language and culture are inextricably tied then this is all the more reinforced by the fact that many languages are interrelated. Languages are often partly constructed through a process of intercultural exchange. Two studies suggest that the majority of English words have foreign origins. Based on an analysis of 80,000 words in the third edition of the *Shorter Oxford Dictionary*, Finkenstaedt and Wolff (1973) report the origin of English vocabulary as follows: 28.3% French and Old Norman; 28.24% Latin; 25% Germanic, although this does include words inherited from Old English; 5.32% Greek; 3.28% derived from proper nouns: and 1% from all other languages. Any given register of academic language may use more or fewer words of foreign origin. Williams (1986), who studied 10,000 words taken from business letters, describes their origins as follows: 41% French (langue d'oïl); 33% 'Native' English; 15% Latin; 2% Old Norse; 1% Dutch, and 10% other. English is certainly engaging with other cultures and languages. Next, we explore the concept of culture.

CULTURE DEFINED

> *'Culture ... is that complex whole which includes knowledge, belief, art, morals, law, custom, and any other capabilities and habits acquired by [...] a member of society.* (Tyler, 1870)

For well over 100 years social scientists have sought to define 'culture'. Definitions abound, but no one definition can be considered definitive. An in-depth review and discussion of definitions of culture would take us too far away from our focus on CLIL essentials. Hence, only a few definitions are explored in this chapter and one is adopted before moving on to more concrete tangible elements that could be a focus for teaching culture in CLIL contexts.

Damen (1987) sees culture as our primary adaptive mechanism, something we need for survival. It is the 'learned and shared human patterns or models for living; day-to-day living patterns. These patterns and models pervade all aspects of human social interaction. Culture is mankind's primary adaptive mechanism' (ibid.). This view is far removed from that of those who view culture as primarily residing in the fine arts.

Useem and Useem (1963) define culture 'as the learned and shared behavior of a community of interacting human beings'. Many definitions refer to culture developing through a process of socialisation. For example, the Center for Advanced Language Acquisition at the University of Minnesota (CARLA, 2012) defines culture as 'the shared patterns of behaviors and interactions, cognitive constructs, and affective understanding that are learned through a process of socialization.' Hofstede (1994) refers to culture as 'the collective programming of the mind'.

In addition to accepting the notion of socialisation, several social scientists stress the ability of the individual to still think for him/herself in the given cultural context.

> Culture is a fuzzy set of basic assumptions and values, orientations to life, beliefs, policies, procedures and behavioural conventions that are shared by a group of people, and that influence (but do not determine) each member's behaviour and his/her interpretations of the 'meaning' of other people's behaviour. (Matsumoto, 1996)

Similarly, Banks (2010) stresses the role of the individual. He points out that culture does not reside in its artefacts or other tangible objects that represent a culture but rather in the way the members of the group interpret, use and perceive these. In other words, despite the fact that culture can be viewed as something shared, it always plays out at the individual level through each individual's interactions with the given cultural elements and other individuals.

We take on board the above conclusions and adopt as a key reference point the definition of culture in the Universal Declaration on Cultural Diversity (UNESCO, 2001):

> [...] the set of distinctive spiritual, material, intellectual and emotional features of society or a social group, and that it [culture] encompasses, in addition to art and literature, lifestyles, ways of living together, value systems, traditions and beliefs.

There is often a tendency in language learning to focus on teaching culture through a study of a given culture's art, customs, dance, family life, food, holidays, meeting people, music, leisure activities, literature, pets, sports, transportation and vocations. These can give rise to valuable lessons. Based on the stated and implied richness of the above definitions of culture, it is possible to suggest a broad range and number of additional reference points for teaching culture. These additional reference points could potentially help students not only to engage with culture as a concept, but to deepen their knowledge of their own and other cultures. The list of reference points is not meant to be in any way prescriptive or exhaustive, or on any level imply that these all need to be covered in a curriculum. This list is simply offered as a series of options for consideration:

abandoned practices	history	public institutions,
architecture	humour	punishments
art (fine, applied, main-stream vs avant garde)	immigration	queuing
attitudes	inclusion	religion
beliefs	informal ways of governing	repression
common assumptions	insults	rituals
concepts of the universe	knowledge	rites of passage
cuisine	legislation	role of nature
customs	literature	roles
education	material objects/artefacts	soap operas
emigration	media	social security
environmental protection	music	social class
events	national budget priorities	spatial relations
exclusion	notions of time	sports
experience	personal space	stereotypes
famous people	perceptions of culture *versus* race	symbols
film	politics	taboos
friendship	politeness	trends
games	possessions	values
gender	practices	ways of giving and receiving feedback
gestures	prejudices	work.
hierarchies	proverbs	

Many of the above are complex constructs, and need to be approached with care. This would involve placing knowledge-building and perspective-taking (looking at the world through another person's eyes) at the centre of the exploration process. Keeping agreed values in mind will also help centre discussions. Moreover, it can be helpful to often return to the fact that no cultural construct is likely to be a monolithic symbol embraced by all members of a language community, and that culture is dynamic and therefore constantly changing and hopefully progressing.

Finally, in an era of globalisation (even if there were a shift to increased localisation), there is and will continue to be no shortage of cross-border matters that will affect us – conflict, disease, exchange of information and knowledge, 'fake news', innovation, migration, ownership, pollution, taxation and trade. It is often said we now live in a VUCA – volatile, uncertain, complex and ambiguous – world. If CLIL is to be fully fit for purpose in this VUCA world, it needs to support not just bi-cultural perspective-taking, but **multicultural perspective-taking**. For if the CLIL language is an international language, it is likely to be used not just with L1 speakers of the CLIL language, but to communicate with people from many other cultures who use the given CLIL language for international communication.

If one of the ultimate aims of learning in and through an additional language is to build students' capacity to take part successfully in intercultural action, then CLIL students need to develop intercultural competence. Next, that construct is broken down into tangible and teachable elements –options, not requirements.

INTERCULTURAL COMPETENCE

> *The first day or so we all pointed to our countries. The third or fourth day we were pointing to our continents. By the fifth day, we were aware of only one Earth.*
>
> Sultan bin Salman Al-Saud, 1985
> (first Arab and Muslim to fly in space)

At its core, intercultural competence is about perspective-taking. More specifically, intercultural competence is the ability that allows a person to think, act and communicate sufficiently effectively to navigate differences between people who hold dissimilar and sometimes opposing views of the world. Spitzberg and Changnon (2009) have a more nuanced view defining intercultural competence as 'the appropriate and effective management of interaction between people who, to some degree or another, represent different or divergent affective, cognitive and behavioral orientations to the world.'

Intercultural competence is a complex construct. What is certain is that developing intercultural competence is a challenging process and no one ever becomes fully interculturally competent (Deardorff, 2014). 'Language fluency is necessary but in itself insufficient to represent intercultural competence' (ibid.). In order to bring greater clarity to the construct, it needs to be broken down into more tangible competences that students and teachers can then seek to develop in themselves. Intercultural competences are usually divided into three or four interrelated categories – knowledge, skills, attitudes and values (Candelier et al., 2012; Deardorff, 2006 and 2013; Council of Europe, 2016; OECD, 2016). Values are sometimes subsumed under knowledge and attitudes.

Below, we draw out a substantial number of intercultural competences. **No CLIL teacher or student would be expected to develop all of these competences**. The discussion below simply seeks to clarify the concept and to create concrete reference points for reflecting on the teaching and learning of intercultural competences.

In the **knowledge domain** (based on Candelier et al., 2012), intercultural competences include knowing:

- that cultures are continually evolving
- that it is often difficult to distinguish one culture from another
- that a given culture is always complex and is itself made up of (more or less) different and conflicting or convergent subcultures
- that one can have a multiple, plural or composite identity
- that every person forms part of at least one cultural community and many persons form part of more than one cultural community
- the characteristics of one's own situation and cultural environment
- some social practices and customs from different cultures, including some which are specific to certain social, regional and generational groupings; cultural practices may vary across and within generational, regional and social groupings
- how culture and identity influence communicative interactions
- strategies that one can use to resolve intercultural conflicts such as knowing that the causes of misunderstanding must be sought out and clarified in common.

Students also need knowledge of alternative interpretations so they can weigh them (Gudykunst, 1993). In addition, they need knowledge of 'oppressions' including 'intersecting oppressions' (e.g. class, gender, race, religion) (Spitzberg and Changnon, 2009). Knowledge of body language is important. It is also important to know how people from diverse cultures have contributed to the development of the world knowledge explored in schools. Finally, in building cross-cultural relationships and understanding, it is helpful to have knowledge about whether a group of people tends to:

- give feedback directly or indirectly
- prefer a confrontational as opposed to a non-confrontational approach to negotiations
- prefer consensual or hierarchical decision-making
- view time as rigid or flexible (e.g. meetings always start on time or 15 minutes late), or
- persuade others by starting with their conclusions or by first detailing how they reached their conclusions (Meyer, 2014).

In the **attitudinal domain**, intercultural competences include having the ability to:

- view difference as a learning opportunity
- consider oneself as an 'outsider'
- be open (and master one's own eventual resistances) to what seems incomprehensible and different
- suspend one's judgment, practices, acquired representations and/or prejudices with reference to other cultures and one's own culture so one can consider other perspectives
- consider all languages as equal in dignity
- allow for plurilingual and pluricultural socialisation
- see loans from cultures as contributing to cultural enrichment
- experience a threat to one's identity including one's individuality
- assume a critical distance from information and opinions produced by media, common sense and one's interlocutors about one's own community and other communities
- construct 'informed' knowledge or representations

- establish a relationship of equality in plurilingual and pluricultural interactions
- be open and empathetic towards the unfamiliar, be that linguistic or cultural
- manage one's emotions and frustrations when engaging with another culture. (based on Candelier et al., 2012)

In the **skills domain**, some core intercultural competences include the ability to:

- use formulae of politeness appropriately in diverse cultural contexts
- tolerate ambiguity and view it as a positive experience
- recognise and identify cultural specificities, references or affiliations
- view and interpret the world from other cultures' points of view
- analyse the cultural origin of different aspects of communication
- analyse the cultural origins of certain behaviours
- analyse misunderstandings due to cultural differences
- identify, analyse and reduce ethnocentrism
- compare one's own non-verbal communication practices with those of others
- explore one's own prejudices, and recognise and name cultural prejudice
- build well-informed and structured arguments about cultural diversity
- resolve conflict arising from different cultural perspectives. (based on Candelier et al., 2012)

In addition, Spitzberg and Changnon (2009) argue that intercultural competence requires skill in identifying and challenging discriminatory acts, as well as being able to assess one's own intercultural performance.

In the **values domain**, intercultural competence includes valuing human dignity and human rights, cultural diversity, democracy, justice, fairness, equality and the rule of law (Council of Europe, 2016). Deardorff (2013) adds to the list, suggesting that global intercultural competence includes: adaptation, cultural humility, listening, relationship building, respect, seeing from multiple perspectives and self-awareness. Stressing the challenges of applying some of these competences, Spitzberg and Changnon (2009) point out that as people seek to adapt to diverse cultural situations, they should not overly compromise their own personal identity. As people often draw their energy for action from the values and attitudinal domains, it is these domains that fuel the implementation of knowledge through the use of mechanisms and the application of skills (Mehisto, 2015).

A first step to developing intercultural competence is building awareness and understanding of some of the core elements of the construct. As there is never a point where one becomes interculturally fully competent, then it is essential to help students build the habit of actively drawing on acquired intercultural competences, and actively reflecting on and continuing to build their reserve of intercultural competence. Next, ways of teaching culture and intercultural competences are discussed.

TEACHING CULTURE AND INTERCULTURAL COMPETENCE

What do we do with a variation?

What do we do with a difference?
Do we stand and discuss its oddity
or do we ignore it?
Do we shut our eyes to it
or poke it with a stick?
Do we clobber it to death?

Do we move around it in rage
and enlist the rage of others?
Do we will it to go away?

Do we look at it in awe
or purely in wonderment?
Do we work for it to disappear?

Do we pass it stealthily,
or change route away from it?
Do we will it to become like ourselves?

What do we do with a difference?
Do we communicate to it,
let application acknowledge it
for barriers to fall down?

(Berry, 1998)

Navigating our own feelings about difference can be challenging as the above poem, which has often been used to discuss identity and belonging as well as fairness in an unfair world, stresses. By virtue of the fact that we all belong to the human race, a discussion of culture can also focus on what binds us together and what is held in common by many cultures. An exploration of commonality is often a key focus in building intercultural understanding. What is common to many of the examples below is that they are focused on knowledge-building and perspective-taking. They are often driven by an ethos that seeks to raise students' awareness of their own personal views in relation to culture and an awareness of their own culture, whilst reducing ethnocentrism and developing a more multicultural view of the world. We discuss:

- ways to make cultural connections in content classes
- critical pedagogy (i.e. funds of knowledge, investigating issues of equity and justice, debunking myths, cultural *faux pas* or mistakes)
- the use of frameworks for navigating cultural similarities and difference
- drama as a tool for co-constructing intercultural learning.

MAKING CULTURAL CONNECTIONS

Knowledge is by its nature multicultural. At the very least, content teachers can help make visible the multicultural nature of the knowledge they are teaching. For example, when discussing the circulatory system, it is possible to identify Ibn al-Nafis (1213–1288) from Damascus, who was the first person to describe the pulmonary circulation of blood. Englishman William Harvey (1578–1657) is generally credited as being the first to describe the circulatory system in detail. To stress the emerging nature of knowledge, it is also possible to point out that there is now evidence showing that the Chinese also knew how the circulatory system worked over 2200 years ago. In addition, the multiculturally constructed nature of knowledge can be drawn out (e.g. the contribution of Egyptian, Greek, Chinese and Indian thinkers to mathematics). This can be done in any discipline.

It is also possible to draw on culture in a much more substantial way in order to drive learning in CLIL content subjects. This is what a CLIL Maths teacher and two English teachers have done in Barcelona with the learning materials and lessons they created. Olivella, Monge and Garriga (2007) took their cue from Do Coyle's 'four Cs' (Content, Communication, Cognition, Culture) model and used culture as driver for student engagement. They make multiple links to culture including their own context and environment, and seek to show how intercultural links from the distant or recent past bring benefit to present-day society.

For example in a unit entitled *To Contain or to be Contained, That's the Question*, students begin with a jigsaw exercise about Pythagoras using the following four sets of cards that they use to teach other: facts about Pythagoras' life; facts about the society he lived in and his work; facts about his ideas; and facts about Pythagorean primes. This was followed by a discussion which covered, among other points, locating Pythagoras' birthplace on a map, why he felt 10 was a perfect number, which prime numbers he discovered, why he was considered the first philosopher, and so forth. There is a link to a UK video about primes and related activities. Students work in groups to discuss why prime numbers are so important, using a graphic organiser to summarise their thoughts. Olivella, Monge and Garriga link the discussion about Pythagoras to how prime numbers are used today to create secret codes for encryption of information. Students analyse different types of secret codes and create one for their own imaginary credit card.

Students are directed to think about core concepts and definitions. In order to help them see the value of what they are studying, there is an explanation about why people receive large sums of money when they find a new prime number. This is accompanied by a 1999 photo of Nayan Hajratwala from India receiving $50,000 for having discovered the first known prime number with more than one million digits. They stress that Hajratwala used a formula by seventeenth-century French mathematician Marin Mersenne to make his discovery, and that since then much larger prime numbers have been found.

Later, students learn about Sieve of Eratosthenes who developed a method for finding prime numbers and then apply that method to solve problems. When students reflect on their learning at the end of the unit, cultural elements are part of that reflection. This specific unit – *To Contain or to be Contained, That's the Question* – can be accessed at http://xtec.gencat.cat by typing the name of the unit into the website's search engine.

FRAMEWORKS

As previously stated, culture is diverse and never a monolithic construct applying to all members of a society. Frameworks that seek to map a culture cannot offer definitive statements about cultures or all members of a culture. What they can offer is reference points for people to explore useful knowledge and skills related to intercultural communication and suggest ways of building intercultural competence. Importantly, an exploration of other cultures is also a way to increase self-reflection where one is called on to think about how others might view us. Thus, frameworks can foster perspective-taking from many angles.

One such framework was created by Erin Meyer (2014) and described in her book the *Culture Map*. The framework offers eight primary frames of reference. These are:

- **communicating:** low-content versus high-context (i.e. the extent to which messages are precise, clear and simple and taken at face value versus messages often being implied and not stated)
- **evaluating:** direct negative feedback versus indirect negative feedback (i.e. the extent to which people prefer direct and clear criticism versus indirect read-between-the-lines criticism)
- **persuading:** principles first versus application first (i.e. the extent to which people prefer to first understand underlying principles, facts and how a conclusion was reached versus wishing to concentrate first on the conclusions and, if those are valued, only then exploring the background information)
- **leading:** egalitarian versus hierarchical (i.e. the extent to which people in positions of authority are deferred to or not)
- **deciding:** consensual versus top-down (i.e. the extent to which decision-making is consensual or relies on people in positions of authority)
- **trusting:** task-based versus relationship-based (i.e. the extent to which trust is built first based on demonstrating competence or building a relationship)
- **disagreeing:** confrontational versus avoiding confrontation (i.e. the extent to which confrontation is seen as harmful or helpful)

- **scheduling:** linear time versus flexible time (i.e. the extent to which people stick to time commitments versus a schedule being just a general indicator of when things will start).

The framework also points out that it is important to understand where each culture stands in reference to the other given culture one is working with. For example, Meyer argues that both 'Americans and British fall toward the low-context end of the Communicating scale. But the British speak more between the lines than the Americans do' (Meyer, 2014). In the early stages of the awareness-building process, students can explore the framework or part of the framework. They can work through case studies to analyse and discuss where disagreements or misunderstandings might arise and how they could be addressed. They can use roleplay to demonstrate misunderstandings and others can suggest solutions to improve intercultural cooperation. They can plan for how they would undertake a project with people from another culture (e.g. how they will determine the wishes of their foreign partners and how they will help their partners to better understand them).

ENQUIRY AND CRITICAL PEDAGOGY

A rich source of cultural learning is having students investigate famous **linguistic and cultural gaffes**. In the linguistic domain they include trying to sell the car Chevy Nova in Spain where *no va* can be understood as 'no go', or a company seeking to sell a package labelled as 'four golf balls' in Japan where the word 'four' sounds like the word for 'death'. In the cultural domain, showing the soles of one's feet, for example when one is sitting with one leg over the other, is considered highly offensive in some countries. Getting right to the point in a business or other work-related meeting is considered rude in several cultures, as is giving someone a watch.

In many communities that have seen considerable immigration, Jim Cummins (2014) suggests that educators 'find ways to enable students to gain access to the linguistic and cultural resources – referred to as **funds of knowledge** – that their parents and communities bring to [a given country] from around the world.' He proposes that students create **identity texts**. Students who are not yet proficient in the language of instruction can create these in part using their first language. The identity texts can include the creation of stories, books and art as well as the discussion of global issues. Students can recount their journey or their parents' journey, or interview others about their journey, as well as about the joys and challenges of settling in a new country or region. To stress the multiple and diverse nature of identity within the country the school is located in, students who come from another region of the country could also explore and share their own experiences.

Students who have not experienced emigration or moving within their own country could be invited to interview others who have. The interviewers can enquire about the interviewees' journey, as well as related practicalities, challenges and feelings. Students can ask about the customs, communities, daily practices, natural environment, well-known figures or about any other aspects of the interviewee's country or region of origin. By raising the visibility of the cultures and/or variants of culture present in one's community, and by accessing local '**funds of knowledge**', these cultures and variants of culture are granted greater status. This is a way of valuing other cultures and languages, as well as regional diversity. It also creates pathways for students to learn more about people from different cultures or people from one's own country who may have diverse views of the given nation's culture. Finally, to better understand the diversity inherent in relatively monolithic societies, students can also investigate the extent to which people who have lived in the school's community for generations hold similar or dissimilar views.

Donna Lee Fields, from the University of Valencia in Spain, works with CLIL secondary teachers on integrating culture and building intercultural competence in their content classes. More specifically, she has worked with teachers on ways of helping students identify, analyse and reduce ethnocentrism. Below she suggests a series of activities for History, Geography or Civics classes. Her guiding principles in creating the following two lessons have been: having the maximum number of students engaged at one time; preparing students for enquiry-based learning; ensuring the regular scaffolding of language, critical thinking and formative assessment; having students reuse content and language several times in different ways; and finding a way for students to connect with the content on an affective level. These activities are offered in the form of key instructions.

1. *Hello. How are you feeling?*
2. *Have a look at this definition of emotions:* 'A strong feeling deriving from one's circumstances, mood, or relationships with others'. *Here is an example*

of the word being used in a sentence: 'When he heard about the disaster, he had to work hard to control his emotions'.

3. *Individually list as many different situations that you have experienced as you can (for example, a funeral, a wedding, your first kiss, an argument with a friend), and list the emotions you experienced.*
4. *Look at this list of 100+ emotions. Which of the emotions on the list are unclear to you? Circle the emotions you listed during the first activity we did. What other emotions on the list have you experienced recently? Circle them as well.*
5. *Compare your list of circled emotions with a partner's list. How many circled emotions do you have in common?*
6. *Here are the learning outcomes for today's lesson and our next lesson.*

Content outcomes

You will have:

- constructed a definition of ethnocentrism
- described how maps can reflect ethnocentrism
- identified some of the consequences of ethnocentrism.

Language outcomes

You will:

- have a wider range of words to describe emotions
- be able to write a concise and clear definition supported with an example.

7. *I am going to show you three maps. Identify the map that is most familiar to you and try to notice how they differ.* (First, show the students a Mercator map of the world with their continent in the centre. Second, show a Mercator map of the world with another continent in the centre. Third, show a Mercator map of the world with yet another continent in the centre. Fourth, show all three maps at once.)
8. *Now, looking at all three maps, please answer these four questions on the handout:*

   a) Which map is most familiar to you?

   b) How do the three maps differ? Why do you think this is?

   c) Imagine you were born and grew up in this country, but spent your last two years of high school in a country on the other side of the globe. What emotions might you feel looking at a map of the world where your native country was no longer front and centre?

d) How might growing up looking at only one of these three maps influence a person's view of the world?

9. *In your groups of three share your answers. How do your perspectives differ? Choose an interesting thought from your group discussion and share it with the class.*

10. *I am going to show you two more maps and you will discuss how these differ from the Mercator maps you have already analysed.* (First, show a Hobo-Dyer equal area projection map. Second, show a McArthur map.)

    Look at the questions on the board and answer them in your group. Each of you needs to be prepared to answer the questions for your group.

    a) How does the centring and size of a country change the viewer's perspective on world powers?
    b) How do maps reflect perceptions of power?
    c) How are political understandings reflected in maps?
    d) Break the word 'ethnocentrism' into pieces and, using our/your observations of the three maps, write a definition.

11. *Let's hear your answers to the three questions.*

12. *Now, each group send someone up to the board to write your definition of ethnocentrism. Let's go through each of these. Which bits are clear and concise? What would you change?*

13. *In your groups of three, please read the following sentences. You'll see that one word in each sentence has been ciphered into Morse Code. Make an educated guess about what these coded words are.*

a) [. - .... -. --- -.-. . -. - .-. .. ... --] can be infused into a society through insidious and unexpected means.

b) In the case of world maps, for instance, in the grand scheme of the universe, it is an arbitrary decision to place one or the other [.... . -- .. ... .--. .... . .-. .] at the top or the bottom of the globe.

(continued over page)

c) There is no universal mandate that requires the 'Prime Meridian' to pass through Greenwich, [. -. --. .-.. .- -. -..].

d) Instead, these are choices based on early cartographers [--- -... .--- . -.-. - .. ...- . ...] and biases.

14. *Now in your group, each take one of the sentences and using a Morse Code chart decipher the coded words. The first person to finish should take the last remaining sentence and decipher the missing word. Finally, compare these deciphered answers with your educated guesses.*

15. *First, please read the following text to yourself. Next, in pairs, write five True or False statements about the text. When finished, work with another pair. Test each other using the True and False statements you just wrote.*

Ethnocentricism and maps

Ethnocentrism can be infused into a society through insidious and unexpected means. In the case of world maps, for instance, in the grand scheme of the universe, it is an arbitrary decision to place one or the other hemisphere at the top or the bottom of the globe. There is no universal mandate that requires the 'Prime Meridian' to pass through Greenwich, England. Instead, these are choices based on early cartographers' perspectives and biases. Like other choices in mapping, they show how individuals in a particular time and place perceived their world.

When Australian Stuart McArthur was 15 years old, he lived in Japan. He was teased by his classmates, who endlessly repeated that people in his country walked upside-down. Years later, when studying at Melbourne University, he produced a new map of the world. This one depicted Australia in the centre and at the top of the map. He offered this as a counterweight to what he considered to be the deep-seated prejudice and misconstrued superiority many people in the Northern Hemisphere had towards those in the Southern Hemisphere. His 1979 map launched a debate about ethnocentrism resulting from geographic positioning on cartographic renderings.

16. *What are some of your favourite True–False statements that you just heard in your group?*

17. *Tomorrow you will work on the following enquiry questions. Here is the hand-out. Let's go through this together:*

In which ways can maps reveal the ethnocentrism of cartographers (map-makers) or those commissioning new maps? Find three examples of contemporary (present-day) maps (or historical maps), and explain how they exemplify ethnocentrism. In your analysis, please use some of the following criteria and **add at least two items to the list**:

- position of the nations
- colouring
- regional specifications or lack thereof (e.g. inclusion or exclusion of Native American reservations in maps of the United States)
- variations in text types and size
- choice of type of map (e.g. Mercator, Hobo-Dyer, MacArthur)
- choice of language(s).

What are the potential negative consequences of ethnocentrism? To be prepared for the next lesson, you need to arrive with your three maps.

18. *Let's go back to the outcomes. What have we achieved today? What do we still have to achieve tomorrow? Are we on track to meet our targets?*
19. *Before we go, what are some of the new phrases or words you learned today?*

CRITICAL PEDAGOGY AND DRAMA

Below, Jane Deluzio discusses two back-to-back 75-minute drama lessons. They explore conflict and oppression. Jane Deluzio is a former drama teacher, drama trainer and consultant, school administrator and curriculum developer. She has worked in Estonia and Kazakhstan in CLIL contexts. In her own Canadian classrooms, she often taught students who were not yet proficient in the language of instruction – English.

She believes drama helps students to: draw out their current knowledge; explore their own feelings and those of others; imagine themselves in different people's shoes so they better understand other people's perspectives; engage so completely with learning that they are driven to express themselves and to learn language *in situ*; experience and notice rich language input such as through the repetition of key language and the use of synonyms; use all four language skills; and use assessment as a tool for learning. She seeks to do all of the above through the lesson she describes below.

Warm-up: focusing the mind

1. *Good morning. Welcome to the circle. How do we start our classes?* (With a warm-up.)

2. *What do you think we are going to be doing with the sheets of newspapers that are spread out on the ground of our drama room?*

3. *We are going to play musical newspapers. You may have played this game with chairs. Has anyone ever played it? How is it played?* (We walk around the room with the music playing. When the music stops everyone has to stand on a sheet of newspaper using both feet. Anyone who cannot find a space on a newspaper has to leave the game.)

4. *Have a look at this list of 100 emotions. Which of these words would you like to ask about? Those who lost, how do you think the winners are feeling? Okay, thanks for that. So, winners, how are you actually feeling? Winners, how do you think the losers are feeling? Why do you think they feel that way? Alright, those of you who lost, how are you* ***actually*** *feeling? Did anyone feel more than one feeling at the same time? Can anyone describe conflicting feelings they had?* (Students can also be asked to write in large letters the emotion they felt on the back of the handout and show everyone what they wrote.)

Exploring the benefits of cooperation

5. *So that was the competitive version of musical newspapers. Now, let's play cooperative musical newspapers. Your goal is to help as many people onto one sheet of newspaper as possible. I am only leaving five sheets of newspaper on the floor. Stand up. I am starting the music.* (Each time the music stops another sheet is removed. The teacher is observing how many sheets of newspaper on the floor will challenge students without frustrating them.) *Now I am going to give you time to plan how you will get everyone onto the remaining sheets within 15 seconds. But first here are some phrases that might help you plan. Look these over.* (The scaffold is given to students as a handout, and includes phrases indicating position with a small drawing – 'on top of', 'below', 'next to', 'behind', and phrases such as 'Let's divide ourselves into …', 'What if we all …', 'We could try …', 'How about piling …', 'Hold onto ….', 'I am falling …', 'Let's try .'). *Alright, you now have two minutes to plan and work out how to get as many people on the last remaining pieces of newspaper within 15 seconds.*

6. *Get ready, I am starting the music.* (The music stops. If students fail to implement their plan, they are asked if they want to try again, or to

create a new plan.) *I am going to observe you and you will tell me when you are ready.* (This is an opportunity to observe and note language learning needs.)

7. *So let's debrief. What strategies did you use? How are you feeling?*

Learning outcomes

8. *Here is what we are trying to learn. Have a look at our planned learning outcomes for today's double lesson.*

Content outcomes

You will have:

- experienced being both being in control and being controlled
- reflected on situations where people have considerable control and where they do not, and some of the consequences
- researched and reflected on examples of oppression in history, Politics or Civics that you have studied.

Language outcome

You will:

- be able to write a short summary describing a situation that your reader will find easy to follow.

By the way in today's lessons I am going to use a lot of synonyms. In other words, I am going to repeat the same thing in different words. At the end of the lesson I will ask you to match synonyms. It won't be a test. It is just meant to help you expand your vocabulary.

Activation of current knowledge and perspective-taking

9. *We are now going to do an exercise called Columbian Hypnosis. It is called Columbian Hypnosis because the exercise was invented in Columbia. It is part of the 'theatre of the oppressed' movement. Can someone remind us what that movement is about? Several of the ideas we are using over the next few days come from the work of the Brazilian theatre director, writer and politician Augosto Boal.*

10. *Could I have two volunteers? Thanks. Who will be 'A' and who will be 'B'? OK, 'A', please place your hand about 30 centimetres from B's face. 'B', consider yourself hypnotised by A's hand. A word of caution, 'A', despite having all the power, you need to remember you are responsible for B's safety. Agreed? 'A',*

move your hand around and safely lead B through all kinds of movements. 'B', maintain the same distance (30 cm) from A's hand. Don't do anything you think is dangerous, not that A would ever put you in such a position. Is that right 'A'?

11. *Now everyone get into pairs. Pick 'A' and 'B'. 'A's, you lead – responsibly.* (Two minutes later …). *'B's, you take the lead.*
12. *How did it feel to be led? How did it feel to lead?*
13. *Now could I have one volunteer? Thanks. Everyone face our volunteer. Our volunteer is going to lead you all with his/her hand. Start.*
14. *How did it feel to lead so many people? How did it feel to be led together by one person? Did anyone think of rebelling? Why didn't you?*
15. *Have a look at these two figures outlined on the wall next to each other. They are exactly the same except 'A' is the leader, the one with the power, and 'B' is the one who is being led.*
16. *Everyone take some blank sheets of paper and some markers. Each of you lists one role, such as a prime minister, gang leader or captain to represent someone who nowadays seeks to lead or control others in some situations. You can also pick figures from history. Tape what you wrote on the wall to the left of Figure 'A'. Read what people have written and add more roles.*
17. *Now, inside the Figure write emotions you think any of these figures who are leading, in power, might feel.*
18. *Let's hear what you have come up with. Did anyone write something similar? Can you tell us why you said that? Interesting, fascinating – Antonio has pointed out that people also use power in positive ways. Does someone want to build on, add to this idea?*
19. *Now write in large letters on a piece of paper the names of one group that might be influenced by any of those roles listed to the left of Figure 'A'. For example, you might write 'citizens', 'sailors', 'children', 'slaves' or 'victims'.*
20. *Go and place theses names to the left of Figure 'B'. Read what others have written. Does this spark any more ideas in you? If yes, write and display more names.*
21. *Now, inside the outline of Figure 'B', write emotions that any of these groups of people might have felt, that is to say experienced, as they were being led or controlled by someone in a role represented by Figure 'A'.*

22. *What conclusions are you drawing from this exercise? Take a few minutes to write your thoughts in your journal.* (Students are given five minutes to do this. The teacher circulates to help students with language if they need it.)

Application of knowledge

23. *We are going to create tableaux.* (This is something the students have done often. A tableau is a drama technique, which in essence is a frozen moment in time – a living picture people make with their bodies.) *Get into groups of four or five. Each group must create a tableau showing a non-physical power struggle or conflict. That means no showing of physical violence. This tableau has to depict/show/demonstrate something the group members have learned about in History, Politics or Civics. You have five minutes to pick a situation and to create your tableau; your frozen moment in time. Other students will have to guess what you are showing, what you are depicting. You will have to tell your story as well, recount your story.*

Assessment *as* learning

24. *Have your group pair up with another group. Each group shows its tableau without saying anything about it. Those observing have to identify and explain the power struggle or conflict being shown/being depicted. If the observers cannot see the power struggle or conflict being shown/being depicted, the observers have to suggest changes to the tableau. The suggested changes, the proposed changes need to be tried out. They need to be tested. The suggested changes, the proposed changes need to be agreed upon.* (The requirement for all to reach agreement is an exercise in power-sharing and helps to ensure a constructive atmosphere. If need be, the teacher intervenes.)

25. *Let's all sit in one circle. Anyone have a surprising or 'ah-ha' moment they would like to share? What are some aspects of conflict or oppression that you had not thought about before?*

26. *Can you match some of these words or phrases we have used today? (They are spread out in the floor in three places in the circle. They include tableau/a moment frozen in time, to depict/to show, suggested/proposed, build on/add to, interesting/fascinating).*

27. *Let's look back at our planned learning outcomes. Which ones have we met? What do we still have to do?*

As follow-up activities, based on any of the viewed tableaux, students could: write up (working alone or with a group) what happened before that moment of after it; choose a character that interests them and write the 'interior monologue' for that character; create a roleplay of the power struggle leading up to the given tableau; conduct improvisations, with students being allowed to replace the character in role by tapping that person on the shoulder and taking over that role.

CONCLUSION

Culture is not easily defined. In part this is because of the diversity inherent within cultures. It is highly unlikely that any cultural construct is a monolithic symbol embraced by all members of a language community. Many people hold a multiple, plural or composite identity. Moreover, culture is dynamic and therefore constantly changing and hopefully progressing. Language and culture are deeply embedded, one within the other. One major purpose for learning a language is to take part in intercultural action. In order to do that, it is helpful to have an understanding of the knowledge, skills, attitudes and values that constitute intercultural competence. Enquiry, knowledge-building and perspective-taking are at the centre of building intercultural competence. In education this involves challenging assumptions be those one's own or other people's, and moving beyond clichés and stereotypes. A key act in perspective-taking can involve supporting students in accessing the funds of knowledge they hold within themselves and which are held by local residents within a community. An exploration of feeling related to cultural matters can act as a stepping stone to developing useful intercultural knowledge and skills. Importantly, as no one is ever fully interculturally competent, it is important for students to develop the habit of actively drawing on acquired intercultural competences, and actively reflecting on and continuing to build their reserve of intercultural competence. Finally, in particular in the VUCA world, CLIL students who are learning an international language have much to gain from moving beyond bi-cultural perspective-taking and exploring multicultural perspective-taking so they are better prepared to communicate with diverse cultures using the CLIL language.

FURTHER READING

Spencer-Oatey, H. (2012). *What is culture? A compilation of quotations*. GlobalPAD Core Concepts. Available at http://go.warwick.ac.uk/globalpadintercultural

7 Assessment

Connections

How this chapter connects to other concepts in the book:

Academic language	Teacher credibility	Learning outcomes	Dialogic learning	High expectations
Academic language is the language of assessment. Students need support in learning this language. In addition, tests need to ensure the language being used is not a barrier to students demonstrating their content learning..	From a student perspective, one of the key markers for teacher credibility is whether teachers are treating all students fairly (Hattie, 2012). For assessment to be fair, students need to know and understand the intended learning outcomes and the assessment criteria.	Intended learning outcomes provide a powerful positive reference point for assessment of learning, if those outcomes are Specific Measurable, Achievable, Realistic, Time bound, Engaging, and Relevant (SMARTER). If they are not SMARTER, outcomes may instead demotivate learners and undermine learning.	Rich opportunities for dialogic learning allow students to test their own thinking. High levels of teacher talk and low levels of student dialogue lead to a reduced sample of student language and verbalised thoughts that a teacher could use to assess teaching and learning needs.	In CLIL schools where teachers and management are 'interested in using [assessment] data to improve their programme and student outcomes [...] we usually witnessed the best school outcomes (high levels of bilingualism and academic achievement along with student, parent and teacher satisfaction)' (Lindholm-Leary, 2016). We should never assume a test score reflects potential. Instead, we need to support students in setting and achieving new heights both when it comes to content and language learning.

In CLIL, if we take off marks for language on content class tests, exams and major assignments, students tend to play it safe. They use the content knowledge and language they are sure they can express in perfect L2. They are less likely to explore diverse lines of reasoning or to use the rich language that they have not yet fully consolidated for regular classroom use. In particular, in my context, I have noticed that if the marking scheme penalises students for taking risks with language and exploring out-of-the-box thinking, girls are more likely than boys to play it safe. In such circumstances, girls get higher marks but are likely to learn less whilst boys get lower marks and are thus more likely to be turned off by school.

(Anne Ontero, CLIL teacher and trainer, Finland)

INTRODUCTION AND CHAPTER NAVIGATOR

Summative and formative assessment drive learning. *Summative assessment* seeks to evaluate student learning at the end of an instructional period such as a unit, a course, a semester, a year or an entire programme. The primary purpose of *formative assessment* is to use assessment as a tool for learning. *Assessment for learning* is 'the process of seeking and interpreting evidence for use by learners and their teachers to decide where the learners are in their learning, where they need to go, and how best to get there (Black et al., 2002). By supporting students in becoming proficient at self- and peer-assessment, teachers help them to become 'assessment literate' (Clarke, 2014). Assessment-literate students are likely to be more autonomous and successful in learning both content and language.

This chapter explores the key concepts of summative assessment or testing, as well as formative assessment including feedback through a CLIL lens. However, the chapter primarily focuses on formative assessment and feedback, as these are core drivers of learning. Consequently, the chapter offers a wide range of suggestions for using formative assessment including feedback to improve teaching and learning of both content and language. More specifically the chapter:

- explains the purpose of assessment
- outlines the foci of assessment in CLIL
- analyses how testing and marking are adapted in CLIL contexts
- provides a repertoire of high-impact formative assessment strategies

- details the characteristics of effective feedback, how teachers can increase student uptake of their feedback, and get feedback from students
- offers an introductory CLIL lesson suitable for several subjects that includes many feedback loops.

PURPOSE OF ASSESSMENT

The key purpose of formative assessment in CLIL is to support the learning of content and language, as well as to foster critical thinking about both, and **ultimately to improve teaching and learning practices**. This aligns with a key conclusion from the analysis of over 1200 meta-studies in education – the teacher's primary role is to know his or her impact on student learning so that learning can be improved (Hattie, 2015b). That requires teachers to assess student learning and the impact of their own teaching practices, and use the results of that assessment to intervene in order to support students' learning. In CLIL that would always include maintaining a dual focus on both content and language.

For students to make the most of assessment as a tool for learning they need to become proficient at assessing their own work and thinking, the work and thinking of others, and their own learning process. Students need to develop '**assessment literacy**' – the capacity to assess effectively their own learning so as to draw conclusions based on that assessment and to take action that will help them to overcome any gap between intended learning and their current state of learning (Clarke, 2014). Assessment literacy is at the core of building learner autonomy.

Effective formative assessment also helps to underpin critical thinking about both content and language as it can encourage students to reflect on what constitutes: high *versus* average *versus* poor-quality work; precise, evidence-based and well-developed arguments *versus* assumptions; and effective *versus* less than effective communication, as well as rich *versus* poor use of language.

In addition, summative assessment can be used to **demonstrate to others that students are achieving intended learning outcomes** (see **Chapter 2**: *The Content Teacher's Perspective*, for a discussion of learning outcomes). This is particularly important in CLIL, as CLIL programmes can come under great scrutiny from individuals and groups who are sceptical of this innovation. The benefit of this greater scrutiny is that when CLIL programmes make public their intended learning outcomes, measure and report on their achievement, plan for and work at addressing shortcomings, and do so on an ongoing basis, they tend to become accountable to themselves and their stakeholders and be more likely to achieve their targets.

FOCI OF ASSESSMENT IN CLIL

As the primary role of assessment is to support learning, and as CLIL calls for the integrated and simultaneous learning of content and language, then assessment in CLIL needs to focus on both the learning of content and language. Assessment data can then be used to identify teaching and learning needs and actions. The following reflect key points that are central to successful CLIL practice:

- **Achievement of intended content outcomes:** Most CLIL programmes seek to teach as much content as is taught in comparable non-CLIL programmes, and thus evidence is required to measure the achievement of that target. This means making a clear distinction between the assessment of content learning *versus* the learning of academic language, be that generic academic language used in many subjects or academic language specific to a given content subject.
- **Baseline language skills in L1 and L2 in both CLIL classes and in comparable non-CLIL classes:** It is helpful to be aware of what students know at the start of a CLIL programme or course. These data can be used to plan learning. In addition, they can serve at a later date as a reference point in order to document the extent of student learning in CLIL versus non-CLIL programmes.
- **Achievement of intended language learning outcomes** pertaining to language awareness, communication, language learning skills and intercultural competence: Language outcomes cease to carry substantial weight if their achievement is not assessed and analysed, and if shortcomings in expected results are not systematically addressed.
- **Ongoing growth of language knowledge and skills**: When CLIL students reach a level where they communicate in their L2 with relative ease, language development may slow down and certain syntax and morphological errors can become fossilised and language may continue to be used in ways that are inappropriate to context (Johnstone, 2002). This may partly be because content teachers do not maintain

high expectations vis-à-vis language (Lyster, 2007) and do not sufficiently guide students in improving the quality of their language. Consequently, measuring progress in language learning provides the data needed for planning continued language growth.

- **Willingness to experiment with language and content:** Students can be adept at avoiding the use of complex language, deciding instead to play it safe using the language they feel comfortable with. This can lead to **an impoverished learning environment**. The same is the case with exploring content concepts. Instead of exploring and testing their thinking about content, students may play it safe, waiting for the accepted explanation in a textbook or from the teacher. Measuring willingness to experiment with content and language helps raise student awareness of their behaviours and the consequences thereof.

> **Going deep: Teacher self-assessment**
>
> **Surface learners** *use memorisation. They are risk-averse. They are concerned about failure.*
>
> **Deep learners** *interrogate content and ideas. They make links between concepts. They are not fearful of mistakes (Fisher et al., 2016).*
>
> *In order to increase deep-level learning Fisher et al. (ibid.) suggest teachers analyse their own assignments. This can help them determine what they believe their students are capable of doing. An analysis of student assignments helps teachers see whether they are having students undertake work that requires surface-level skills or deep learning. Asking students to interrogate ideas, create concept maps, and/or develop and follow a line of enquiry are likely to encourage deep learning whereas assignments that ask students to simply find and directly copy answers to questions from a text are likely to do the opposite.*

- **Use of language for various purposes** (e.g. group work, social discourse, reading academic texts, writing assignments in diverse subjects such as History or Maths using the disciplinary language of that given subject): Reflection on language use helps ensure that students understand what they have learned and still need to learn in order meet curriculum expectations.

- **All four language skills** (listening, speaking, reading, writing): Each of these skills reinforces the other. We understand ideas and content concepts differently and possibly less deeply if we have simply heard about them, *versus* if we have heard and spoken about them, *versus* if we have heard, spoken and read about them, *versus* if we have heard, spoken, read and written about them (Doidge, 2007). A balanced and proficient use of the four skills helps ensure that information and knowledge are processed and used in different ways. This should deepen understanding. Assessment makes visible what has been accomplished and where future effort might be concentrated.

- **Ability to work with authentic materials, as well as with native and non-native speakers of the CLIL language:** Ultimately, language is being learned for the purpose of authentic communication, hence it is important to assess progress being made in meeting this target, both when using materials from the media and when doing projects with other schools who use the same CLIL language or for whom the CLIL language is an L1.
- **Current capacity to apply learning gained through the L2 in L1 contexts:** Students should be able to apply what they have learnt through CLIL in contexts where they are using their first language. Assessment can help raise awareness of this key factor and be used to suggest any needed improvements.

In addition to the above core drivers for planning assessment in CLIL, there are additional factors worthy of consideration. These additional factors also have a substantial influence on student learning in CLIL contexts. Thus, they merit assessment so students and teachers can be better-placed to manage these factors and improve learning:

- **Attitude regarding content, language and learning in general:** Learning always takes place through an affective filter that can hinder or enhance learning. If a student's attitude is influencing learning negatively the first step in dealing with the issue is to identify it (e.g. status or value accorded each school language, openness and willingness to experience 'otherness', acknowledgement and development of a bilingual identity).
- **Generic learning skills and language learning skills:** As learning skills are powerful tools for fostering learning of both content and language and learner autonomy, it is important for students to think critically about their own use or non-use of learning skills. Students can use that reflection to plan for how they will expand their repertoire of learning skills strategies (see pages 169–182).
- **Level of engagement and effort:** It is difficult to learn content and language without actively engaging with the learning process. Moreover, **effort** invested in the learning of both content and language is central to success, as is teacher feedback about effort. Feedback regarding effort is considered much more powerful in helping students move forward than evaluative feedback (see page 237).

- **Current understandings and interests:** These are gateways to new learning, and can give teachers an understanding of what content and language students need to learn, as well as what they would like to learn. This is central to maintaining learner motivation.
- **Day-to-day communication including out-of-class communication in the CLIL language:** By reflecting on the extent and quality of communication both in and out of class, students will be better placed to make a conscious effort to become more effective communicators in the CLIL language.
- **Pair and group work:** The focus needs to be maintained on the learning process, as well as language use. This does not mean group work always has to be done entirely in the CLIL language.
- **Extent to which feedback about both content and language is *understood* and applied:** (See the section below entitled *Student uptake of feedback*).

All of the above are not necessarily assessed for a mark.

TESTING

Although this chapter focuses primarily on formative assessment, some advice is offered about summative assessment. The discussion on summative assessment begins in this section with a relatively generic review of testing and then moves on in the next two sections to advice on adapting tests and marking in CLIL contexts. .

First and foremost a test needs to be a fair and valid instrument for measurement and decision-making. Fair tests are impartial in nature, meaning that the test items should carry the same meaning and have the same consequences for all students. This means that the tests should avoid cultural or gender bias. They should only test what has been taught and be clearly tied to intended content and language learning outcomes. Moreover, students have the right to know how they will be tested. That would include knowing the type of test that will be used, its length, the marking scheme and the criteria for judging their answers/work. To understand these elements students need to be supported in building test-taking skills. Numerous concrete suggestions about how to do this effectively are offered in this chapter's **formative assessment** section.

'Validity is the hallmark of quality', and the 'ultimate purpose of [valid] measurement' is to improve learning (Newton and Shaw, 2014). To be valid, a test and the criteria used to evaluate the test answers must actually measure what is taught. If this is the case, it allows the teacher to infer what the students have learnt and how learning can be further improved. The importance of the validity of measurement instruments may seem obvious but it is not always easy to achieve. The Centre for the Enhancement of Learning & Teaching (2017) offers the following example of a Science question given to 14-year olds which is not fully valid – 'Name the products of the **combustion** of carbon in an adequate supply of oxygen', versus 'Name the products of the **burning** of carbon in an adequate supply of oxygen'. If the latter produces 'a much higher number of correct answers, [...] [t]he original question had problems of validity in that it was, to some extent, testing language and vocabulary skills rather than the basic science involved'. Furthermore, if combustion is a key academic term and it has not been learned well enough to recall it on a test, this also means that sufficient attention may not have been drawn to the term during lessons. The term may also have not been used enough times for it to be remembered. It is generally believed that new terms must be used in diverse meaningful contexts some seven times over several days before they can be recalled at a later point.

It is also important to take into account that assessment tends to drive learning. If we do not assess group work skills, skills in answering enquiry questions, learning skills such as planning for content and language learning, self-assessment skills, or attitude and effort, students are unlikely to give these elements the attention they deserve (see remainder of this chapter for ways in which this can be done). Instead, students and teachers are likely to concentrate on what is being assessed by tests. Scott (2010) and Stobart (2008) argue that, in particular, high-stakes assessment can have serious unintended negative consequences often referred to as 'negative washback effects'. These can occur at the macro level affecting an entire system or at the

High-stakes assessment and affect

High-stakes assessment also has an impact on student affect: eagerness/motivation to learn and academic efficacy. With this in mind, assessment in CLIL needs above all to take on a formative orientation. That is, it should allow students the opportunity to learn, show mastery even after a given assessment takes place and most importantly involve the students in the assessment process. CLIL assessment also needs to provide immediate, specific feedback to the learner and the teacher to inform instructional decisions by the teacher and learning decisions by the student.

(Dr Dina Tsagari, Advisory Board Member, CLIL Centre, Cyprus)

micro level affecting the individual. Scott argues that on the macro level over an extended period of time high-stakes tests can lead to a reduction in the knowledge, skills and dispositional states that we value and teach, and that this leads over time to an impoverished learning environment (see the figures below).

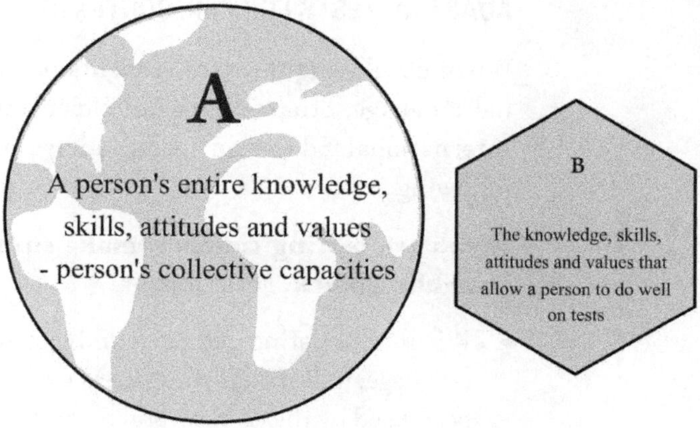

Over time, in high-stakes situations, A is transformed so that it becomes more like B.

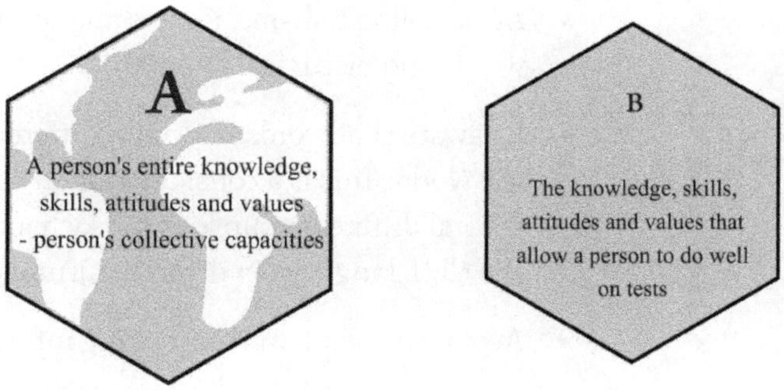

(drawing on Scott, 2010)

Finally at a micro level, test marks can have a profound negative effect on students (Wiliam, 2016). This is because the mark can equate with a student's own self-image – I am a 'C' student – and therefore become self-limiting (ibid.). This view is reinforced by research showing that a student's prior achievement (average mark) is a strong indicator of future performance (Hattie, 2012), unless teachers have higher expectations for students. Teachers that believe in each student's capacity to improve his or her performance in achieving intended content and language learning outcomes are likely to see improved student achievement of both (see the discussion on the affective side of learning in **Chapter 5**: *Scaffolding Content and Language Input and Output*).

ADAPTING TESTS FOR CLIL CONTEXTS

When developing tests for students being assessed through an additional language, Stuart Shaw and Helen Imam of Cambridge Assessment International Education (2015) advise educators to keep in mind the following:

If you are testing content, make sure language does not act as a stumbling block. For example:

- When formulating questions and instructions, avoid using difficult language, unless that language is well-known to the students and has been used by them on several occasions.
- Check that the successful completion of a task does not depend on a single word that may be difficult to understand (rarely used by students). Replace this word or explain its meaning.
- Avoid colloquialisms, idioms and unfamiliar cultural references in both words and pictures.
- Be aware that words may have different meanings in different parts of the world. This is a consideration in contexts where students come from several different countries or teachers in a given school have learned the CLIL language in diverse cultural contexts.
- Avoid irrelevant and distracting information.

Ensure instructions are precise and convey exactly what the student is expected to do. For example:

- Use simple language, 'straightforward' vocabulary, standard command words and short sentences.
- Avoid questions with two functions such as *'describe and explain'*. If you want students to do two tasks, break the question into two parts.

Avoid long or structurally complex sentences. For example:

- Ensure that long sentences are broken up for clarity. Use short, simple sentences.
- Eliminate superfluous words.

Avoid phrasal verbs, as they are colloquial and potentially difficult to process. For example:

- Students may have difficulty with expressions such as 'put up with'. This could be replaced by 'tolerate'.

Preserve the flavour of source texts. However, sensible editing can benefit all students. For example:

- Avoid **structurally** complex source materials or consider simplifying the structure of complex texts.
- Consider whether sources are colloquial or culturally opaque. For example, cartoons often contain colloquial language and cultural features, which can cause difficulties. Photographic sources may be safer for diverse, international audiences.

Try to standardise instructional language and command words. For example:

- Aim for consistency in the command words used across a syllabus.
- Make any specific requirements as transparent as possible. For example, some students see the question 'Is X true?' as a 'Yes/No' question. If an explanation is also required make the requirement explicit: 'Is X true? Please justify your response.'

Use line spaces to separate points and to assist reading. For example:

- Factual points can be made in single sentences, separated from the question by a line space.

Consider offering visual support. For example:

- Diagrams, graphs and pictures can break up text and lessen the reading load.

It is important not to expect students to use language in tests that they have not been taught and practiced using in class. One of the best ways to analyse whether a test is asking students to write using language they have not been taught is to answer all test items yourself and then reflect on whether students have used this language in your class on several occasions.

It is noteworthy that some school systems fostering bilingualism have all high-stakes examination questions in two languages. This is the case in Wales, where students can answer any given exam question in either Welsh or English, but not both (Lewis, 2015). Similarly, in Malta, on the matriculation examination in four subjects, 'students may answer any given examination question in either Maltese or English, but are not allowed to code-switch within the same answer' (Camilleri Grima, 2015).

MARKING OR GRADING IN CLIL CONTENT CLASSES

A major concern for content teachers is whether, on a content test or assignment, points should be taken off for language. In our experience most CLIL content teachers do not take off marks for language errors *per se*, although students may lose marks if they lack the language needed to show what they have learned in the content class. Language teachers have a similar concern when it comes to deciding whether to assign marks for the cultural, geographic or other content that is being used to carry the language points that are being taught. CLIL language teachers often do not assign marks for the content being used to carry the language points. That said, many CLIL content and language teachers do use low-threat, yet effective ways of giving marks for language that help students maintain a dual focus on content and language. Some of the most common strategies used by CLIL teachers for marking language use in addition to content learning on tests or assignments include:

- assigning marks for language on content class tests and assignments, but not including those in the students' final grades for the course. Students also self- and peer-assess language use. Students are still regularly supported in planning for language learning. For example:
    - Students are always assigned a mark out of 10 or 100 for language on all major assignments or tests. They are asked to chart the mark in a graph, and set targets for how they will improve their language learning. Language learning is discussed in class as a whole, as well as in teacher-student and parent-student-teacher interviews.
- assigning marks for the accurate use of content being used to carry the language learning in language classes, but not using these marks in the final assessment.

- assigning 10% of all marks on major content class assignments or unit tests for language, but doing this with a twist. The teacher indicates where marks have been lost for language and provides clues such as *Br* for bridging problems, *Gr* for grammar errors, *Im* for the imprecise use of words or terminology, and *So* for the use of social language when academic language is called for. The students then have one or two days to fix the errors and resubmit their work. If they fix the language errors they get back the lost marks. This means that potentially no marks are lost for language, while students are still encouraged to reflect on and improve their use of language. To facilitate the use of this strategy it would be helpful to agree as a school on the abbreviations that everyone will use.
- assigning 10% of all marks on major language class assignments or unit tests for the content. The marks are deducted but students can correct their mistakes within one or two days of getting their work back in order to retrieve the lost points.
- regularly offering up to 5% in bonus points in content classes for meeting language criteria. For example:
    - Some content teachers provide students with key language they expect students to use and reward students with bonus points if they do so.
- giving a small percentage (e.g. 5%) of marks in content classes for language use. In particular, marks could be gained for using key discourse patterns, phraseology and terminology from a given unit. Marks could also be lost for making mistakes in using this key language. The key language that students must learn is recorded in a class database or document before starting a new unit. Students are told at the start of the given unit that they must learn this language and that 5% of their final mark will depend on how well they use this language. A teacher can use the database entries to assess student use of this language. In addition, students can use the database to self-assess or peer-assess language use during oral presentations.

All of the above require that marking schemes be as transparent as possible. Care needs to be taken to ensure marking schemes for language do not penalise students for taking risks with language. In fact, some points or bonus points might also be awarded for students taking risks with language.

While marks or grades are an essential part of schooling, not assigning marks for language **does not mean that language is not assessed**. The sections below detail formative assessment strategies designed to help students become more assessment-literate and thereby improve their capacity to learn both content and language. This will be followed by a discussion of feedback, and feedback strategies that seek to move learning beyond the use of grades.

FORMATIVE ASSESSMENT

Formative assessment helps students to become knowledgeable partners in the learning process. This should result in high levels of assessment literacy among students and encourage them to take greater control of their own learning of both content and language. Formative assessment and other strategies that foster assessment literacy have been consistently found to be among the most powerful positive influences on student achievement (Wiliam 2011, Hattie 2012, Clarke 2014).

In order to become more proficient at assessing progress in the achievement of intended content and language outcomes against success criteria (e.g. exemplars of excellent work), students require rich opportunities to assess and reflect on their own work and the work of others. In addition, the intended learning outcomes need to be challenging. In other words, they need to embody high but realistic expectations for content and language learning. Students need to understand both the intended learning outcomes and the criteria that will be used for measuring success. Activities and content and language scaffolding all need to support students in working effectively with each other and with materials to accomplish meaningful tasks. Students also need to build their repertoire of learning skills, including language learning skills, so that they have the tools needed to become more autonomous learners. Teachers need evidence of student learning or lack thereof to make decisions about the teaching and learning of both content and language. Students need feedback on how to move forward in order to achieve the intended learning outcomes.

A collection of high-impact formative assessment strategies is discussed below. They are offered as options for consideration. For those ideas that come from other publications, references are provided, but the ideas are adapted for CLIL contexts:

- **Pre-assessments:** Conduct a pre-assessment to find out what students already know about the topic, and the language they have acquired.

  Without this, teachers do not know what the students have already learnt. Moreover, giving students a pre-test prior to starting to teach a unit has been shown to lead to higher achievement on the end-of-the-unit test (Carey, 2014).

- **Reflection on the learning process:** Ask your students what is stopping them from achieving the mark they need in the content subject.

  More specifically, a teacher can ask students what is stopping them from learning the language they need, or how they can help themselves or how someone else can help them to learn what is needed. Frequently ask students how they will know they are successful (Wiliam, 2011).

- **Exam preparation strategy 1:** Instead of giving students exam questions from previous years or having them sit a practice exam, ask them to create exam questions and answer them (Black et al., 2009 referring to King, 1992 and Foos et al., 1994).

  In CLIL, it is advisable to encourage students to review their answers twice – once from the perspective of making certain the content is accurate and a second time to check for the language (e.g. precise use of words and phrases, grammar, spelling, punctuation). *Exam creation has been shown to be more effective than practice exams, giving students study guides or just letting them study on their own* (Wiliam, 2011).

- **Exam preparation strategy 2:** To prepare students for the final exam, give a practice exam, but do it with a twist. Instead of collecting and marking these exams, have students get into groups of four. Give the students back their practice exam papers and an empty copy of the same exam paper. The students' task is to analyse all four of their completed exam papers, and collectively answer the exam questions again. The exam paper is then reviewed as a class (Black et al., 2009).

  If the exam paper has marks for both content and language, students are more likely to focus on both even if they know the language marks will not be included in the final mark.

- **Exam preparation strategy 3:** Group student work into piles of four. For each group of four, write feedback about both content and language on four separate pieces of paper. Return the exam papers to the group of four students, along with the feedback on four separate pieces of paper. The students must match the feedback to the work (Black et al, 2009).

  This requires students to read each other's work, and think about the strengths and weaknesses of each piece of work. In addition, knowing that others will see their work and the teacher's feedback may also motivate the students to work harder.

- **Exam (or test) preparation strategy 4:** Have students take a mock test and then compare their test answers with model answers provided by the teacher (Huxham, 2007).

  This makes the students do the analysis and saves the teacher time. Model answers need to show how they are linked to the marking scheme and/or the assessment criteria.

- **Student-created evaluation criteria:** Take some examples of student work from the previous year (e.g. essays, lab reports, paintings, video presentations) and have students analyse them to create content and language criteria for evaluating their own creation of a similar product.

  To be effective this activity requires scaffolding such as having students first only focus on one or two aspects of the work – for example, the introduction and conclusion. This can be done in groups. Two groups can then compare their criteria and develop a common list. Then the class agrees on one list. The teacher would add missing criteria. As the students become more adept at this type of activity they could be encouraged to look at additional aspects of the work such as accuracy of content, creativity, quality of thought, quality of language and structure. *If students have determined the criteria, they are more likely to understand them and take them into account.*

- **Student-developed marking scheme:** Give students the questions and ask them to develop marking schemes.

  Students must justify their marking schemes when they present their conclusions to the class. *This requires students to identify and think through the elements of high-quality answers that demonstrate conceptual understanding and that are correct from both a content and language perspective.*

- **Student assessment of drafts:** After receiving draft essays, select the three best ones. Give all students copies of these three essays along with their own essay. The class first works in groups and then through full class discussion to try to understand why these essays are good from both a content and language perspective, and to identify whether there is anything the authors could do to improve them. The students are then asked to revise their own essays and hand them back in again (Wiliam, 2011).

  This should lead to improved product and a lightening of the marking load.

- **Improving the quality of student feedback:** Ask students to use sticky notes to give feedback on various parts of other students' work and then have students analyse the quality of that feedback.

  More specifically, the sticky notes are pulled off the student work and a document camera is used to project the feedback. The class can then vote on whether they would find that feedback useful. Students could also explain how they might use the feedback. Where necessary, they can discuss how to make the feedback more helpful (Wiliam, 2011).

- **Feedback logs:** Have students create a feedback log of the comments they receive about content and language, and analyse how these comments are or are not changing (see the section below entitled *Student uptake of feedback*).

  If there is no change, there is no uptake in feedback.

- **Traffic lights 1:** At any point during a lesson, have students reflect quickly on how they are feeling about the topic under study by raising a green, yellow or red laminated strip of paper to indicate the following:
  - *Red:* I feel lost.
  - *Yellow:* I feel unsure of some points.
  - *Green:* I understand the topic.

  As an extension option, students may be asked to explain the reasoning behind their self-assessments to partners or groups. Those listening need to suggest concrete steps that can be taken and then check to see if the feedback has been understood. In addition, when studying, students could place green, yellow and red dots on pages of their notes to assess how well they have mastered the material. They then concentrate on mastering the pages marked red and yellow (Wiliam, 2011). The same could be done with the key discourse patterns, phraseology and terminology from a given unit that is in a class database and that must be learned.

- **Traffic lights 2:** Have students reflect quickly on their work and label it red, yellow or green using the follow scale:
  - *Red:* I feel lost.
  - *Yellow:* I feel unsure of some points.
  - *Green:* I understand this.

  Greens raise their hands. Yellows go to the greens for support. Greens are encouraged first to determine what the yellows understand and do not understand, and only then to provide the necessary explanations. Greens are encouraged to finish by having yellows explain their understanding of the topic. Reds come to the teacher (Black et al., 2009). Teachers can then check with the rest of the class to ensure that everyone has understood the topic.

- **Traffic lights 3:** When students have finished individually preparing a draft version of their presentations, have them get into groups of four. Each member presents his/her work. The three students viewing the presentations use laminated red, yellow and green strips of paper to indicate their evaluation of the work:
  - *Red:* I have suggestions to make.
  - *Yellow:* No major mistakes or omissions.
  - *Green:* Better work than mine. I learned something.

  The feedback can be given in writing or orally. There can also be a short whole-class discussion to have students explain what they now think they need to do to improve their work. Anyone who receives one or more yellows or reds must work on improving his/her presentation. If someone has received only greens, s/he is given a new task (Black et al., 2009).

- **Coloured cups:** Give the students three paper or plastic cups (one green, one yellow, one red) that can be used to communicate with you.

At the start of the lesson, the green cup is stacked on top of the yellow and red cups, and placed on the corner of each student's desk. If a student feels the teacher is going too quickly, he or she can put the yellow cup on top of the stack of cups. If the student wants the teacher to stop in order to ask a question, he or she can display the red cup (Wiliam, 2011).

- **Using a rubric:** In order to get a quick sense of where students are in understanding a topic, have them use a self-assessment rubric (based on Fisher et al., 2016).

  This encourages the habit of reflecting on what has been accomplished and what needs to still be done.

Self-assessment of learning
I do not **yet** understand. ⇨ I need coaching.
I am starting to understand. ⇨ I need coaching, but first want to try some more on my own.
I understand. ⇨ I am making some mistakes, but think I can work through these on my own.
I understand well. ⇨ I can coach someone else without just telling him or her the answers.

- **Looking for the mistakes:** When marking tests for students, instead of identifying specific mistakes, only write on the test that the student has made X number of errors (e.g. *You have made 3 calculation errors and used 1 unsuitable formula*).

  The students then search for and correct their errors. When it comes to language, dots can be placed next to a sentence that needs work, or additional prompts can be provided such as *Br* for bridging, *Gr* for grammar, *Im* for imprecise word use, *Sp* for spelling and *So* for the use of social language when academic language is called for (Wiliam, 2011). The entire text or a section of text can be preceded by a dot with *St* for structure if the student needs to revisit the structure of a text.

  This requires students to think deeply about each question and helps them better understand what they do not know. If there are some students with no errors, they can help other students find and correct their errors. The students acting as teachers are encouraged to make sure the students they are coaching can explain the process for getting the right answer.

- **Buddy sign-off:** Before work can be handed in, a class 'buddy' must check the work against an agreed list of success criteria.

  If the work does not meet the criteria, it is returned to the buddy, not to the student who wrote it (Wiliam, 2011).

- **The affective side of learning:** Have students analyse their mindset to see if they tend to have a fixed or a growth mindset.

  Growth mindset students usually have higher levels of resilience and achievement. The mindset analysis can be done by asking the following five questions: How do you feel and what do you do:

  - when you are faced with a problem or obstacle
  - when you are faced with a challenge
  - when you are criticised
  - when you are asked to expend a lot of effort, or when you see someone else succeed? (Dweck, 2007)

  Key here is not how one reacts immediately after any of the situations listed above, but how one reacts in the long-term. If the student can soon move on, learn from the situation and make the best of it, they can be said to have a growth mindset. In addition to undertaking the self-assessment, students can be shown pictures of neurons and learning can be discussed as both a social and a biological process. Students can read a short text on how their capacity to think can be improved. Also, in challenging situations, students can be supported in exploring growth mindset solutions.

- **Analysis of one student's work:** Randomly select a student to present his or her work in progress, projecting it and constructively analysing it as a class.

  Possible steps to do this can include:

  - explaining the rationale and asking students for permission to do this
  - agreeing on criteria that will be used to analyse the work in progress, and what sorts of feedback are acceptable and unacceptable

  - letting students know on what day this will happen
  - having a student pick at random (e.g. a name from a baseball cap) the student whose work will be presented
  - having all students, including the person whose work was picked, use the agreed-upon criteria to individually analyse the work and write down their feedback
  - having students share their ideas in groups of three or four and come up with concrete suggestions for improvement
  - discussing the feedback as a whole class and working in class right then and there to apply the feedback in order to improve the work
  - asking the student whose work was analysed which suggested improvements they found particularly helpful. The student can also conclude if there is something else he or she feels still needs to be improved and how that will be done.

- **Checklists**: Provide students with a checklist to review work before it is turned in. There is a separate section on language.

  Alternatively ask students to first create a checklist to review work before it is submitted for marking.

- **Assessment exemplar**: A few days before an assignment is due, place an exemplar of previous student work with feedback on content and language on the class website, along with an improved version of that work.

  Students can ask follow-up questions about the feedback and next steps or even add their comments. Students will then hopefully have a better sense of how to polish their own work before handing it in.

- **Using email:** Provide initial feedback about content and language on student draft work via email. Next, have the students resubmit their draft together with the improved piece of work using the Track Changes function to show their changes.

  Time permitting, meet the student face-to-face to discuss the final piece of work and only at the end of the discussion give the student a grade. If student numbers and time do not permit, students can be given time in class to discuss with their peers teacher feedback and how they plan to implement it on future assignments.

- **Portfolios:** Have students develop portfolios. Students select their best work.

  This includes their analysis of how their work (both language and content) has improved. A face-to-face teacher and student discussion takes place once per semester (see the insert on portfolio assessment below and on the following page).

- **Feedback discussions 1:** Give students an opportunity to discuss with peers the feedback they have received from you.

  The students would need to explain to their peers what they plan to do to take teacher feedback into account. Their peers could make additional suggestions.

- **Feedback discussions 2:** As homework, students mark and comment on one or two student papers, PowerPoint presentations, tests, etc.

  These can be from a previous year. In class, students work in groups of three or four to discuss the marks and comments. The final results are discussed in the class as whole.

- **Feedback discussions 3:** Have students learn the basic skills of effective feedback.

  In groups of three, students work through a list of the characteristics of effective feedback and analyse a series of feedback statements to determine which ones are effective and which ones are not. Then students work in groups of three to analyse a piece of their work. One student gives feedback, the second student receives it and the third assesses whether the feedback respects the agreed-upon effective feedback guidelines. (See page 236 for the characteristics of effective feedback.)

- **Student-directed feedback:** On a draft assignment, have students tell their peers and/or the teacher what aspects of their work they would like to receive feedback on.

PORTFOLIO ASSESSMENT:

What is a portfolio?

A portfolio is a presentation of a student's best work. It is evidence, collected over a considerable period of time, of a student's knowledge, skills and progress made in achieving learning content and language outcomes. It is a tool for learning (see figure opposite).

***Binder, box, folder* and/or *electronic file* containing**

- *a monthly selection of student work (e.g. writing, reports, art, tests, sound and video recordings) from one or several subjects*
- *student reflections on why a work was chosen*
- *student reflections on their progress that cites evidence from their own work*
- *student reflections on lessons learnt in producing work*
- *student plans including learning strategies and goals that will be used to move forward*
- *peer and teacher (and possibly parent) reflections on the student's analyses, work process, results, long-term development, strategies or plans*

Selection criteria for student work

- *linked to intended content and language learning outcomes*
- *based on results achieved and/or progress made*
- *collected at regular intervals (e.g. once a month) and representative of student's best work, demonstrating progress, effort and results*

Aimed at helping students

- *to assess personal growth/progress*
- *to become assessment literate (the capacity to assess effectively learning, use of learning skills and attitude, to conclude and take action to overcome any gap between intended learning and their current state of learning)*
- *to become more autonomous learners*
- *to develop critical thinking and learning skills*
- *to build educational partnerships with peers, teachers and parents*
- *to work with peers, teachers and parents in seeing learning as a holistic, cross-curricular and longitudinal process*
- *to receive positive reinforcement and feedback about how to move forward*
- *to set realistic goals*
- *to build self-confidence, as well develop presentation and dialogue skills*

Ultimately all of the above implies that eventually students should lead these conversations with teachers and parents.

For discussion at or during

- *at peer-assessment meetings*
- *at student-teacher meetings*
- *at parent-teacher-student meetings*
- *during preparation for exams*
- *at report card time*
- *when students want to share their work with others*
- *in the middle of or at the end of a major project.*

VIEW FROM THE FIELD:
Demystifying assessment

Mary Richardson

Mary Richardson is a Senior Lecturer in Educational Assessment at the UCL Institute of Education, London. She has worked in assessment research for policy-making agencies, a national awarding body and in academia. Mary's work includes two core themes – assessment and education for social justice – and she uses empirical and philosophical approaches to explore ideas. From 2015–2017, Mary was the director of the UCL support project for the development of textbooks for a trilingual education context in Kazakhstan. She has also directed multilingual projects in Europe, using Citizenship and Art syllabi to research shared ideas of citizenship and belonging.

As a teacher, it is important to demonstrate to your students that you too are always learning, and using assessment to help you to do that. A particularly problematic aspect of contemporary education is the compartmentalisation of learning – by this I mean learning a 'bite size' piece of information in readiness for an exam, and then, usually, forgetting it. Such practice has a reductive effect on the idea of education as a continuous process. I appreciate that students will need, and indeed want, to pass particular assessments at certain times in their lives and that such assessments are very important, but this need not be at the expense of their overall relationship with education. This is where you, the teacher, come in!

Your students will be better placed to learn both content and language if they have their own, personal (inner) formative assessment toolkit. This is well described by Wynne Harlen (2012). Formative assessment has a symbiotic relationship with the learner – the more motivated they are, the more confidence a student will develop. Harlen presents a persuasive argument that is focused on building students' self esteem and their 'locus of control' – these two ingredients are key to a student being able to use feedback in a positive and educationally sustaining way.

You can help your students to be more effective learners if they:

1. look to you for guidance rather than instructions,
2. are willing to take risks, and
3. are able to use errors to develop ideas and learning.

You may be concerned that here is another list of 'things to think about', but they integrate with the practical tasks already outlined in this chapter. For example, when students are reviewing their own work or the work of peers, ask them to find a 'risky' solution – how might they find a really challenging way to come to the same answer? Ask them to discuss, in pairs or small groups, what would happen if an assessment resulted in a FAIL. They can draw up a list of outcomes related to personal/emotional responses, educational outcomes and then a practical list of ideas for learning from this.

Share some examples of what may initially be termed as 'failures' and how they resulted in 'success'. It is helpful to use general examples rather than a specific person (e.g. in scientific research, many major breakthroughs have been discovered 'by accident' and due to continuous practice, persistence and the dogged behaviour of scientists. Sports people achieve by practicing to overcome what they are 'bad' at and honing those skills for years before they hit the Olympic stadium; there are many more examples of 'failure/set-backs' being turned into success that are likely to be specific to your locale and culture, so do some research to make this an effective means of getting students engaged).

The best thing you can do is model your expectations regarding both content learning and language use – discuss your lessons with students, and talk about their learning and your learning. Try being more open about what the students and you are doing. Be open about assessment – we often use the term 'transparency' without fully explaining assessment processes, criteria and related concerns. Finally, demonstrating to students through empathy and concrete actions that you are their ally is the best way to demystify assessment.

FEEDBACK DEFINED

The verb phrase 'to feed back' was first used in Mechanical Engineering whilst the noun 'feedback' was first used in the field of Electronics. Both imply that the engineer is getting some form of information back from the mechanical and/or electronic device that can be used to adjust and/or improve the functioning of the device (*Cambridge Advanced Learner's Dictionary*, 2014).

The term 'feedback' has entered education through the field of psychology. Building on Black et al. (2009), we define feedback as **verbal and non-verbal reactions to performance** of a task that are based on evidence and previously discussed performance criteria, and that are used as a basis for improvement.

For feedback to be effective, Sadler (1989) proposes certain 'indispensable conditions'. We have slightly adapted these for CLIL contexts. For feedback to be deemed effective, the learner has to:

a) understand the ***standard*** (or intended content and language learning outcomes and criteria/benchmarks) being aimed for,

b) compare the ***actual*** (or current) ***level of performance*** with the standard, and

c) engage in appropriate ***action*** which leads to some closure of the gap.

In order to achieve closure of the gap, teachers may wish to keep two things in mind:

(1) Giving feedback does not mean it is taken on board. Hattie (2012) reports that 70% of teachers say they give their students feedback, but only 45% of their students report receiving feedback.

(2) Teachers need feedback about their own teaching in order to improve their teaching and student learning (see the section below entitled *Teacher Uptake of Feedback*).

NATURE OF EFFECTIVE 'FORMATIVE' FEEDBACK

Building on Bransford et al (2000), Coe et al. (2014) and Hattie (2009), we suggest that effective feedback:

- **is focused on process, self-regulation** and/or **task** (e.g. **process:** *You are almost where you need to be. If you systematically compared your work with the success criteria you could find the things you need to improve. This would mean double-checking your work against each criterion, and if necessary asking for advice about how to make improvements;* **self-regulation:** *Next time you get frustrated with the group, maybe you could sit back for a minute. Breathe in deeply a few times, and think about how you could help the group get back on track;* **task**: *You are moving in a different direction than discussed. It would be wise to reread the instructions.)*
- **is direct, factual and uses examples** *(e.g. In your next debate avoid one-line rejections of your opponent's logic. You need to explain in another sentence or two why your opponent's logic is flawed.)*
- **does not focus on the person** *(e.g. It avoids any mention of the student's personality or temperament and/or does not make comparisons to other people.)*

Unintended feedback

Providing feedback as a reward 'enhances ego rather than task involvement' (Black et al., 2009).

Telling a student they are intelligent tends to lower their performance as students then become invested in protecting that image and not taking risks in exploring their thinking (Dweck, 2007).

Moving on from and not returning to key knowledge that students need to learn after they have demonstrated their understanding may leave them the impression that that knowledge has been well learnt and will be easily retrieved when required. Returning to key knowledge and having students reuse it in diverse meaningful ways helps students not only to experience how well encoded or not that knowledge was in their long-term memory, but also to better encode it.

Finally, ending a conversation with a student after the language error has been corrected can leave the impression that the substance of what a student is saying is not important. As students are usually most interested in expressing and discussing their thoughts, it is wise to continue the dialogue for at least another sentence after the language error has been repaired. This will help show that the student's thoughts are being listened to and that they are valued. This is likely to improve language learning as well, for it is meaningful dialogue and related language that is more likely to be remembered than a decontextualised discrete point about language.

- **is non-threatening**, which means that it does not evaluate, label or judge, but is instead informational and focused on the next steps to be taken *(e.g. do not say you are intelligent, lazy or that the work is poor; instead, explain what improvements need to be made – You have obviously worked hard on this, and you are almost where you need to be. There is one major problem which has to be corrected so that this becomes a first-rate piece of work. The problem is .... To address this you could ...)*
- **acknowledges the strengths of the student's work** *(e.g. Your laboratory report is much improved. You have used the agreed upon structure. In particular, the 'results' section is very clear, detailed and follows a logical sequence. In addition, throughout the report you used many of the new phrases and terminology that we learned this week.)*
- **is focused on effort** *(e.g. You have clearly worked hard at improving the quality of your writing. Your paper is well organised. You defend your ideas well. Finally, you have very few spelling and grammar mistakes. Can you explain to the class how you achieved this result?)*
- **is aimed at creating reflective and self-directed learners** *(e.g. Are you satisfied with this outcome both when it comes to the geography and your use of language? Do you think there is room for improvement? If yes, what would you improve and how?)*

- **is timely.** Feedback needs to reach students early enough so that they can do something to close the gap between the state of their current work/knowledge/skills and the expected standard.
- **is related to what students:**
    - **are expected to learn** (content and language), and
    - **have already learnt**, and
    - **helps students take greater responsibility for improving their own learning and performance** *(e.g. So, looking at the criteria and your own work, what do you think can be improved?)*

STUDENT UPTAKE OF FEEDBACK

Progress hinges on the capacity to learn from mistakes.
(Syed, 2015)

It is one thing to provide feedback to students and quite another for students to take on board and apply that feedback. Hence, it is essential to make a conscious effort to not just provide feedback to students about what they have done well and how they could move their thinking and the quality of their work forward, but also to check whether the feedback has been understood and if and how it is being applied.

The following are some thoughts on how to improve student reception of feedback:

- **Check to see if feedback has been received** not by asking if feedback has been understood, but rather by exploring how it has been understood. This can be done by giving students a moment to think and then having students explain how they would apply the given feedback. Students can be asked to do this in writing as well.
- **Use recasts with care and avoid overuse**. 'Recasting' (a teacher mirroring back a corrected version of a student's incorrect utterance) is a frequently used tool to provide feedback on language. This is because it is an easy way for teachers to feel a mistake has been corrected so they can go on with the lesson. However, recasts do not necessarily lead to student processing of the intended feedback. Lyster (2007) reports that recasting is more effective in classrooms where teachers have the habit of getting students to reflect on the correct use of language. In addition, to make optimal use of recasts Lyster suggests that they be

short so only the key part of the student's response is recast. They need to be focused by, for example, vocally stressing the change. The recast can also be quickly written on the board.

- **Use prompts**. Prompts involve giving students clues such as asking questions to help them to improve the accuracy of content and language usage. For example, when it comes to content a teacher might ask if there might be another cause for a given reaction, whilst when it comes to language the teacher might ask – 'Do we say the temperature '*rised*' or the temperature '*ro…*'?' –, hoping the clue of a first syllable is sufficient for the student to correct his/her mistake. Prompts can be used to reduce the use of recasting and increase learner engagement with assessing and correcting their own work (Lyster, 2007).
- **Provide oral feedback in the form of audio files**. Audio is preferred by some students and may lighten teacher workload.
- **When writing feedback, not writing it on the student work, but instead having students keep an ongoing interactive feedback log**. A feedback sheet (see below) is added to each assignment of a similar type or maintained electronically. The first column is for two concrete suggestions about how the given student can improve his or her work. In the second column, the student indicates measures he or she has taken to apply in the next assignment the previously provided feedback.

Teacher feedback	**Student report**
Assignment 1 – incl. suggested next steps	Explanation of how you applied Assignment 1 Feedback on Assignment 2
Suggestions	I took the following steps: …
Assignment 2 – incl. suggested next steps	Explanation of how you applied Assignment 2 Feedback on Assignment 3
Suggestions	I took the following steps: …
Assignment 3 – incl. suggested next steps	Explanation of how you applied Assignment 3 Feedback on Assignment 4
Suggestions	I took the following steps: …

- Have students **hand in their previous essay or lab report with their new one** so it is easy to see if previous feedback was taken into account.
- **Avoid giving general feedback to the entire class** as this is thought to have a low level of uptake.
- **Direct feedback at student misinterpretations of facts or concepts** as this is highly specific and personal, and therefore more likely to be recalled.
- **Have students graph their marks**. The visualisation of the rise and fall of achievement is thought to be a powerful positive influence on motivating action.
- **Support the development of engaged listening skills** (see section on learning skills on pages 169–182) as this can support student uptake of verbal feedback.
- **Provide students with feedback on both content and language on drafts** of projects, essays, presentations, WebQuests, and so on. Students are more likely to take this into account than is the case when feedback is received along with a final mark. The next section provides further advice on how to do this.

Classroom catchphrases:
If you are not getting better at this, it is because we haven't yet figured out how to do that. We will figure it out.

FEEDFORWARD

Marshall Goldsmith (2007) argues that in addition to feedback about the past, people in business need support in moving forward. They do not just need feedback (input about the past), but 'feedforward' – concrete advice about the next few steps that can be taken to move forward. Providing feedback about the past does not necessarily lead to solutions. Furthermore, providing large amounts of advice about how to move forward is likely to overwhelm working memory, and reduce the possibility that the advice will be recalled and taken into account. In education,

Black et al. (2009) stress in a similar way that an essential part of feedback is providing students guidance about the next few steps they need to take.

One way of helping students to reflect on and improve their work is to create assignments that include numerous opportunities for feedforward. Smythe (2006) argues that building in feedback loops, or as Goldsmith would likely call them feedforward loops:

- reduces the possibility of students doing rushed work at the last minute
- provides students more opportunities and encourages them to take more time to reflect on their work
- is likely to reduce intentional and unintentional plagiarism.

If feedback/feedforward loops are combined with self-reported grades they are likely to have an even greater impact on student learning. Having students suggest their own grades along with a rationale for their proposed grade has been shown to be one of the most powerful learning strategies ever researched: it has a very positive impact on student achievement substantially accelerating learning (Hattie, 2012). This is likely because systematically assessing in particular one's own draft work against agreed criteria fosters assessment literacy. Students gain a stronger grasp of the assessment criteria and are encouraged to take greater responsibility for reflecting on and improving their own work. It may be time-consuming, but it tends to be highly effective.

For example, the major assignment for a term such as an essay or a research project can build in several feedback loops. Several of the strategies presented below have been discussed in isolation in the section on formative assessment, but here they are presented as constituent elements of an entire process (a learning progression) requiring students to revisit, reflect on and improve their work over an extended period of time.

Step 1: Students are introduced to the idea that they will be asked to hand in a draft version of their work to which, based on given assessment criteria, they will have assigned grades to various aspects of their work and explained why they deserve those grades. They are told the teacher will then agree or disagree with those grades and provide feedback on the draft with at least two suggestions for improvement. The students will first practice doing this on a small assignment such as creating a

PowerPoint presentation using the rubric below and in addition using agreed upon assessment criteria. The teacher will use the same rubric to provide feedback, expecting students to improve their work and hand it in once again with the previously filled out rubric and a newly filled out one. Step 1 is intended to scaffold for students what they will be expected to do with a major assignment.

Step 2: To further prepare for the self-assessment of a major assignment, students analyse in groups an excellent and poor essay, lab report or composition to determine performance criteria that refer to content as well as language. These are discussed and criteria are agreed upon with the whole class.

Step 3: Students create the draft essay, lab report or composition and assign grades to the various agreed upon aspects of their draft referring to the assessment criteria. They also write an explanation of why they deserve those grades. They could also assign themselves one global final mark for their work.

Step 4: A fellow student reviews the draft, grades it and justifies the grades, and suggests ways to improve the work. The original student then weighs the feedback and applies it as he or she sees fit.

Step 5: The students hand in the work to the teacher along with the grades they think they deserve for the various agreed upon aspects of their work along with a rationale for assigning themselves those grades. They could also assign themselves one global final mark for their work. Students could also hand in the feedback they received from a fellow student without the suggested mark.

Step 6: The teacher provides feedback to the student that includes ways to improve the work.

Step 7: The student improves his/her work and hands in the assignment for final marking along with his/her suggested grades and related rationale for those grades and the final global mark.

Finally, if a teacher feels students are not making the effort required on their first drafts, he or she can assign marks to both the draft and the final copy. For example, 40% of the mark can be given for the draft and 60% for the final product (Wiliam, 2011).

Self-reported grades: looking forward

Name: ____________________

Date: ____________________

Quality of thought

Student's assessment

0									10

Rationale:

____

____

Teacher's assessment

0									10

Teacher's feedback/forward

____

____

Accuracy of content

Student's assessment

0									10

Rationale:

____

____

Teacher's assessment

0									10

Teacher's feedback/forward

____

____

Organisation

Student's assessment

0									10

Rationale:

____

____

Teacher's assessment

0									10

Teacher's feedback/forward

____

____

Quality of language

Student's assessment

0									10

Rationale:

____

____

Teacher's assessment

0									10

Teacher's feedback/forward:

____

____

VIEW FROM THE FIELD:
Fostering reflection after receiving a mark

Eva-Jo Jylhä, Oulu, Finland

Eva-Jo Jylhä teaches English at secondary school in Oulu, Finland in a programme for students in Grades 10–12 who study approximately 85% of their content subjects through English, which is for them an additional language. Students are admitted to the programme through a competitive process.

As students tend not to reflect on either the quality of their essays or how they created them after receiving their grade, Eva-Jo Jylhä has developed the following counterweight. In class, she has her students use the tool below to encourage them to draw lessons from the writing of one marked essay so that those lessons could be applied on their next essay. The first essay was entitled *Comparative Textual Analysis*. It involved the comparison of two texts.

Capturing your own learning in order to enhance future performance

These tasks are designed to help you:

- analyse what you achieved or did not achieve with your first paper (and to do so in reference to the marking scheme and performance criteria)
- capture what you have learned from this analysis
- plan for the application of that learning to improve your next paper.

As you work through the following questions or tasks, please take some notes so you will be able to return to these before writing your next paper.

1. Read the performance criteria we have for writing papers, and the marking scheme for this paper on comparative textual analysis. What is your general impression? To what extent did you take into account the criteria and the marking scheme?
2. Re-read your own paper looking for the things mentioned in the marking scheme and the performance criteria.

- Have you highlighted key points and developed well-structured arguments?
- Are you supporting your arguments with examples and evidence?
- Have you paid enough attention to context (text type, time and place of writing/publication, etc), audience and purpose?
- Are you simply observing or are you also analysing the observations you make? Do you move beyond simply reporting on what you see to writing about purpose?

3. Analyse the organisation of your paper.
    - Skim the paper and measure the extent to which you discuss each of the two texts – text 1 and text 2. Do you discuss the two texts in a balanced way?
    - Is there a balance in depth of insight you offer in reference to both texts or are you actually saying more about one text than the other?
    - Do you introduce the two texts or do you dive right into your analysis?
    - Can you trace how your line of argument holds the text together?
    - Have you written solid paragraphs, complete with topic sentence, evidence, unpacking of evidence and a concluding/transitional sentence?
    - Do you integrate examples into your line of reasoning?
4. How do you hold the reader's interest and support him/her in reading your text?
5. Examine your use of language and the marks you have received or lost for it.
    - What sorts of mistakes are you making?
        - Grammar – articles, prepositions, subject/verb agreement, etc.
        - Vocabulary – imprecise word choice, vagueness, etc.
        - Sentence construction – sentence fragments, run-on sentences, etc.
    - Are there words or phrases you repeat a lot? Could you replace some of them with another word or phrase? Are there words you know that could make your writing more precise?
    - Are there places where your register is inappropriate/too simplistic/too casual/more appropriate for social situations?
6. Now go through the notes you have taken. Highlight points that you will take into account before you write your next paper. File these notes in your *Planning* folder under *Term papers*.
7. Finally, now that you have completed your analysis, how accurate was your initial impression of the extent that you took into account the criteria and the marking scheme?

Another way of feeding forward is to have students, who have just finished taking a test or an examination, take the time to write some notes on what they have just experienced. Post-test reflections are used in the trilingual Nazarbayev Intellectual Schools of Kazakhstan. These schools have embraced CLIL. The post-test reflections consist of informal notes, but could take a much more structured form. Students could be given a fresh copy of the test or exam. They could write notes next to questions about how they prepared, why they felt or did not feel able to answer a question, or, if they thought some question was unfair, why that was the case. These annotated tests could be sealed in an envelope that is opened and discussed only after the tests or exams are marked. Alternatively, students could be asked to provide feedback on the test on an anonymous electronic platform. The teacher would share and discuss this feedback with the class to draw conclusions.

TEACHER UPTAKE OF FEEDBACK

Nuthall (2005) suggests that 'teachers depend on the responses of a small number of key students to make their instructional decisions and are unaware of what most students are thinking'. As a counterweight, **it is essential to seek feedback from all students** so that decisions about how to co-construct the learning environment with the students are based not just on classroom questions posed to a few students, but on a wide range of evidence. This would allow for teachers and students to adjust their practices so student learning is improved well before summative assessments.

In order to gain deeper insights into what all students think and know, teachers can have all students take 1–5 minutes to answer **anonymously** in writing **one** of the questions below. These questions can be used as exit slips at the end of a lesson (i.e. students hand their answers the teacher as they exit the classroom). As part of the introduction to the exit slip concept, it would be important to explain to students why you are asking these questions, and how you will report and take action on what you learn. It may also be useful to show samples of past student answers to demonstrate that in most cases you are looking for more than a one-word answer.

Language

- What percentage of what I said in the CLIL language today did you understand?
- Which new words or expressions did you learn today?
- Do you feel safe to try to say something in the CLIL language, if you are not exactly sure how to do that? What might help you to speak up?
- What are some words or phrases you would like to learn in the CLIL language?

Content and/or language

- What was the main point being taught in today's class?
- What is the main thing you learned in class today?
- How might you use what we learned in class today in your future job?
- Identify a question that still remains unanswered for you.
- What else do you want to learn about this topic?
- What else do you need to learn about this topic?
- Can you identify one point from the class that is still unclear to you?
- What do you need more practice on?
- Which evaluation criteria are you unsure about how to meet?
- What mistakes did you make on your last assignment/essay/lab report/presentation that you did not make this time?
- How should we change our success criteria for this project?

Learning process

- What mark are you expecting to achieve in this class and how do you plan to achieve it? *(Try giving students a full five or more minutes to answer this question, and signalling to them that you are looking for some deeper order thinking on this matter.)*
- Do you feel safe to express your opinion in class? Why or why not?
- What was the most useful thing we did today and why?
- Who spoke more today, the teacher or the students?
- What do you wish you had been taught sooner?

- What is something a classmate has done that has helped you learn?
- What is something you have done to help a classmate learn?
- Which app or piece of technology do you love the most and why?
- What do you fear the most about this class/this semester?
- Did you get a chance to summarise what we learned today for anyone else? If yes, for whom and how?
- At what moment during the class did you feel most/least engaged?
- What distracted you during today's class?
- What if anything did we do today that was unhelpful? Why?
- What is one thing another teacher does that helps you learn?
- What is one thing you would prefer that I stop doing?
- What is something your classmate(s) does (do) that makes it hard for you to learn?
- What study habits do adults suggest you develop? How does your personal experience align with these suggestions?
- Where do you study? *(Current advice is that studying in diverse places increases recall.)*

Online survey tools can be used to survey and quickly synthesise and display student feedback. For students to take exit slips or surveys seriously, they need to know what conclusions the teacher has drawn from the student feedback, and they need to see changes in teaching practice that are based on that feedback. Over time, students will become more adept at answering the above questions as they see the benefit of being precise. Black et al. (2009) discuss a teacher named Ceri whose students initially responded to teacher questions about their learning with very general blanket statements such as 'I can't do quadratics', but eventually through the regular use of formative assessment became more aware of what they know, and more precise in stating what they don't know – 'I can't do quadratics when there's a minus in front of the x squared'.

A teacher's own openness to receiving feedback or resistance to receiving feedback has a major impact on student achievement. Since CLIL places substantial additional demands on students, it is essential that best practices be applied in teaching and learning. In order to take feedback onboard, someone needs to offer that feedback. Having teachers film and discuss their own lessons with colleagues (and even with students) is among the ten most powerful known ways of improving student achievement (Hattie 2012, 2015a). This is called 'microteaching' as it focuses teacher attention on a specific lesson or part of a lesson in order to analyse the impact teaching is having on the students. Thus, in microteaching it is helpful to turn the camera on the students.

When viewing and discussing the recording with colleagues and possibly even students the teacher's aim is to learn as much as possible about how to improve teaching and student learning. It is important to supress any impulse to justify actions or behaviour. The discussions can focus on part of the lesson and concentrate, among other points, on: learner autonomy; student engagement; critical thinking; the use of sustained dialogue; the richness or paucity of student language output; scaffolding; wait time; teachable moments (moments that represent an unexpected good opportunity for learning); learning skills; and student self-regulation. Input from colleagues and oneself are then used to improve teaching, and later, to reflect on what impact any change made to teaching is having on student learning.

The video/digital recordings are made with student (and where required, parental) permission, students are made aware of their purpose, and it is agreed in advance that recordings are kept secure, used only for the stated purpose and permanently deleted after use.

ONE LESSON WITH SEVERAL FEEDBACK LOOPS

The following lesson has been used successfully as the first lesson at the start of Biology, Chemistry, Geography and Physics courses for 16–18 year olds. It is meant to set the tone for the courses as it encourages students to examine assumptions and think critically. It also includes numerous feedback/feedforward loops, which is a way of signalling that in these courses, whether students are seeking answers to enquiry questions or doing laboratory work, their thinking will be challenged, and they will acquire useful new knowledge, skills and language. The feedback loops include several opportunities:

- to assess one's thinking against a group's thinking
- to assess one's thinking and the group's thinking against an expert opinion
- to self-assess the quality of one's group work skills
- to receive feedback from and provide feedback to group members.

The lesson also encourages a high level of student engagement and team-building. Links to the various content subjects can be made during the debrief of the exercise and over the weeks to come, as the activity tends to be highly memorable. The lesson has been adapted for and used in CLIL contexts through the inclusion of several scaffolds to support the students in processing the content and language input. Language is highlighted through the provision of labelled visuals of key terminology, through the provision of discussion frames for doing group work and through the adaptation of the original answer key. Students are also supported in building context, and the content and language input is broken into small digestible chunks.

The learning outcomes for the 75-minute lesson, which focuses on winter survival, are as follows:

Content

You will:

- be able to discuss in detail common items that will help you survive or put you at risk of not surviving outdoors in the winter.

Learning skills

You will:

- have experienced and reflected on the benefits and pitfalls of group work
- have learned to test your assumptions, and drawn conclusions about how to improve decision-making.

Language

You will:

- be able to manage group work using the CLIL language.

Students are told that they will shortly find themselves above the Arctic Circle in Lapland in the winter and will need to find a way to survive in the wilderness. They are told they will work in groups of four. As a first step, they can ask an expert in the field of winter survival one question. In their group of four, they are given three minutes to come up with the question.

1st feedback loop

As a second step, the teacher takes on the role of expert and answers the students' questions. Some groups come up with more than one question in case another group has asked the same question they had decided upon. Asking the question acts as a warm-up and begins to scaffold critical thinking about the topic. This is the first of several feedback loops – it is an opportunity for students to compare their questions (their thinking) with those of other students.

After the questions are asked and answered, a series of photographs of winter in Lapland (taken from the Internet) are projected on the screen. The students are asked to list any important observable facts that they can identify from the pictures that might help them in their upcoming discussion about winter survival. They are asked to take notes. The pictures are intended to act as a scaffold in order to build context and ground student thinking in some of the realities of Lapland in the winter.

Next, the students are shown the following facts:

You are in Lapland in the winter. Your four-seater plane has crashed in an isolated unpopulated area. You are all physically OK.	
The snow is 60 cm deep.	There is no radio coverage.
It is -7 degrees Celsius.	There is no black box in the airplane.
The plane is well off its flight plan.	No one is injured.
You are 120 km from the nearest road.	It is 14:00.
It is 14 February.	The plane caught fire and blew up.

Students are given a document containing labelled images of a can of vegetable fat, gauze, lighter fluid, rope, a sectional air map, ski poles, several types of alcohol showing their alcohol content – 6%, 12%, 40% or 85-proof, and steel wool. The students are also provided on a sheet of paper with the language for doing group work (see page 109). Next, they are instructed orally and and in writing to do the following:

1. **Individually**, decide whether you will walk out of the wilderness or stay where you are and wait for help.

2. **Individually**, rank in column 1 the items on the following page by importance (1 – most important, 15 – least important). You have 15 minutes (see page 254).

3. **In your group of four people**, plan how you will work as a group (e.g. How will you use your time? Will each person be given an opportunity to explain his/her choices? How will you test the quality of your thinking?). You have 7 minutes. Look at the group work assessment tool on page 255. This might help you be more effective in working with your group. Also, near the end of today's lesson you will be asked to use this tool to assess how you worked in your group. Group members will also assess your performance.

> ***2nd feedback loop*** allowing students to compare their opinion and justifications with those of other group members. The group conclusion will be taken forward for future application and assessment.

4. **As a group**, decide whether you will walk out of the wilderness or stay where you are and wait for help. You have 5 minutes.

> ***3rd feedback loop.*** As students work to justify their own opinions or challenge other students' opinions, they are constantly getting feedback about their own thinking. They are also likely providing feedback to others.

5. **As a group**, rank (put in order) in column 2 the same items by importance (1 = most important, 15 = least important). Make sure each member of the group has been listened to and that you test your assumptions. You have 30 minutes.

> ***4th feedback loop*** allowing students to compare their opinions and justifications with those of the expert. They are likely to take on board many of the expert's justifications.

6. **Compare your thinking with that of the expert in the field.** Write the suggested order into column three. Everyone should have the same numbers in the same order in column three. Then, individually calculate the difference between columns 1 and 3. This is simply the difference between your score and the expert score. No negative numbers are used. Add up the total.

> ***5th feedback loop*** allowing students to compare their personal opinions and justifications with the group's opinions and justifications. These are also compared with the expert's opinions and justifications.

7. **Compare the group's thinking with that of the expert in the field** (see page 256–257). Calculate the difference between columns 2 and 3. Everyone in the team should get the same score. Add up the total.

Items for survival	1 Individual order/ ranking	2 Team's order/ ranking	3 Suggested order/ ranking	4 Difference between columns 1 & 3	5 Difference between columns 2 & 3
Cigarette lighter without the fluid					
Compress kit (with 5 metres of 10mm gauze)					
Newspaper (one per person)					
Two ski poles					
Sectional air map made of plastic					
Family-sized chocolate bar (one per person)					
Litre of 85-proof whiskey					
Can of vegetable fat					
Ball of steel wool					
Loaded .45-calibre revolver					
Compass					
Knife					
10 metres of rope					
Flashlight with batteries					
Extra shirt and trousers for each person					
		Total points			
		The smaller the number the better the result		Personal	Team

Winter survival exercise expert ranking

The following ranking of the survivors' items was suggested by Mark Wanig drawing on Rulstrum (1958). Wanig was an instructor in survival training in the US Army. The text has been abridged.

1. **Cigarette lighter (without fluid).** The biggest danger facing the group is exposure to the cold. The greatest need is for a source of warmth. The second greatest need is for signalling devices. This makes building a fire the first order of business. Even without fluid, the cigarette lighter can be used to produce sparks. The fire will provide warmth. During the day, the fire will also provide smoke for signalling. At night, the firelight can act as signalling.
2. **Ball of steel wool.** A ball of steel wool can catch the sparks made by the cigarette lighter. Steel wool is the best substance to catch a spark and support a flame. It works even if it is a little bit wet.
3. **Extra shirt and trousers for each survivor.** Clothes are probably the most versatile items one can have in a situation like this. They help people stay warm. They can be used for shelter, signalling, bedding, bandages and tinder to start a fire.
4. **Family-sized chocolate bar (one per person).** The large chocolate bar would supply the energy needed to survive for a long time. Chocolate is high in carbohydrates. Carbohydrates are easy to digest. They supply energy.
5. **Can of shortening or vegetable fat.** This item has many uses. The bottom of the can reflects light. It can act as a mirror-like signalling device. In sunlight, a simple mirror can generate 5 to 7 million times that of candlepower. The reflected sunbeam can be seen beyond the horizon.

   Other uses for the item are as follows: The shortening can be rubbed on the body to protect exposed areas, such as the face, lips and hands, from the cold. In desperation it could be eaten in small amounts. When melted into oil, the shortening is helpful in starting fires.

   The can is useful in melting snow to produce drinking water. The body loses water through perspiration, respiration and shock. Dehydration affects the ability to make decisions.
6. **Flashlight with batteries.** At night, the flashlight can act as a signalling device. In the cold, however, batteries lose power very quickly. The batteries must, therefore, be kept warm. They must be kept close to someone's body.
7. **Piece of rope.** The rope could be used to pull dead limbs off trees for firewood. When cut in pieces, the rope will help in constructing shelters. When frayed, rope can be used as tinder to start fires. When unravelled, it will make good insulation from the cold if it is stuffed inside clothing.

8. **Newspaper (one per person).** The newspaper could be used for starting a fire. It can also serve as an insulator. When crumpled or rolled up, it can be placed under clothes. The newspaper can provide dead-air space for extra protection from the cold. Dead air is a good insulator.

9. **45-calibre revolver.** This revolver provides a sound-signalling device. The international distress signal is three shots fired in rapid succession. There have been numerous cases of survivors going undetected because they were too weak to make a loud enough noise to attract the attention of a nearby search party.

   The availability of a lethal weapon can be a real danger. Anger, frustration, impatience, irritability, and lapses of rationality may increase as the group waits to be rescued. Although the revolver could be used for hunting, it would take a highly skilled person to kill an animal.

10. **Knife.** A knife is a versatile tool, but it is not very important in a winter setting. It could be used for cutting the rope into desired lengths and making shavings from pieces of wood for tinder.

11. **Compress kit (with gauze).** Feet and hands are probably the most vulnerable to frostbite. The gauze can be used to wrap around feet and hands to keep them warm. The gauze would also make effective tinder. The small supply of the gauze is the reason this item is ranked so low.

12. **Ski poles.** Their likely most useful function would be as supports for a shelter. The poles are useful as a flagpole for signalling. A person walking through snow to collect wood can use them for stability. The ski poles can also be used to test the thickness of the ice on a lake or stream.

13. **Litre of 85-proof whiskey.** The whiskey can be used in fire building. If a piece of clothing is soaked in the whiskey and attached to an upright ski pole it can be set on fire. The danger of the whiskey is that someone might drink it when it is cold. Whiskey takes on the temperature it is exposed to. A drink of whiskey at -30 degrees would freeze a person's oesophagus and stomach and do considerable damage to the mouth. Drinking it warm will cause dehydration. The bottle, kept warm, would be useful for storing drinking water.

14. **Sectional air map made of plastic.** This item is dangerous because it will encourage individuals to attempt to walk to the nearest road or town. This will lead to almost certain death.

15. **Compass.** Because the compass may also encourage some survivors to try to walk to the nearest road or town, it is the most dangerous item. The only positive feature of the compass is the possible use of its glass top as a reflector of sunlight to signal search planes. There are already other potential signalling devices.

Self-assessment of group work							
Grading scale: 3 = very much 2 = a fair amount 1 = a little 0 = not at all							
I listened to different opinions.	I encouraged people to speak.	I provided useful ideas & relevant information.	When necessary, I challenged opinions.	I stayed focused on the task.	I contributed to decision-making.	I used the CLIL language.	**Points earned**
3 2 1 0	3 2 1 0	3 2 1 0	3 2 1 0	3 2 1 0	3 2 1 0	3 2 1 0	
What are some words and phrases in your first language that you need to learn in the CLIL language in order to conduct more of your group work in the CLIL language?							

6th feedback loop with an opportunity to feedforward. This could involve taking forward the conclusion that an effectively functioning group can usually achieve a better result than an individual working alone. It could also include a conclusion about how to work more effectively next time both as an individual and as a group to ensure a better group score.

The act of trying to first decide the importance of various items for survival under winter conditions, and only then seeing the expert opinion is likely to make the learning of facts about winter survival more memorable than if students had simply worked through these on their own or with the teacher (Carey, 2014). Students who find the language used in the expert opinion challenging have been observed asking other students for the meaning of some terms and using dictionaries. The motivation to understand the text has been high. Normally the group gets a lower score than the individual. A lower score is the better score, as it is more closely aligned with the expert opinion. If there is anyone who worked more effectively as an individual than in a group, this is a moment of reflection for all involved. The scores and the students' conclusions are discussed as a class. Students are encouraged to draw conclusions about quality decision-making. In addition, connections can be made to Biology or Physics or to other subjects.

7th feedback loop with an opportunity to feedforward about how to improve group work. This is also an opportunity to identify missing language needed for future use.

Students are then asked to use the above rubric to assess how they worked in the group. The rubric is intended to act as a scaffold for preparing and conducting group work. Once the self-assessment is completed, students are asked to share the self-assessment with the group and the group is asked to assess each member of the group. The rubric also includes a feedforward element regarding language. Students are asked to list words and phrases they still need to learn in order to do more of the group work through the CLIL language. All students could be asked to write at the same time any needed words and phrases on the board. Students who know this language can use another colour of marker or chalk to add the translations in the CLIL language. The teacher can fill in missing pieces. Students can write down the phrases they need in their notebooks. The teacher can photograph the board for future use. As a further reflection on language students can be asked to identify new words and phrases including interesting turns of phrase that they noticed in the expert's opinion text. As an extension, students can be asked to use this language to summarise six major pieces of advice for anyone who gets lost in the wilderness in a Northern Hemisphere winter.

8th and 9th feedback loops, which constitute an opportunity for students to feed forward to the teacher.

Finally, the intended learning outcomes can be returned to at the end of the lesson. Students can use their thumbs to show the extent to which these have been achieved. If students indicate one of these has not been well achieved a discussion about how to achieve it can be undertaken. Before leaving, the students are asked to give the teacher an exit slip answering the question 'What is an unanswered question you have about the expert ranking?'

Several teachers have adapted the above winter survival exercise in order to offer their students numerous feedback loops. Oscar Chueca Segura, who teaches 16 to 20-year old students in a vocational CLIL programme in Catalonia, Spain, has adapted the above activities for his course entitled *Basics on Computer Systems Architecture*. Students used the adapted activity to discuss and assess their learning before a summative assessment. The students were completing a unit where they were expected to be able to identify, configure and test the interconnections between computers and networks. In the language domain they were expected to be able to have a polite, detailed and frank discussion about proposed solutions in reference to customer needs. Oscar gave the following items to his students in a scrambled order and the students first placed them in a logical order individually and then in a group, as well as finally comparing their answers with the teacher's suggested ranking.

- Define the purpose of the computer for its users
- Choose devices taking into account technical features and requirements
- Check compatibility between devices
- Select a case
- Prepare specific tools and consumables
- Assemble power supply unit in case
- Assemble hard disk + DVD + other storage devices
- Assemble CPU on motherboard
- Assemble heatsink + fan on CPU
- Assemble motherboard and RAM on case
- Assemble extra cards (graphic, Ethernet, sound, extra ports, etc.)
- Undertake internal cabling
- Turn on power supply
- Check POST messages

The winter survival exercise has also been adapted for another CLIL ICT course to explore the steps for writing and testing code. It has been adapted for a secondary CLIL Electrical Engineering course to have students plan for the construction of an electrical panel. Ildar Iahkin in Tatarstan, Russia, has used it for CLIL students to analyse and discuss organelles in human tissues.

CONCLUSION

Students possessing a high degree of assessment literacy are likely to be effective autonomous learners of both content and language. Assessment literacy goes hand-in-hand with the exploration of intended learning outcomes for both content and language, with the exploration of performance criteria, and with rich opportunities for students to practice assessing exemplars of poor, good and excellent work, as well as their own work and the work of peers. Feedback that helps students focus on the next steps is part of this mix, as is the development of students' understanding of the characteristics of effective feedback and how to provide that to themselves and others.

Finally, if assessment is going to serve as a tool for the learning of content and language, then conclusions drawn from assessment of both need to be discussed by educators and students, and this **must lead to changes in teaching practices and/or student learning practices.**

ADDITIONAL RESOURCES

The following standards offer broad benchmarks for assessing language learning. These would need to be adapted to a given context and descriptors will likely need further definition or exemplification.

American Council on the Teaching of Foreign Languages (ACTFL) proficiency guidelines for listening, speaking, reading and writing (see https://www.actfl.org/publications/guidelines-and-manuals/actfl-proficiency-guidelines-2012)

Cambridge ESOL proficiency standards (see www.cambridgeesol.org.uk)

Centre for Applied Linguistics (CAL) Oral Proficiency Exam and Student Oral Proficiency Assessment Rating Scale (see www.cal.org for additional instruments)

Common European Framework of Reference for Languages details six levels of foreign language proficiency standards (see http://www.coe.int/t/dg4/ linguistic/cadre1_en.asp)

WIDA (world-class instructional design) English Language Development (ELD) Standards (see https://www.wida.us/standards/eld.aspx)

8

Learning progressions: Bringing it all together

I was taught that the way of progress was neither swift nor easy. (Marie Curie)

I don't know how to do it today, but I will know how to do it tomorrow and do it. (Shu Hattori)

Connections

How this chapter connects to other concepts in the book:

Formative assessment

Regular opportunities for students to get and give feedback, which directs them to reflect on what they have done and what they could do next to learn needed content and language, are central to maintaining momentum in a learning progression.

Learning skills

Generic learning skills and language learning skills constitute powerful tools that students can use to move their learning forward.

For example, knowing how to self-regulate attention, behaviour and feelings is a key skill CLIL students can use to stay focused on tasks and move through a challenging learning progression, rich in 'new' content and language.

Critical thinking

A step-by-step learning progression is not intended to make learning unchallenging and simple. Instead, it is meant to help students to engage critically with and learn core subject matter content and new related language.

Ultimately, an effective learning progression helps students to go further in their thinking than they could working through a topic on their own without the support of materials or other people.

Cognitive load

If heavy new content and academic language are being learned at the same time, this is likely to overwhelm working memory. Breaking the planned learning process into a more manageable series of steps can accelerate learning. An initial series of steps can consist of doing a few short tasks in the L2 that introduce some key 'new' language, but that are light on content, before moving to a task that is heavy with new content that uses the 'new' language.

Academic language

Academic language is a challenge to learn in one's mother tongue. When working through an L2, students need language input and output scaffolded in a logical progression. This involves among other things ensuring that at any one time students are not overloaded with new language and content. Instead a thoughtful step-by-step systematic approach is required to help students first see, understand and then use new academic language in a manner that facilitates their deep-order engagement with new content.

INTRODUCTION AND CHAPTER NAVIGATOR

This chapter has two aims. The first is to show how good CLIL practice can guide the development of a complete **learning progression** of one short unit. The second aim is to help readers experience a CLIL learning progression from a student's point of view.

In order to achieve the above aims, the chapter provides the reader with an opportunity to step into a student's shoes and work through a series of tasks on the *human heart*. The tasks constitute a unit that was designed for 16-year-olds[1] studying Biology. The learning tasks and materials are accompanied with some explanatory notes and an analysis of how the tasks and materials exemplify CLIL good practice.

More specifically, this chapter will:

- define the term 'learning progression' and provide one short example of part of a learning progression
- detail an entire learning progression for a short unit on the human heart which will:
  - provide an introduction to the tasks and materials
  - offer a series of tasks and related materials, and provide an explanation of their use and an analysis of how these tasks and materials support learning in a CLIL context
  - concurrently offer additional tasks which can be used for differentiation[2]
- summarise key points from the chapter.

---

1 The materials presented in this chapter have been adapted from the original for which Y. L. Teresa Ting received the 2013 ELTons Education Award for Innovative Writing from the British Council and Macmillan, an international award which recognises excellence in educational materials and initiatives (http://englishagenda.britishcouncil.org/eltons). The original version of these materials and accompanying analyses of the tasks can be found in *Into the Heart of CLIL: Materials and Methods*, Rende: Centro Editoriale e Librario, Università della Calabria, 2015.

2 'Differentiation is ... the process of identifying, with each learner, the most effective strategies for achieving agreed targets' (Weston, 1992). In this chapter, differentiation consists of offering additional tasks in order to keep all students engaged in working toward the achievement of the intended learning outcomes.

WHAT IS A 'LEARNING PROGRESSION'?

A learning progression is a pathway that students travel as they seek to achieve intended short and long-term content and language learning outcomes that have been set for them.

Planned learning progressions consist of the purposeful sequencing of teaching and learning. More specifically, a **planned learning progression seeks to structure step-by-step how students' understanding of and competence in using the core concepts, explanations, reasoning and practices of the given discipline (e.g. History, Music, Science) grow over time** with the help of best teaching and learning practices. In CLIL, a well-planned content class learning progression seeks, in addition to structuring content learning, to integrate when and how the needed new language will be processed (the input), used to produce something (the output) and learned.

One cannot assume that a teaching progression is a learning progression. Instead, ideally, we plan lessons based on evidence about our students' learning progress. This planning represents what a teacher believes is the best sequencing of content and language learning. To ensure that the planned teaching progression aligns with the actual learning progression, the learning process needs to include many multi-directional feedback loops – rich opportunities for formative assessment. These feedback loops are used to reinforce learning of content and language, and to determine what students do not yet understand or what they are not yet able to do that they need to be able to do. Teaching and learning are then adjusted accordingly. In other words, the teacher and the students are advised to constantly check if the students are actually experiencing learning as you planned it. If not, then the teaching and learning progression likely needs to be adapted.

CLIMATE:
An example of part of a learning progression

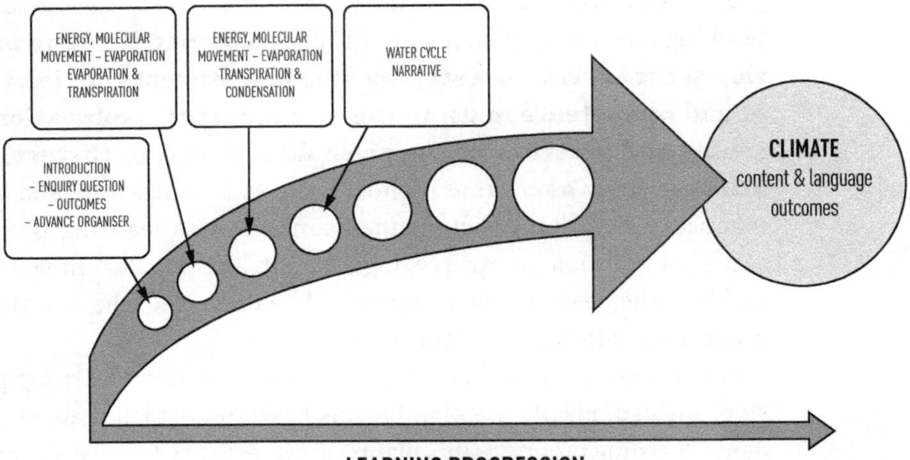

The above figure illustrates some of the elements that are essential to understanding the water cycle. These elements form only part of the progression towards developing a deep and holistic knowledge about *climate*.

To develop a strong grasp of the topic '*climate*', students would need to understand and use a series of concepts and/or ideas such as *precipitation, altitude, latitude, climate classifications and their types, human activities, climate models* and *climate change*. Eventually they would need to discuss and create a narrative about *climate*.

A learning progression about the new topic (*climate*) can begin with presenting an enquiry question. In this case it might be 'what is a healthy climate?' A question of this nature aims to engage students in thinking about the topic at hand. The students can be told that they will be asked to answer this question at the end of the unit. Next, the intended content and language learning outcomes for the given unit can be shared and discussed with the students so they understand what will be expected of them. An advance organiser depicting the water cycle can be shown and students can be told that they will begin the unit on climate by reviewing the water cycle. This advance organiser can help students to visualise the primary concept that will initially be studied. Teachers can then guide students through a series of well-scaffolded tasks which help them expand their language knowledge and build an increasingly deep-order and complex understanding of climate. The application of that learning may eventually involve students developing plans for ways of reducing people's negative impact on climate.

INTRODUCTION TO THE LEARNING ACTIVITIES AND TASKS

In the next section of this chapter, there is a series of learning tasks that should enable students to meet the upper secondary curriculum expectations regarding the human heart. It normally requires 150 minutes of class time for students to complete the tasks, and for these tasks to be debriefed by the class as a whole. By working through these tasks and materials the students will be able to:

Intended content outcomes

- describe the structure of the heart (its anatomy)
- describe how the heart pumps and oxygenates blood (its physiology)

Intended language outcome

- clearly and concisely summarise their learning using scientific terminology.

Please work your way down the tables which guide you, the reader, (1) to work through some of the *student tasks*, and then (2) to *reflect* on what you have experienced, and to read through an *analysis* of the student tasks.

The tasks that follow are organised like this:

Student tasks
First, take on the student's role and do the tasks.
Reflection and analysis
Next, resume your teacher role.

You will be asked to alternate between working through a few tasks, reflecting on what you have just experienced and reading the analysis of these tasks. Then, you will be asked to do the same again with a few more tasks. We encourage you to complete the entire unit on the heart. Differentiation options are offered as suggestions for helping students who may be struggling or need additional challenges to stay engaged.

By first working through the tasks, you will hopefully be able to 'see learning through the eyes of the student' – to personally experience 'learning through CLIL'. Next, reflecting on what you have experienced and by working through the accompanying analyses, we hope to make visible the learning process, including the use of various task-types and task-sequences. The task-types and task-sequences as well as related strategies are offered as models for adaptation and use in your own contexts.

Student tasks

Task 1:

Read through the following learning outcomes for the unit on the heart.

Learning outcomes

By the end of this unit you will be able to describe:

Content

- the structure of the heart (its anatomy)
- how the heart pumps and oxygenates blood (its physiology)

Language

- clearly and concisely summarise your learning using scientific terminology.

Task 2:

Here is a question that I will be asking you at the end of the unit.

Why could heart valve disease lead to fatigue and shortness of breath?

Task 3:

Please watch the 1-minute video I will play for you with no sound. Try to keep track of how blood flows in and out of the various parts of the heart.

The video can be accessed here: https://www.youtube.com/watch?v=JAoWb3gc4mE

Reflection and analysis

Reflection:

In what ways, if any, did seeing the outcomes and the video help prepare you (the reader) for the unit on the heart?

Explanation and analysis:

A helpful first step in a learning progression is to clarify what needs to be achieved. By displaying the intended learning outcomes, teachers can help make visible to students what content and language they need to learn. From a student's perspective, even if they do not yet fully grasp the concepts to be learned, seeing the intended outcomes can give them a sense of what will be happening in the class and what they will have to achieve. By contrast, keeping students in the dark about what is expected of them can lead to a sense of discomfort or even anxiety about what will be happening in class, and about what they will be expected to be able to do. Being in the dark about what needs to be achieved would also make it more difficult for the students to take responsibility for their own learning. It is difficult for a student to take control of his or her own learning if he or she does not know what the teacher expects. In other words, students can use outcomes to structure their thinking, focus their own learning and measure progress.

From a teacher's perspective, intended learning outcomes give a clear focus to lesson planning. They allow a teacher to be more transparent about what needs to be achieved. Transparency in outcomes also makes it easier to evaluate student progress and the teacher's own work.

After students have been given a few moments to read the outcomes, it is important to probe whether students have broadly understood the terms *human circulatory system* and *human respiratory system*. The students are given an opportunity to ask any questions they wish.

The Task 2 enquiry-type question is offered to capture students' attention and invoke their curiosity. It aims to encourage critical thinking and the practical application of what will be learned about the heart. When asked again at the end of this unit, the question also becomes a vehicle for checking how deep student understanding is of the role of the heart and how the heart relates to the respiratory system.

The viewing of the video as a whole class with no sound is intended to act as an advance organiser. Advance organisers, even if they are not fully understood when initially viewed tend to foster learning. In this case, they can help students to visualise the heart and blood flow. This is a scaffold showing in broad terms what needs to be learned. The scaffold can contribute to the construction of a cognitive schema on which to hang the upcoming learning about the heart.

Student tasks

First read the instructions for Exercises 1 and 2. Then do these exercises.

Exercise 1 (individual work): Circle the right italicised words or phrases in order to indicate the correct form of the questions.

Questions	**Answers** (see **Exercise 2**)
1. How *many/much* chambers does the heart have?	
2. How *many/much* blood does the heart pump each minute?	
3. What are the upper chambers *named /called*?	
4. How are the ventricles, the lower chambers of the heart, *different from/different by* the upper chambers?	
5. *Is it true/Is true* that the heart shows approximate left-right symmetry?	

Exercise 2 (individual work): Match the following correct answers to the questions above. There are two extra answers that cannot be used.

1. Yes, it is.	5. They are larger.
2. Yes, there are.	6. Four to six litres a minute (4–6l/min) for the average person while at rest and up to 30l/min for endurance athletes while doing sports.
3. 'Atrium' in the singular, 'atria' in the plural.	
4. There are four.	7. Yes, it does.

Reflection and analysis

Reflection:

Was the cognitive demand placed on you (the reader) sufficient to keep you engaged with the task? Did you learn any new content or terminology and how did that occur?

Explanation and analysis:

The heart is a new topic for the students. Understanding the structure and functions of the heart is demanding even when this topic is studied through the L1. When studied through the L2, the cognitive demand is substantially increased. In such situations, if considerable new content and language are presented simultaneously, the students may be cognitively overwhelmed.

As discussed in the chapter on academic language, academic texts are often 'lexically dense', meaning that they contain many terms and concepts. When it comes to the content being learned, students must understand and be able to correctly use discipline-related terms and underlying concepts in order to speak, read and write about the topic at hand.

Two primary strategies are used in these two exercises to support students in navigating the challenges inherent in learning the topic through an L2. First, the exercises are intentionally short, as, in the initial stages of this learning progression, it is important for students to build a sense of interest in the topic and confidence that they can cope with the new unit. Second, as the content is unknown, students need to become familiar with the new language. The materials follow the principle that when the cognitive demand regarding the content is heavy, the cognitive demand being created by the language must be light.

This first exercise is primarily a language task. Students have to choose between frequently used words they would have already learnt in language class. This is language that would be used in all school subjects. To make the correct choice students need to understand the question, not answer it. Hence, the cognitive demands regarding the content are relatively light. The students' attention is drawn to the correct use of language (e.g. *many* versus *much*). The language tasks were chosen because they reflect typical errors that Italian speakers make while they are learning English. For example, no distinction is made between *named* and *called* in Italian. The Italian verb *chiamare* includes in it both concepts – *named* and *called.* Also, the Italian preposition *da* can mean both *by*, *of* and *from*.

The first exercise also provides some of the important subject-specific terminology that will be used in the unit. First, students are introduced to the word 'chambers' – a word which students may have previously heard in reference to various types of rooms. In question 4 of the first exercise, the students learn that the lower chambers of the heart are called ventricles. In other words, the students are being introduced to and having to use more academically demanding language one step at a time while also learning about the anatomy of the heart. Thus, the language exercise can also be considered as a scaffold preparing for the introduction of 'new' information on the heart.

To do **Exercise 2**, students have to deduce the meaning of new terminology based on clues about the new terms and concepts (e.g. chamber, ventricle, atrium, atria, left-right symmetry, mirror images). Students are being exposed to the new content, but are also clarifying the meaning of words/terms.

Each question and answer gives progressively more information (The heart has 4 chambers; the heart pumps 4–6L/minute; atrium in the singular, atria in the plural, etc). Some questions and answers help students acquire the knowledge needed to answer the other questions. At the same time, students are exposed to basic facts regarding the structure of the heart and blood flow.

Students are having to use 'new' terminology that is needed to discuss the heart before approaching a more substantial text on the heart that is heavy in new language and content. This is what experts in CLIL would refer to as the 'pre-use' of language prior to fully delving into a topic rich in new content and language. Having students 'pre-use' language for a meaningful task is thought to be much more effective than simply pre-teaching language before students work with a new topic and text.

Student task

Differentiation option: (Assigned only to individuals who finish exercises 1 and 2 well before the rest of the class.)

Here are notes on the heart that contain one CONTENT mistake per sentence. Find and correct the mistakes.

The heart is composed of five chambers. The two upper chambers are called atrium in the singular and atriums in the plural while the two lower chambers are called ventricles. The upper chambers (the atria) are larger than the lower chambers (the ventricles). In addition, the heart shows top-down symmetry so there is a right upper atrium and a right lower ventricle which is approximately symmetrical to a left upper atrium and a left lower ventricle.

Reflection and analysis

Reflection:

To what extent did this activity engage you and why?

Explanation and analysis:

This exercise is given to those students who finish the first two exercises well before others. Students can check each other's corrections. Finally, they can be provided a corrected version of the text to compare it with their work.

The exercise serves the following purposes:

- It helps keep all students engaged in learning by providing an additional more challenging task to those who need it.
- It requires students to read the text critically and to focus on meaning and new language (an opportunity to revisit both new language and concepts).
- It is an opportunity to self- and peer-assess what was learnt and/or not learnt through doing the first two exercises.
- It helps students build a narrative about the structure of the heart.

Student task

Exercise 3 (individual work): A young astronaut from a distant galaxy has recently returned home from a year-long 'intercultural' exchange on Earth. The astronaut reports back to his boss on the heart of Earthlings. Complete the intergalactic astronaut's conversation with his boss.

Reflection and analysis

Reflection:

In what ways is this task more challenging with regard to content and language than the previous exercises? What strategies did you use to cope with the increased level of difficultly?

Explanation and analysis:

This step in the learning progression **invites students to revisit what they have done,** but this time **with a new purpose in mind**. More specifically, to complete this exercise, most students would likely need to re-read **Exercise 1** and **2** several times and their answers to those exercises before writing out academic terms such as *atria, atrium* and *ventricles*, or phrases such as *different from*. These become potential acts of both assessing and consolidating learning.

The exercise is more challenging than many cloze or otherwise known as fill-in-the-blank exercises. Instead of just filling in one word into a blank, **Exercise 4** has many blanks and in several cases requires the use of more than one word. This discourages 'mindless copying' because students will need to test out several options before they can create a logical answer.

The seemingly simple act of writing a word by hand calls for an intricate cognitive process. The word we see 'in our mind's eye' can emerge onto paper only if we have very precise motor control not only of the muscles in our hands but of those in much of the rest of our body (e.g. eyes, arms, shoulder). Since such fine motor control must last for as long as necessary to transfer 'words in the mind' into words on paper, the writing out of any word requires a level of cognitive engagement that is more complex and requires more 'attention' than simply reading a word or circling the correct choice. This is all the more the case when learning through an L2.

In addition, when we listen, speak, read or write, different areas of the brain experience heightened activity. It is thought that this means we understand things differently if we have only read about them, as opposed to having read and spoken about them, or as opposed to having read, spoken and written about them (Doidge, 2007). Using all four language skills to work with meaningful content is likely to lead to a deeper understanding of the topic at hand. Gaining a deeper understanding also implies that the new content and language are more likely to be retrieved and available for later use.

Student task

Exercise 4 (pair work): Using what you have learned from the previous three or four exercises, choose the schematic diagram which best represents the heart. Justify your choice.

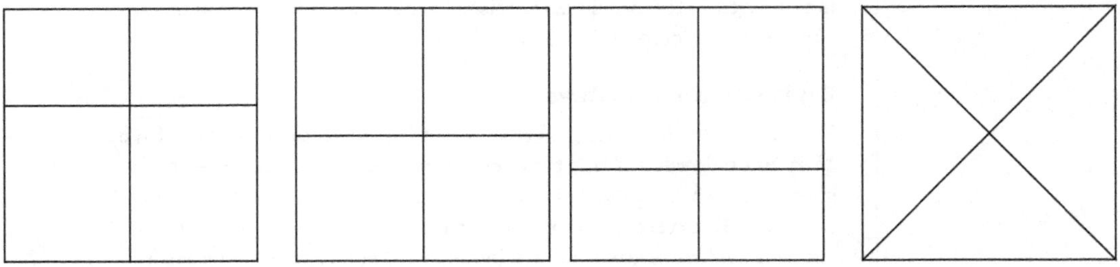

Differentiation option: You could ask those students who have finished the exercise well before others to:

- explain why at least one of the other diagrams does not represent the human heart.

Reflection and analysis

Reflection:

In what ways does this task represent a new step in making visible students' understanding of and competence in describing and explaining the structure of the heart?

Explanation and analysis:

The learning of the academic language of Science was scaffolded through the previous three exercises as was the learners' understanding of the structure of the heart. In the previous exercises, students had to use both content and language knowledge one piece/step at a time.

In **Exercise 4**, students are expected to progress to the synthesis of previous learning (content and language) and its application as one entire concept that they can also describe.

To do this task students must focus on the abstract meaning of the images and use both the content and language they have learned.

In order for a learner to decide which image best represents the heart, and then to justify that choice, the learner must take several steps:

a) first recall or review the previous exercises to extract what has been stated about the structure of the heart

b) extract **content-specific terminology** such as *atrium* and *ventricles*

b) recall generic common language such as *lower, upper* and *larger*

c) reorganise these words (*atrium/atria, upper, smaller*) into meaningful phrases. '*The atria are the upper chambers. They are smaller than the ventricles*'.

The differentiation option requires a use of the same language and concepts, but with a twist. This is a way of further reinforcing new learning and encouraging critical thinking.

Student task

Exercise 5 (individual work): Referring to the information in the previous exercises, divide this square to create a visual representation of the heart. We will call this visual representation *Figure 1*. Later, not now, based on a series of exercises you will be asked to label *Figure 1*.

Figure 1: *The human heart*

Reflection and analysis

Reflection:

Why not simply give the students a handout that has already been divided into the four chambers?

Explanation and analysis:

Here, students are asked to recall and draw the image of the heart they chose in the previous exercise. They are simply replicating the image from the previous exercise.

To complete this seemingly simple task, the students will have to actively engage again with the information. We have observed that after drawing the two lines, almost all students (and teachers that have worked through these materials) go back to glance at the image in the previous exercise. It is a moment of self-assessment that reinforces learning. Also, the students now have a figure or schematic drawing of the heart that they can 'call their own'.

Student tasks

Exercise 5:

Step one (individual work): Complete the following text using *'a/an'* (the indefinite article), *'the'* (the definite article) or nothing (simply leaving the line blank).

> *Now pretend you are ____ surgeon. _____ heart you are looking at is ___ heart of ___ patient lying on his/her back.*
>
> *Right and left refer to what __ patient would describe as his or her left or right side.*
>
> *Now label ____ Figure 1: write 'right' below _____ right side of the patient's heart and 'left' below ____ left* side.

Differentiation options: Some students might benefit from a **scaffold**. Students can be asked to explain the difference between the definite and indefinite articles before starting the exercise. If they have difficulty explaining the difference, they could be asked where they might find the answer. For students who are particularly challenged by the task, an explanation of the difference between the two articles can be projected on the screen: e.g. Use *a* when speaking about something in general such as a car (**in**definite article). Use *the* when speaking about one specific object such as **the** car that is parked next to you (definite article).

Step two (individual work): Now the teacher will either read or play an audio recording of the text you just worked with so you can check your work.

Step three (individual work): Now begin to label *Figure 1*. Write 'right' below the right side of the patient's heart and 'left' below the left side.

Step four (individual work): You have already identified the right and left sides of the heart. Now, use what you have learned from the previous exercises to label the four chambers of the heart. Write the following on *Figure 1*:

i. right ventricle
ii. left atrium
iii. right atrium
iv. left ventricle

Step five (individual work): On the same Figure, use a thick line **(_____)** to indicate the two 'new' anatomical structures:

- the **inter-atrial septum** which separates the two atria
- the **inter-ventricular septum** which separates the two ventricles.

Step six (pair work): Compare what you have done with what another student has done. Now your teacher will show you how *Figure 1* should look.

If you made a mistake, where did your thinking go wrong?

Reflection and analysis

Reflection:

About step one – what are the potential benefits of leaving out the definite and indefinite articles in this exercise, and requiring the students to insert these in the text? About step five – why ask students to identify something (i.e. the septa) that they have not been taught?

Explanation and analysis:

The six steps of the exercise represent an important collective step in the **learning progression** for this unit. Students are being asked to integrate what they have already been taught about the atria and ventricles with an important convention of the medical community – anatomical structures that an individual would refer to as being on his or her right side are illustrated on the left-hand side of an image, and structures on the individual's left side are represented on the right-hand side of the image. By teaching this important 'convention of the community', the exercise also seeks to cultivate 'spatial literacy' in students. This is the ability to negotiate space and conceptualise distance in order to effectively use visual information in one's work.

The first step of the exercise requires students to decide on the correct use of the definite and indefinite article. This is one of the most challenging language choices faced by second-language speakers of English. To be able to choose the correct article students may need to read the text several times to understand what is being said before they can make the right choice. **This seemingly simple language exercise forces students to deeply process the text.**

Step-by-step additional demand is placed on the students (e.g. in step five, students must use new information about the heart to deduce what the *septa* are and where they are located).

Finally in step six, students are asked to check their own work. This is a way of encouraging the students to develop the habit of always checking their work before they consider it finished. This is a learning skill. To scaffold this checking process and in order to ensure it is sufficiently systematic, the students can be asked to explain how they will check their work. Alternatively, one student could write the steps of her/his checking process on the board, and it could be discussed and enhanced.

Students are also expected to compare their work with someone else's work. This is intended to foster the habit of cooperating with others to improve one's work. For those students who have found a mistake in their work, the final question in step six is intended to help them reflect on and improve their own thinking about the structure of the heart. Effectively planned learning progressions build in numerous feedback loops.

Importantly, the correctly or incorrectly labelled *Figure 1* makes immediately visible to the teacher how well students are understanding and assimilating the content and language input, which has all taken place in the students' L2.

At this point, having engaged several times in diverse ways with the structure of the human heart and the related scientific terminology, the students are likely to have a firm grasp of both the content and the language. They should now be ready to progress towards learning how the heart functions.

Student task

Exercise 6 (pair work): Use the following instructions and work with a classmate to label *Figure 1*.

	information	labels for your diagram
1.	Blood from the body enters the heart at the top of the **right atrium** via a vein called the **superior vena cava**. • Draw an arrow to represent the superior vena cava and position this arrow in the correct location on *Figure 1: The human heart*.	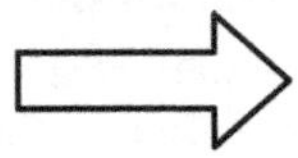
2.	• Add the words 'FROM BODY' to the tail of the arrow you just drew.	**FROM BODY**
3.	This blood from the body is rich in **carbon dioxide** waste produced by cells in the body. • Add the label '**CO_2**' inside the arrow representing the superior vena cava.	**CO_2**
4.	• Label the outside of this arrow with 'superior vena cava'.	**superior vena cava**
5.	When the atria contract, blood is pumped from the right atrium into the right ventricle *through a one-way valve* called the **tricuspid valve**. • Add the image of the valve to the correct location on *Figure 1*.	
6.	When the ventricles contract, this one-way valve prevents **CO_2**-rich blood from flowing backwards to the atria. • Insert this no 'U-turn' symbol into your drawing to show that blood does not return to the atria.	
7.	When the right ventricle contracts, blood is pumped out of the heart to the **lungs**. This **CO_2**-rich blood is carried from the heart to the lungs via the **pulmonary artery**. • Use another arrow to represent this information. Have your arrow exit the left side of the right ventricle.	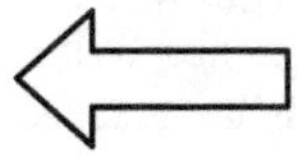
8.	• Add 'TO LUNGS' at the head of the arrow. Also, add the label '**CO_2**' inside the arrow representing the pulmonary artery. • Label the outside of this arrow appropriately.	**TO LUNGS** **CO_2** **pulmonary artery**

Reflection and analysis

Reflection:

Why have students started to build a figure showing how blood flows through the heart before they have read an entire text on the topic?

Explanation and analysis:

In this exercise students are being asked to process substantially more new content than was the case in the previous exercises, and to integrate that with what was learnt in the first exercises. The students are now not just expected to learn about additional structures of the heart, but also to explore how blood flows through these various structures. In other words, the students are now progressing to learning about how the heart functions (its *physiology*). In addition, as students work through each step of the exercise, they are expected to demonstrate their learning.

In **Exercise 6**, the content and language 'information' is differentiated from the instructions. The instructions are bulleted. If we leave aside the instructions, the new content and language information can be merged into the following standard academic paragraph which is dense in information:

> Blood from the body enters the heart at the **right atrium** *via a vein* called the **superior vena cava**. This blood from the body is rich in **carbon dioxide waste** produced by cells in the body. When the atria contract, blood *is pumped from* the right atrium *into* the right ventricle, *through a one-way valve* called the **tricuspid valve**. When the ventricle contracts, this one-way valve prevents **CO_2**-rich blood from flowing backwards to the atria. When the right ventricle contracts, blood *is pumped out of* the heart to the **lungs**. This **CO_2**-rich blood is *carried from* the heart to the lungs via the **pulmonary artery**.

In a class taught through the L1, it would not be unusual to give students one or more such challenging paragraphs. When learning content through a second language, CLIL students can find this type of paragraph, which is dense with information and new language, difficult to process. However, if this type of text is broken into small segments, as is the case in **Exercise 6**, the text becomes easier to process. The same is the case with the tasks. Here they consist of several short tasks as opposed to one long and complex task. The shorter segments of text and tasks both act as a scaffold on two levels. First, the short texts and tasks are unlikely to overburden working memory. Instead, the act of breaking up the text and shortening the tasks helps build students' confidence in their ability to cope with both. Second, the tasks require students to immediately engage with each small piece of text (input) in order to transform the information in the text into the various constituent elements of a figure of the heart (output). This means that students have to deeply process what they are reading. Under these circumstances, the students are likely to be mentally engaged with the tasks and operate within their ZPD – going further than they could on their own if the material and tasks had not been broken into pieces. It is also noteworthy that content information is not simplified or compromised in any way, and an academic register of language is maintained throughout.

Finally, the 'half-finished' figure provides students and teachers an efficient way once again to assess what has been learned. If all learners have not succeeded with the task, then some discussion is needed to find out what has not been understood so students can be guided in gaining the knowledge they need to complete the task.

At this point, the student's 'half-finished heart' is designed to foster continued progression along the learning path toward understanding the structure of the heart, blood flow and the relationship between the circulatory and respiratory systems. Having understood how the right side of the heart is structured and how it functions has hopefully created curiosity and speculation about the left side of the heart.

Student tasks

Exercise 7:

Step one (individual work):

Listen to a text about oxygenated and deoxygenated blood. Which one of each of the following pairs of italicised words did you hear?

> In the **lungs**, de-oxygenated blood becomes re-oxygenated, *enriched/rich* with oxygen. De-oxygenated blood is dark red but oxygenated blood is *light/bright* red. This re-oxygenated blood leaves *lungs/the lungs* and returns to the heart *through/true* the **pulmonary vein**. *Like/Unlike* all other veins in *body/the body*, the pulmonary vein is the only vein carrying oxygenated blood. The pulmonary vein carries re-oxygenated blood from the lungs to the heart, entering via the left atrium. When the atria *contract/contact*, this re-oxygenated blood is pushed from the left atrium *to/into* the left ventricle, through the **bicuspid valve** which, like the tricuspid valve, is a one-way valve that prevents blood from flowing *back/backwards*. When the ventricles contract, this richly oxygenated blood is pumped from the left ventricle *into/to* the **body**, leaving *heart/the heart* via
> the very *large/wide* artery called the **aorta**.

Step two (individual work):

Compare your work with your partner's. Finally, check your work against the teacher-suggested answers.

Step three (individual work):

Now, use the information in the above text to complete labelling *Figure 1*.

Step four (individual and pair work):

In what way(s) if any, does your figure differ from your neighbour's? Now, compare your labelling of the left-hand side of the heart with the teacher's *Figure 1*. Make any necessary corrections to your figure.

Reflection and analysis

Reflection:

What makes this exercise more challenging than the previous one and how has it been scaffolded?

Explanation and analysis:

In the previous exercise both the text and the tasks were in bite-size pieces. The students were asked to follow a detailed step-by-step process. Now, the students are expected to progress to working with an entire text at once and with only minimal instructions. However, the previous exercise and more specifically the concrete results of that exercise (the labelled figure) are intended to act as scaffolding for this exercise. We now analyse this exercise in greater detail.

The first step in **Exercise 7** is a simple listening comprehension task. By asking students first to skim over each pair of italicised words the exercise models a simple test-taking skill – always skim-read a text before taking a listening test. Choosing between each pair of italicised words is challenging primarily because it is in the students' L2.

As students do the second step (checking their answers) they need to reread the text or at the very least parts of the text. Both the first and second steps help scaffold the act of independently reading the entire text and labelling the figure of the left side of heart.

As previously implied, the third step, requiring independent reading followed by labelling the left-hand side of the heart gives students greater responsibility. The labelled right side of the heart can act as a scaffold.

Step four is not just another moment for self-assessment, but as the students' figures may vary to some extent, it is also an opportunity for a brief discussion about those variations and about how a figure or diagram may differ from the given object. Of course, hopefully this is a moment where students can enjoy a sense of satisfaction at having completed a figure and labelled 'their heart'.

Not only are the various steps of this exercise an opportunity to learn about the left side of the heart, this exercise fosters the development of the ability to interpret, negotiate, and to make meaning and use of visual information. Such productive visual literacy is an increasingly important skill. As contemporary media regularly use succinctly written text and visuals that allow for information to be processed at a glance, it is also logical to help students learn how to organise information in the same manner.

Finally, if students are asked to visually represent (e.g. in a drawing or figure) what they have understood about a complex Science concept, their understanding tends to be more complete and durable than if they are simply asked to work with text and answer questions.

Student tasks

Exercise 8 – Step one (individual work):

Let's build on what we know. Put the following sentences in a logical order to form a well-sequenced paragraph:

a. In the lungs, CO_2 is exchanged for O_2.

b. This system ensures that the blood circulating throughout our body contains enough oxygen (O_2), which our cells need for survival.

c. The heart and the lungs form the circulatory system.

d. This relationship between the heart, lungs, body and O_2/CO_2-rich blood is shown in Figure 2.

e. To do this, the heart receives blood that contains high concentrations of CO_2-waste from the body and pumps it to the lungs.

f. This O_2-rich blood returns from the lungs to the heart where it is then pumped back to the body.

g. In addition, the circulatory system also removes the carbon dioxide (CO_2) waste produced during cell metabolism.

Differentiation option: If some students need an additional challenge, they can first be given the above sentences cut into two pieces each. After they have joined up each set of two pieces to create the seven sentences, they can be asked to put the sentences in a logical order to form a well-sequenced paragraph.

Exercise 8 – Step two (in groups of 3):

What language in the sentences helped you decide on the correct order? Work in groups of three to answer these questions.

1. Give two reasons why sentence C is the best way to start the paragraph.
2. Which two words in sentence B helped you see that B follows C?
3. What words in sentence G helped you to see that it follows sentence B?
4. Which words helped you see that sentence E follows sentence G?
5. Why is sentence E before sentence A?
6. Which words tell you that sentence F follows sentence A?
7. Why is sentence D a good concluding sentence?
8. Why would sentence D not be a good starting sentence?
9. Which word could you change so that sentence D could become a starting sentence?

Reflection and analysis

Reflection:

Can you identify texts you have already used to teach where questions like those in step two of **Exercise 8** could help your students see and use academic language?

Explanation and analysis:

As throughout much of the entire learning progression about the heart, students in this exercise revisit what they have done, but using what they have learned for a different purpose whilst also extending their knowledge about the heart.

The first two steps in **Exercise 8** have three primary aims which are to help students:

1. to consolidate previously learnt knowledge
2. to learn a substantial amount of new language
3. to build academic literacy.

Step one of **Exercise 8** exposes students to considerable new language, but very little new content. Thereby, step one avoids placing an excessive cognitive load on students. As there is, metaphorically speaking, heavy lifting to do with the language, heavy lifting of subject matter content is avoided. Therefore, the students' cognitive resources can be used to focus on the new language while previously learnt content is being implicitly consolidated.

The sentences from step one are presented below in the correct order. The underlined text is academic language that is not typically encountered in language classes. Collocations are italicised. The dotted lines show the links between the sentences.

> The heart and the lungs form the circulatory system. This system ensures that the blood circulating throughout our body contains enough oxygen (O_2), which our cells *need for* survival. In addition, the circulatory system also removes the carbon dioxide (CO_2) waste *produced during* cell metabolism. To do this, the heart receives blood which contains *high concentrations of* CO_2-waste from the body and pumps it to the lungs. In the lungs, CO_2 is *exchanged for* O_2. This O_2-rich blood *returns from* the lungs to the heart where it is then pumped *back to* the body. This relationship between the heart, lungs, body and O_2/CO_2-rich blood *is shown in Figure 2*.

Students can deduce the meaning of the new or infrequently encountered words by using their now existent understanding of how oxygenated blood is pumped from the heart to the rest of the body. The now-familiar content helps students decode the 'new' academic language that would have been difficult to comprehend if it had been presented at an earlier moment in the learning progression.

There is one new piece of content – carbon dioxide is waste that is produced during cell metabolism. As the term 'CO_2-waste' is repeated and then explained in the next sentence, students are usually able to understand this new content.

Step two, which asks students to re-examine the text in step one, aims to make visible several aspects of academic language (e.g. antecedents, connectives, structure such as starting with a topic sentence, using full terms with symbols or acronyms in parentheses before switching to only using symbols or acronyms). The final sentence follows a formulaic pattern – the relationship between X and Y is shown in *Figure 1*. This is a pattern that is common to many disciplines. When students' attention is drawn to it, they are more likely to learn it. Asking students to reflect on how a text like this has been formed helps make visible how academic texts can be constructed. This is a small step on the road to cultivating the academic literacy needed to not only read but produce academic texts.

Exercise 8 – Step three (individual work):

Using the information above, complete *Figure 2* with: CO_2, CO_2, O_2, O_2 and HEART and LUNGS.

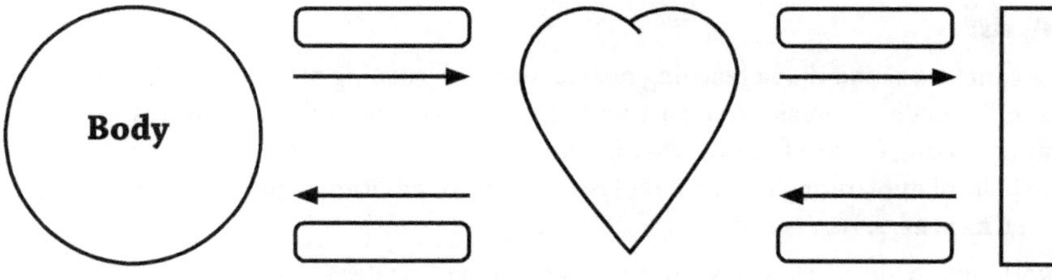

Figure 2: *The relationship between the BODY, the HEART and the LUNGS and O_2/CO_2-rich blood.*

Step three of **Exercise 8** provides both the students and the teacher an opportunity for rapidly determining whether the students have learned the key point that was taught during the lesson. It also fosters diagrammatic literacy.

Student tasks

Exit slips and homework

To finish today's lesson, please take a minute to answer the following question in writing:

- What is one key fact that you learned today about how the heart functions?

Leave the answer on my desk without putting your name on it.

Here is tonight's homework assignment – **Exercise 9:**

The following notes were written carelessly. Consequently they are full of content errors! The number of errors per sentence is indicated in parentheses (brackets). Please rewrite the text making the necessary corrections.

> According to scientific convention, the anatomy of the heart is presented in illustrations with the right side of the heart on the right and the left side of the heart on the left (2). This convention helps dentists learn about the heart and perform surgery correctly (1). De-oxygenated blood from the body enters the heart on the left, at the left atrium, via the superior vena cava (2). From the right atrium, this oxygenated blood is pumped to the left ventricle, passing through the one-way valve called the bicuspid valve (3). The strong muscles of the right ventricle pump this de-oxygenated blood to the lungs, via the pulmonary vein (1). In the body, this de-oxygenated blood is re-oxygenated (1). Once re-oxygenated, this oxygen-poor blood returns from the lungs to the heart and re-enters the right side of the heart (2). *(The pressure that pumps blood from the heart to the lungs and back to the heart is established by the left ventricle* (1)!) Oxygen-rich blood from the lungs re-enters the heart via the pulmonary vein which enters the heart at the left ventricle (1). The left atrium pumps this oxygen-poor blood to the right ventricle, pushing the blood past the bicuspid valve (2). From the left ventricle, oxygenated blood leaves the heart via the aorta and is pumped to the lungs (1). *(Imagine the strength of the muscles of the left ventricle. When the left ventricle contracts, it generates enough pressure to pump de-oxygenated blood to all parts of the body and back to the heart!* (1)).

Reflection and analysis

Reflection:

What is the benefit of having students write exit slips? What principles do you use to guide you in assigning homework?

Explanation and analysis:

As previously stated, we cannot assume that a teaching progression is a learning progression. Exit slips are written by students individually whereas several activities in this lesson were done in groups. Thus, exit slips are a quick way of getting feedback about what individuals have learned during the lesson. That information can be helpful in planning for the next lesson. A list of additional questions to elicit feedback can be found in **Chapter 7:** *Assessment.*

The **Exercise 9** homework text, which is riddled with errors, encourages students to revisit both the new content they have been learning and the related new language. Thus, this step in the learning progression is primarily focused on the consolidation of learning.

Homework at the secondary school level has been shown to be highly effective if it is used to consolidate learning (Hattie, 2012). By contrast it is thought that giving substantial amounts of new information for students to process as homework is not effective.

Hence, there is only one piece of new important information embedded in the homework. This information is in italics and parentheses. It states that there is only one source of pressure which moves the blood towards the most remote ends of the body and then back to the heart. This central idea is a stepping stone in the learning progression to understanding the circulatory system.

Student tasks

The second 75-minute lesson can begin with **the class watching once again the short video on the heart** from the day before. You can stop and start the video, asking the students to explain in pairs what they have just seen, or by having one student at a time comment on what he or she has seen.

Next, students are asked to exchange their homework with each other. The correct answers to the homework are displayed. Each student is asked to underline errors in a classmate's work before guiding the classmate to fix the error(s).

Finally, the intended learning outcomes, which were discussed at the start of this unit, can be displayed.

Learning outcomes

By the end of this 2-day unit you will be able to:

Content

- describe the structure of the heart (its anatomy)
- describe how the heart pumps and oxygenates blood (its physiology)

Language

- clearly and concisely summarise your learning using scientific terminology.

Students could be asked to use their thumbs as a meter to show the extent to which each of these outcomes has been achieved (i.e. a scale from thumbs pointing straight up = 100% achievement to thumbs straight down = 0% achievement of the given outcome).

Reflection and analysis

Reflection:

Why revisit the intended learning outcomes?

Explanation and analysis:

Starting with the same video and asking students to work in pairs to describe the circulation of blood in and out of the heart is an opportunity to recall and consolidate learning from the previous day's lesson and from the homework. It is also an opportunity for students to assess their learning and identify any shortcomings.

Having students check each other's homework will encourage them to revisit it with care. Instead of having each student correct a classmate's homework, asking students to guide their classmates in fixing work can help reinforce a culture where students are expected: (a) to regularly reflect on their own and other students' work, (b) to cooperate with classmates in order to support learning, and (c) to take greater responsibility for their own learning.

Both the adding of student explanations to the video and the analysis of outcomes achievement serve as benchmarks of achievement. Revisiting the video and the intended learning outcomes helps students to better see how they are moving towards meeting these outcomes. When learning targets are visible and discussed, it is also an opportunity to discuss, reflect upon and better manage the learning process/progression.

Student tasks

Exercise 10 (individual work): Read the text and complete the two tasks.

The life and adventures of a little red blood cell ...

The Dutch scientist Antonie Philips van Leeuwenhoek (1632–1723), known as 'the Father of Microbiology', made significant improvements to the microscope. He was also the first to describe with precision the red blood cell, estimating it to be '25,000 times smaller than a fine grain of sand' (adapted from Wikipedia).

Red blood cells (RBC) live for about 4 months. A single RBC will travel about 1500 kilometres in its brief 4-month lifetime! Using information from the Internet, find a city or other geographical site which is approximately 1500 kilometres from our community.

- If the diameter of a red blood cell is 7μm or micrometres (= one millionth of a metre) and a red blood cell travels 1500 kilometres in its lifetime, what is the ratio of **RBC-size** to **the distance a RBC travels in its lifetime**?
- The ratio of size: distance travelled is 1:______

Below are elements of the roadmap depicting how blood moves from your heart to your toes and back to your heart. Using numbers, trace the order of the movement of red blood cells from the left ventricle to your toes and back to the heart:

- aorta
- down the legs
- into the capillaries in the lungs
- into the left atrium
- into the left ventricle
- into the right atrium
- into the right ventricle
- past the bicuspid ('mitral') valve
- past the tricuspid valve
- out of your toes
- releases CO_2 and picks up O_2
- releases oxygen and picks up carbon dioxide
- through the inferior vena cava
- through the pulmonary artery
- through the pulmonary vein
- into your toes
- turns from bright red to dark red
- turns from dark red to bright red
- up the legs

Differentiation option: The elements of the roadmap depicting how blood moves from the heart to the toes and back again can be cut into strips and students can place these in the correct order in a circle.

Reflection and analysis

Reflection:

The learning progression has moved on to make connections to other concepts and disciplines. How has this been done and what is the potential benefit?

Explanation and analysis:

Connections create meaning. At this stage in the learning progression, small steps are being taken to help students make connections between the heart and other concepts and subjects. Learning about the heart is situated in the historical and cultural context of the development of science (e.g. a seventeenth- and eighteenth-century Dutch scientist improving the microscope). Students are being helped to understand the magnitude of what is happening inside their own bodies by marking a geographical site that is approximately 1500 km from their own community). The Maths problem helps reinforce the utility of Maths, but it also helps reinforce for the students the magnitude of what is happening inside their own bodies. The ratio is $1:2x10^{11}$ or, in other words, a RBC travels 200 billion times its own size. This is like a two-metre tall man running around the equator 10,000 times.

Students are also guided in thinking about how blood moves beyond the heart. This begins to lay the way for future topics in Biology.

It is noteworthy, that the introduction of a Maths problem is possible at this stage because the students are not faced with unknown concepts and considerable new detail. If students were given this problem in a situation rich in new language and content they would have had to direct their attention and cognitive resources to decoding not just the text, but the key concept(s). When working hard to process new text and concepts, it is difficult to be curious about anything besides the matter at hand.

Thus, only once the learning progression has ensured that students understand the key concepts and related details at hand is it logical to encourage students to take on an additional task such as the Maths problem.

The differentiation option allows students to better see the road travelled by red blood cells leaving and returning to the heart. Having the students put the strips in the correct order in a circle helps reinforce the fact that this is a circuit with no real start or finish.

Student tasks

Exercise 11: Read the text below. After watching the video on the heart, fill in the blanks.

About the size of your **fist**, the human heart is the most important muscle in the body ... It can beat more than a hundred thousand ______________ a day, pumping about 2-______________ **gallons*** of blood through a 60-______________ **mile**** **network** of vessels in the ______________...

**7600 litres ** 96000 kilometres*

The video can be accessed at: https://youtu.be/H04d3rJCLCE

Differentiation option: Students who could benefit from an extra challenge would get the same text but without text in bold.

Reflection and analysis

Reflection:

Why might watching this video at this point during the learning progression help build student confidence?

Explanation and analysis:

At this point in the learning progression, students are being asked to listen to a native speaker of English speaking quickly about the heart. It is likely that the learners will be able to easily follow what this native English speaker is saying. This is because the key concept – the heart being a muscle that pumps blood – has been worked with several times. New words are in bold. The imperial measures 'gallon' and 'mile' have been footnoted with comparable metric measures which should allow students operating in the metric system to understand that both terms refer to a form of measurement. The video provides further clues to new language. At the same, time the minor new linguistic challenges should help keep students engaged as they seek to understand these words.

The video is also likely to help consolidate learning and build student confidence in their ability to understand content in English. If the video had been used in the same manner much earlier in the learning progression, students would likely have had difficulty in following it – too many new concepts and words.

Finally, this exercise also provides additional information about the heart (quantity of blood pumped and the length of network of blood vessels). The act of writing down this new information should help reinforce it.

Student tasks

Exercise 13:

So far we have learned about the **anatomy** of the heart. Now, we are going to move into exploring the **physiology** of the heart to understand how it functions. (Physiology describes the way in which a living organism or bodily part functions.)

Step one (individual work):

Look at diagram 1 (opposite) and circle the structures you **already know**.

There are three new structures: **write** them here.

- ____________________
- ____________________
- ____________________

How many valves does the heart have?

- ____________________

Each chamber can be considered to have its own valve. Associate each chamber with its valve:

chamber	**valve**
right atrium	
right ventricle	
left atrium	
left ventricle	

Are these valves at the **outlet** of the chambers or at the **inlet** of the chambers?

Step two (individual work):

Look at the figure on the right – there are five 'new' structures. Make a list of these five 'new' anatomical structures:

- ____________________
- ____________________
- ____________________
- ____________________
- ____________________

diagram 1

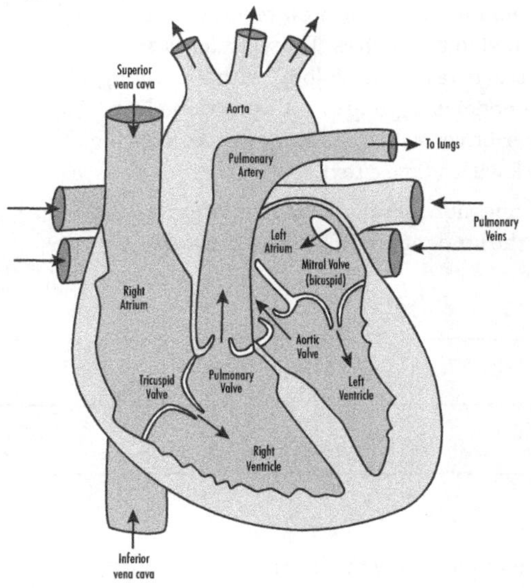

diagram 2

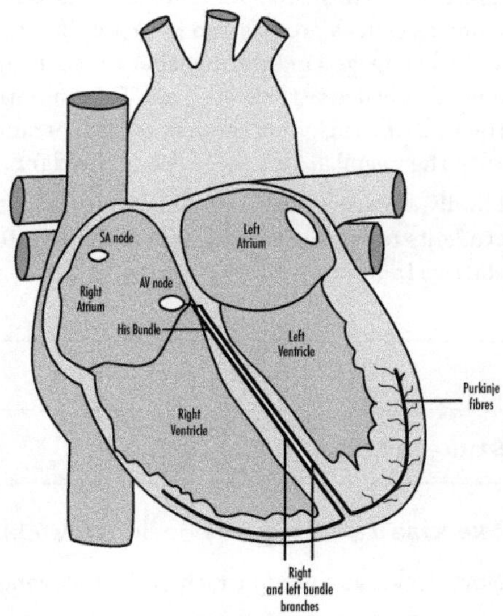

Reflection and analysis

Reflection:

What is the benefit of asking students to engage with two figures instead of one when they are doing an exercise?

Explanation and analysis:

In this exercise the students are progressing from previously having interpreted a very basic schematic representation of the heart (a square divided in four) to using two substantially more detailed traditional figures of the heart. In step one, by identifying the three 'new' valves and identifying those valves associated with each of the four chambers, the materials aim to reinforce the students' understanding of the importance of one-way valves for ensuring that blood flows only in one direction throughout the circulatory system.

The second step in the exercise focuses students' attention on the anatomical structures that control heart physiology. Students are thus supported in shifting from discussing anatomy to being prepared to begin to discuss physiology. This shift from anatomy to physiology was scaffolded by first having students work through the previous exercises in order to learn basic facts about the anatomy of the heart. Next, a clear signal was given students at the start of the exercise that, having studied the anatomy of the heart, they would now also begin to focus on the physiology of the heart. These two terms are capitalised to draw attention to them. To ensure comprehension, the term *physiology* was defined – i.e. the way in which a living organism or bodily part functions. This was done despite the fact that the term was briefly explained in the intended learning outcomes. In particular when operating in a foreign language, students need to use a term several times in a meaningful context if it is going to be retained, and recalled when required. Hence, in CLIL contexts when terms are initially introduced it is better to repeat the terms where possible and avoid the use of pronouns to replace them.

It is noteworthy that the figures are not simply used to illustrate accompanying text about the anatomy of the heart, but instead as stated students are required to *extract* new terminology from, as well as process and interpret information contained in the figures. Thus, students are actively engaged in locating what for them are the new 'structures of physiology' without relying on lexically dense texts such as: 'The sino-atrial node (SA node) is a group of cells positioned on the wall of the right atrium, near the entrance of the superior vena cava'. In other words, working with the visual at this stage is a scaffold for eventual work with a dense text.

Finally, the use of two complementary images instead of one more detailed image invites the students to engage more deeply with the information as the students compare and contrast the two images.

Student tasks

Exercise 14 – Step one (individual work):

Now, decide as a group which of the following sequences represents how the heart works.

Hint – think of where the blood **would go** if the sequence **were** correct.

1. Both right and left atria contract and then, after a short delay, both the right and left ventricles contract.
2. The chambers contract in the following order: right atrium contracts ⇨ then the right ventricle contracts ⇨ then left atrium contracts ⇨ then left ventricle contracts.
3. The right side of the heart contracts (both right atrium and right ventricle) and then the left side of the heart contracts (both left atrium and left ventricle).
4. Whichever chamber can contract contracts; there is no coordination.

Exercise 14 – Step two (individual work):

Now use the following sentences to explain why the incorrect sentences in step one are incorrect. Write these under the correspondingly incorrect explanation from above:

- If this were the case, we would probably be very different animals.
- If this were the case, the heart would be half as efficient as it really is and we would probably be less intelligent than we are.
- If this were the case, the blood from the atria would have nowhere to go since the corresponding ventricle would also be contracted.

Exercise 14 – Step three (individual work and later pair work followed by full class discussion):

You will watch the first 1.20 minutes of a video to check your answer. Here is the link:

https://www.youtube.com/embed/RYZ4daFwMa8?&end=87

However, before this, there are two new terms you need to learn – **diastole** and **systole**. To help you understand the video, first read the following text. Try to learn the meaning of these two new terms and practice pronouncing them.

Each heartbeat has two basic parts: diastole (di-AS-toe-lee), or relaxation, and systole (SIS-toe-lee), or contraction (to remember these two terms, try associating **di**astole with **di**late and **s**ystole with **s**queeze).

During diastole, the atria and ventricles of your heart relax and begin to fill with blood. At the end of diastole, both atria contract (atrial systole) and pump blood into the ventricles. The atria then begin to relax. Next, both ventricles contract (ventricular systole) and pump blood out of your heart.

This coordinated pumping of atria and then ventricles means that there must be a ***delay*** between the moment the atria contract and the moment that the ventricles contract. This is possible thanks to ***electro-physiology*** ... which we learn about in our next class.

Reflection and analysis

Reflection: What is the benefit of having students hypothesise about heart contraction sequences?

Explanation and analysis: At this stage of the learning progression students are being asked to use both the knowledge they have gained about the anatomy and the physiology of the heart. More specifically, the first two steps of this exercise invite students to use their prior knowledge to evaluate the feasibility of four heart contraction sequences. In step one, sentence 4 is intended to boost students' sense of confidence as it is easily rejected. Sentences 2 and 3 suggest a right-left sequence of pumping while sentence 1 (the correct answer) is the only choice that suggests an atria-ventricle sequence. The writing task in step two helps make clear both the content knowledge and some of the language needed to discuss the decisions made in step one.

In step three, the students are asked to listen to a native speaker discussing the physiology of the heart. In addition to offering an opportunity for students to check their work, step three allows students to experience, albeit indirectly, contact with a native speaker. It is central in CLIL contexts for students to become accustomed to and comfortable with hearing different people speaking the CLIL language.

In addition, step three requires students to follow the discussion about two new concepts – *diastole* and *systole*. Thus students are being kept on a path of always learning new content and language.

Student task

Exercise 15 (individual work, then group work, then whole-class work):

Create a text to describe both the anatomy and physiology of the heart. Summarise clearly and concisely: (a) the structure of the heart, (b) how the heart pumps blood in and out of itself, and (c) when and where blood is oxygenated.

You have 5 minutes to list the important points that you think should be mentioned in this summary. Then work with a classmate to create a joint text about the heart.

Finally, we will work as a class to create a text that the class as a whole believes will help you all to meet the intended learning outcomes.

Reflection and analysis

Instead of providing the students with a summary text about the anatomy and physiology of the heart, their task is to create such a text. This is an intellectually demanding task that will require students to:

- recall newly learned content and language
- summarise their learning clearly in a logical sequence and to do so concisely
- assess and improve their work several times.

During the whole class discussion, before signing off on the text, students can be asked to discuss one more time in pairs if there is a place in the text where clarity needs to be improved, and if so, how that could be done.

This student-produced text can become part of the students' learning materials. Having students sign off on a text and having them place it in the hallway or on a class webpage gives student-produced thinking and language a valuable platform. Teachers often report that students invest considerably more effort into work that they know will be displayed as opposed to work that is not.

Student tasks

Task 1: Let's have a look at the intended learning outcomes, which were discussed at the start of today's class.

Learning outcomes

By the end of this 2-day unit you will be able to:

Content

- describe the structure of the heart (its anatomy)
- describe how the heart pumps and oxygenates blood (its physiology)

Language

- clearly and concisely summarise your learning using scientific terminology.

After I read each of these, on my count of 1, 2, 3, all of you at the same time, use your thumbs as a meter to show me the extent to which each of these outcomes has been achieved. Thumbs pointing straight up = 100% achievement to thumbs straight down = 0% achievement.

Task 2: Let's return to the question I asked at the start of the unit. Take a minute to think – does anyone have an idea about why heart valve disease could lead to fatigue and shortness of breath?

Task 3: Finally, your homework is to figure out how Ibn al-Nafis (1213–1288) and William Harvey (1578–1657) are tied to this unit on the heart. I will ask you this at the start of the next class.

Reflection and analysis

Reflection:

Why revisit the intended learning outcomes yet again?

Explanation and analysis:

The students discussed the intended outcomes at the start of the unit and this class, and despite the challenging nature of the materials most students are likely to have achieved the outcomes. Returning to the learning outcomes at the end of a lesson or unit helps make visible to the students and the teacher what they have or have not accomplished. The achievement of goals or intended learning outcomes is thought to act as a motivator for students as it can provide a sense of accomplishment. If the intended learning outcomes have not been achieved, it becomes important to discuss what has not been achieved, what the obstacles have been and how these could be addressed and the outcomes achieved.

The question requires students to draw on their learning from the unit and to infer why fatigue or shortness of breath are some of the consequences of heart valve disease. This is a further opportunity to apply their newly acquired knowledge and learn a few new facts at the same time.

Finally, the homework seeks to make a multicultural connection by showing students that the knowledge they have acquired has been co-constructed across cultures and over centuries.

CONCLUSION

This chapter has briefly discussed learning progressions in general. It has then presented one learning progression in detail and sought to integrate many of the best practices discussed in the book. The intended content and language learning outcomes were discussed with the students. An initial video aimed to act as an advance organiser in order to help students visualise what they will be learning. An enquiry-type question was asked to capture student interest. The progression itself sought to avoid a situation where students must process substantial amounts of new language and content at the same time. Instead, students were supported in using some of the new language in a meaningful context before having to delve into content-rich texts that were also rich in new language. As key concepts and related details were learned, students were encouraged to think critically about them. It was generally not possible to copy answers from texts. Instead, students had to often draw conclusions, and make and test inferences, as well as apply their learning. Some activities focused expressly on developing awareness of academic language. Numerous opportunities were offered for re-using newly learnt content and language for different purposes and doing so using all four language learning skills. This fostered the consolidation of learning. Scaffolding was offered throughout. Several opportunities were also provided for students to discuss and assess their learning of both content and language. The learning outcomes were returned to several times to assess progress. Students also had to summarise their learning in writing and orally, working alone, in pairs and then with the class as a whole. Finally, several cultural connections were made.

Shining light on CLIL practice

How about first testing one lesson per semester on a couple of colleagues who do not teach your subject? If non-experts engage with and learn from the tasks and materials you plan to use with your students, then there is a good chance that your students will too. If colleagues struggle at some point, that creates an opportunity to rethink and improve the planned lesson. In any case, colleagues are bound to offer suggestions.

References

Alexander, R. (ed.) (2010). *Children, their world, their education: Final report and recommendations of the Cambridge Primary Review*. London: Routledge.

Baddeley, A. (2004). *Your memory: A user's guide*. London: Carlton Books.

Baddeley, A., Eysenck, M.W. and Anderson, M.C. (2015). *Memory*. Hove, UK: Psychology Press.

Baetens Beardsmore, H. (2016). Personal verbal communication.

Bailey, F. and Pransky, K. (2014). *Memory at work in the classroom: Strategies to help underachieving students*. Alexandria, VA: ASCD.

Baker, C. (2006). *Foundations of bilingual education and bilingualism* (4th ed.). Clevedon: Multilingual Matters.

— (2011). *Foundations of bilingual education and bilingualism* (5th ed.). Clevedon, UK: Multilingual Matters.

Banks, J. A. (2010). 'Multicultural education: Characteristics and goals'. In J. A. Banks and C. A. McGee (eds), *Multicultural education: Issues and perspectives* (*7th* ed.). Boston, MA: Allyn & Bacon, 3–30.

Barnes, J.D. (2008). 'Exploratory talk for learning'. In N. Mercer and S. Hodgkinson (eds), *Exploring talk in schools*. London: Sage, 1–15.

Bartolomé, L. I. (1998). *The misteaching of academic discourses: The politics of language in the classroom*. Oxford: Westview Press.

Berry, J. (1998). *When I dance*. New York, NY: Harcourt Brace Jovanovich.

Bialystok, E. (2007). 'Cognitive effects of bilingualism: How linguistic experience leads to cognitive change'. *The International Journal of Bilingual Education and Bilingualism*. 10/3, 210.

Black, P., Harrison, C., Lee, C., Marshall, B. and Wiliam, D. (2002). *Working inside the Black Box: Assessment for learning in the classroom*. London: King's College.

— (2004). 'Working inside the Black Box: Assessment for Learning in the Classroom'. *Phi Delta Kappan*, 86 (1) 8–21.

— (2009). *Assessment for learning: Putting it into practice*. Berkshire: Open University Press.

Bolam, R., McMahon, A., Stoll, L., Thomas, S. and Wallace, M. (2005). *Creating and sustaining effective professional learning communities: DfES Research Report RR637*. Bristol: University of Bristol.

Boroditsky, L. and Gaby, L. (2010). 'Remembrances of times east: Absolute spatial representations of time in an Australian Aboriginal community'. *Psychological Science*, 21 (11) 1635–1639.

Bourdieu, P. and Passeron, J.-C. (1994). 'Introduction: Language and the relationship to language in the teaching situation'. In P. Bourdieu, J.-C. Passeron and M. de Saint Martin (eds), *Academic discourse*. Cambridge: Polity Press, 1–34.

Bransford, J. D., Brown, A. L. and Cocking, R. R. (eds) (2000). *How people learn: Brain, mind, experience, and school.* Washington, DC: National Academy Press.

Brinton, D. M. and Masters, P. (eds) (1997). *New ways in content-based Instruction.* Alexandria, VA: Teachers of English to Speakers of Other Languages.

Brinton, D., Snow, M. A. and Wesche, M. (2011). *Content-based second language instruction.* Ann Arbor, MI: The University of Michigan Press.

Brown, H. D. (2007). *Principles of language learning and teaching.* New York, NY: Pearson Education.

Brown. G. and Wragg, E. C. (1993). *Questioning.* London: Routledge.

Cambers, G. and Sibely, S. (2015). *Cambridge IGCSE Geography.* Cambridge: Cambridge University Press.

Cambridge University Press (2014). *Cambridge advanced learner's dictionary.* Cambridge: Cambridge University Press.

Cammarata, L. (2016). 'Foreign language education and the development of inquiry-driven learning programs'. In L. Cammarata (ed.), *Content-based foreign language teaching: For developing advanced thinking and literacy.* New York, NY: Routledge, 123–146.

— (2009). 'Negotiating curricular transitions: Foreign language teachers' learning experience with content-based instruction'. *The Canadian Modern Language Review,* 65 (4) 559–585.

Cammarata, L., Tedick, D. J. and Osborn, T. A. (2016). 'Content-based instruction and curricular reforms: Issues and goals'. In L. Cammarata (ed.), *Content-based foreign language teaching: For developing advanced thinking and literacy.* New York, NY: Routledge, 1–21.

Camilleri Grima, A. (2015). 'Malta: Bilingual education for self-preservation and global fitness'. In P. Mehisto and F. Genesee (eds), *Building bilingual education systems: Forces, mechanisms and counterweights.* Cambridge: Cambridge University Press, 215–224.

Candelier, M., Camilleri-Grima, A., Castellotti, V., de Pietro, J. F., Lőrincz, I Meißner, F.-J., Noguerol, A. and Schröder-Sura, A. (2012). *The framework of reference for pluralistic approaches to languages and cultures: Competences and resources.* European Centre for Modern Languages: Graz.

Carey, B. (2014). *How we learn: The surprising truth about how, when and where it happens.* Macmillan: London.

CARLA (Center for Advanced Eesearch on Language Acquisition) (2014). *What is culture?.* Retrieved on 06/07/2014 from www.carla.umn.edu/culture/definitions.html

Cenoz, J. (2015). 'Content-based instruction and content and language integrated learning: the same or different?'. *Language, Culture and Curriculum,* 28 (1) 8–24.

Centre for the Enhancement of Learning & Teaching (2017). Retrieved on 12/02/2017 from www2.rgu.ac.uk/celt/pgcerttlt/assessing/assess3.htm

Chabris, C. F. and Simons, D. J. (2011). *The invisible gorilla: And other ways our intuition deceives us.* London: HarperCollins.

Chen, K. (2012). *Could language affect your ability to save money*? New York, NY: TED.

— (2013). 'The effect of language on economic behavior: Evidence from savings rates, health behaviors, and retirement assets'. *American Economic Review,* 103 (2) 690–731.

Christodoulou, D. (2016). *Making good progress? The future of assessment for learning.* Oxford: Oxford University Press.

Clarke, S. (2014). *Outstanding formative assessment: Culture and practice*. London: Hodder Education.

Claxton, G., Chambers, M., Powell, G. and Lucas, B. (2011). *The learning powered school: Pioneering 21st century education*. Bristol, UK: TLO.

Cloud, N., Genesee, F. and Hamayan, E. (2000). *Dual language instruction: A handbook for enriched education*. Boston, MA: Heinle & Heinle.

Cobb, T. and Horst, M. (2004). 'Is there room for an AWL in French?'. In P. Bogaards and B. Laufer (eds), *Vocabulary in a second language: Selection, acquisition, and testing*. Amsterdam: John Benjamins, 15–38.

Coe, R., Aloisi, C., Higgins, S. and Major, L. E. (2014). *What makes great teaching?*
Review of the underpinning research. London/Durham: Durham University and Sutton Trust.

Council of Europe (2016). *Competences for democratic culture: Living together as equals in culturally diverse democratic societies*, Strasbourg: Council of Europe.

— (2007). *From linguistic diversity to plurilingual education: Guide for the development of language education policies in Europe*, Strasbourg: Council of Europe. Retrieved on 24/01/2010 from www.coe.int/t/dg4/linguistic/Guide_niveau2_EN.asp

Coyle D., Hood P. and Marsh D. (2010). *CLIL: Content and language integrated learning*. Cambridge: Cambridge University Press.

Crehan, L. (2016). *Cleverlands: The secrets behind the success of the world's education superpowers*. London: Unbound.

Cumming, J. and Lyster, R. (2016). 'Integrating CBI into high school foreign language classrooms'. In L. Cammarata (ed.), *Content-based foreign language teaching: For developing advanced thinking and literacy*. New York, NY: Routledge, 77–97.

Cummins J. (2000). *Language, power, and pedagogy: Bilingual children in the crossfire*. Clevedon: Multilingual Matters.

— (2001). *Negotiating identities: Education for empowerment in a diverse society* (2nd). Los Angeles: California Association for Bilingual Education.

— (2014). 'Teaching through a multilingual lens: Classroom resources for global education'. In D. Montemurro, M. Gambhir, M. Evans and K. Broad. (eds), *Inquiry into practice: Learning and teaching global matters in local classrooms*. Toronto, ON: Ontario Institute for Studies in Education of the University of Toronto.

— (2017). 'Pedagogies of powerful communication in CLIL and bilingual education'. Presentation at *Evidence-based strategies to support bilingual education in Spain and the US*. Salamanca: University of Salamanca.

Damen, L. (1987). *Culture learning: The fifth dimension on the language classroom*. Reading, MA: Addison-Wesley.

Davison, C. and Williams, A. (2001). 'Integrating language and content: Unresolved issues'. In B. Mohan, C. Leung and C. Davison' (eds), *English as a second language in the mainstream*. Harlow, UK: Pearson Education Ltd., 51–70.

Deardorff, D. (2006). 'The identification and assessment of intercultural competence as a student outcome of internationalization at institutions of higher education in the united states'. *Journal of Studies in International Education*, 10: 241–266.

— (2013). *Promoting understanding and development of intercultural dialogue and peace: a comparative analysis and global perspective of regional studies on intercultural competence*. Paris: UNESCO Division of Cultural Policies and Intercultural Dialogue.

— (2014). *Some thoughts on assessing intercultural competence.* Retrieved on 11/06/2017 from https://illinois.edu/blog/view/915/113048

Doidge, N. (2007). *The brain that changes itself.* London: Penguin.

Donato, R. (2016). 'Sociocultural theory and content-based foreign language instruction: Theoretical insights on the challenge of integration'. In L. Cammarata (ed.), *Content-based foreign language teaching: For developing advanced thinking and literacy.* New York, NY: Routledge, 25–50.

Doran, G. T. (1981). 'There's a S.M.A.R.T. way to write management's goals and objectives'. Management Review, 70 (11) 35–36.

Durlak, J. A., Weissberg, R. P., Dymnicki, A. B., Taylor, R. D. and Schellinger, K. B. (2011). 'The impact of enhancing students' social and emotional learning: a meta-analysis of school- based universal interventions'. *Child Development,* 82 (1) 405–32.

Dweck, C. S. (2007). *Mindset: The new psychology of success.* New York, NY: Random House.

— (2010). 'Mind-Sets and Equitable Education'. *Principal Leadership,* January, 26–29.

Eccles, J. S., and Gootman, J. A. (eds) (2002). *Community programs to promote youth development.* Washington, DC: National Academy Press.

Elder, L. and Paul, R. (2001). *The aspiring thinker's guide to critical thinking.* Dillon Beach, CA: Foundation for Critical Thinking.

Ellis, N. C. and Robinson, P. (2008). 'An introduction to cognitive linguistics, second language acquisition, and language instruction'. In P. Robinson and N. C. Ellis (eds), *Handbook of cognitive linguistics and second language acquisition.* London: Routledge, 3–24.

Ericsson, A. and Pool, R. (2016). *Peak: How all of us can achieve extraordinary things.* London, UK: Vinatge.

Finkbeiner, C. and Koplin, C. (2002). 'A cooperative approach for facilitating intercultural education'. *Reading Online,* 6 (3). Retrieved on 21/07/2010 from www.readingonline.org/newliteracies/finkbeiner/

Finkenstaedt, T. and Wolff, D. (1973). *Ordered profusion: Studies in dictionaries and the English lexicon.* Heidelberg: C. Winter.

Fisher, D., Frey, N. and Hattie, J. (2016). *Visible learning for literacy, grades K-12.* London: Corwin.

Foos, P. W., J. J. Mora and S. Tkacz (1994). 'Student study techniques and the generation effect'. *Journal of Educational Psychology,* 86, 567–76.

García, O. and Li Wei. (2014). *Translanguaging: Language, bilingualism and education.* London: Palgrave Pivot.

Gardner, R.C. (1985). *Social psychology and second language learning: The role of attitudes and motivation.* London: Edward Arnold.

Garrett, N. (1991). 'Theoretical and pedagogical problems of separating "grammar" from "communication"'. In B. F. Freed (ed.), *Foreign language acquisition research and the classroom.* Lexington, MA: D. C. Head, 74–87.

Genesee, F. (2005). 'Second language immersion: A summary for teachers, administrators and parents'. In R. McConnell (ed.), *Immersion handbook.* Tallinn: Estonian Language Immersion Centre, 5–26.

Genesee, F. and Fortune, T. (2014). 'Bilingual education and at-risk students'. *Journal of Immersion and Content-Based Language Education,* 2 (2) 165–80.

Genesee, F. and Hamayan, E. (2016). *CLIL in Context Practical Guidance for Educators.* Cambridge: Cambridge University Press.

Gibbons P. (2009). *English learners, academic literacy and thinking: learning in the challenge zone*. Portsmouth, NH: Heinemann.

— (2002). *Scaffolding language, scaffolding learning: Teaching second language learners in the mainstream classroom*. Portsmouth, NH: Heinemann.

Gibbs, J. (1995). *Tribes: A new way of learning and being together.* Sausilito, CA: Center Source Systems, LLC.

Goldsmith, M. (2007). *What got you here won't get you there.* London: Profile Books.

Good, C., Aronson, J., and Inzlicht, M. (2003). 'Improving adolescents' standardized test performance: An intervention to reduce the effects of stereotype threat'. *Applied Developmental Psychology*, 24, 645–662.

Gudykunst, W. B. (1993). 'Toward a theory of effective interpersonal and intergroup communication: An anxiety/uncertainty management (AUM) perspective'. In R. J. Wiseman and J. Koester (eds), *Intercultural communication competence*. Thousand Oaks, CA: Sage, 3–71.

Halliday, M. A. K. (1993). 'Some grammatical problems in scientific English'. In M. A. K. Halliday and J. R. Martin (eds), *Writing science: Literacy and discursive power.* London: Falmer.

Hardwick, S. W. and Davis, R. L. (2009). 'Content-based language instruction: A new window of opportunity in geography education'. *Journal of Geography*, 108 (4–5) 163–173.

Harlen, W. (2012). 'On the relationship between assessment for formative and summative purposes. In J. Gardner (ed.), *Assessment and learning*, 2nd edition. London: Sage, 87–102.

Harrington, M. and Sawyer, M. (1992). 'L2 working memory capacity and L2 reading skills'. *Studies in Second Language Acquisition*, 14 (1) 25–38.

Hattie, J. (2009). *Visible learning: A synthesis of over 800 meta-analyses relating to achievement*. New York: Routledge.

— (2012). *Visible learning for teachers*, London: Routledge.

— (2015a). *Hattie Ranking: 195 Influences and effect sizes related to student achievement*. Retrieved on 24/02/2017 from https://visible-learning.org/hattie-ranking-influences-effect-sizes-learning-achievement/

Hattie, J. (2015b). *What works best in education: The politics of collaborative expertise*. London: Pearson.

Hattie, J. and Yates, G. (2014). *Visible learning and the science of how we learn*. London: Routledge.

Heugh, K. (2016). Presentation at the 'Trilingual Education: National and International Experience' Conference held in Astana, Kazakhstan, 23–24 November.

Heugh, K., Li, X. and Song, Y. (2017). 'Multilingualism and translanguaging in the teaching of and through English: rethinking linguistic boundaries in an Australian University'. In B. Fenton-Smith, P. Humphries and I. Walkinshaw (eds), *English medium instruction in higher education in Asia-Pacific: issues and challenges from policy to pedagogy*. Dordrecht: Springer, 259–279.

Hofstede, G. (1984). 'National cultures and corporate cultures'. In L. A. Samovar and R. E. Porter (eds), *Communication between cultures*. Belmont, CA: Wadsworth.

Hopwood, V. and Gallaway, C. (1999). 'Evaluating the linguistic experience of a deaf child in a mainstream class: A case study'. *Deafness and Education International*, 1 (3) 172–187.

Hu, M. and Nation, I. (2000). 'Vocabulary density and reading comprehension'. *Reading in a Foreign Language*, 13 (1) 403–430.

Huxham, M. (2007). 'Fast and effective feedback: are model answers the answer? Assessment and evaluation'. *Higher Education*, 32 (6) 601–611.

Immordino-Yang, M. H. and Damasio, A. (2007). 'We feel, therefore we learn: The relevance of affective and social neuro-science to education', *Mind, Brain, and Education*, 1 (1) 3–10.

Johnstone, R. (2007). 'Characteristics of immersion programmes'. In O. García and C. Baker (eds), *Bilingual education: An introductory reader*. Clevedon: Multilingual Matters, 19–32.

Kasper, G. (2008). 'Discourse and socially shared cognition'. In J. Cenoz, N. H. Hornberger (eds), *Encyclopedia of Language and Education, Volume 6*. New York: Springer, 59–78.

King, A. (1992). 'Facilitating elaborative learning through guided student generated questioning'. *Educational Psychologist*, 27, 111–26.

Klein, G. (2014). *Seeing what others don't: The remarkable ways we gain insights*. New York, NY: PublicAffairs.

Kramsch, C. (1998). *Language and culture*. Oxford: Oxford University Press.

Knouzi, I., Swain, M., Lapkin, S. and Brooks, L. (2010). 'Self-scaffolding mediated by languaging: Microgenetic analysis of high and low performers'. *International Journal of Applied Linguistics*, 20 (1) 23–49.

Lambert, W. E. and Tucker, G. R. (1972). *The bilingual education of children: The St. Lambert experiment*. Rowley, MA: Newbury House.

Legenhausen, L. (2009). 'Autonomous language learning'. In K. Knapp and B. Seidlhofer (eds), *Handbook of foreign language communication and learning*. London: Mouton de Gruyter, 373–400.

Lewis, W. G. (2015). 'Wales: Towards a national strategy'. In P. Mehisto and F. Genesee (eds), *Building bilingual education systems: forces, mechanisms and counterweights*. Cambridge: Cambridge University Press.

Liaw, M. (2007). 'Content-based reading and writing for critical thinking skills in an EFL context'. *English Teaching and Learning*, 31 (2) 45–87.

Lightbown, P. (2014). *Focus on content-based language teaching*. Oxford: Oxford University Press.

Lightbown, P. and Spada, N. (2013). How languages are learned (4th ed.). Oxford: Oxford University Press.

Lindholm-Leary, K. J. (2001). *Dual language education*. Avon, UK: Multilingual Matters.

Lindholm-Leary, K. J. and Borsato, G. (2006). 'Academic achievement'. In F. Genesee, K., Lindholm-Leary, W. Saunders and D. Christian (eds), *Educating English language learners*. New York: Cambridge University Press, 176–222.

Little, O. and Boynton, L. (2004). Personal communication.

Lyster, R. (2007). *Learning and teaching languages through content: A counterbalanced approach*. Philadelphia, PA: John Benjamins.

— (2016). 'Intentionally drawing attention to language in meaningful contexts.' In F. Genesee and E. Hamayan, *CLIL in context: Practical guidance for educators*. Cambridge: Cambridge University Press, 34–35.

MacIntyre, P. D. (2002). 'Motivation, anxiety and emotion in second language acquisition'. In P. Robinson (ed.), *Individual differences and instructed language learning*. Philadelphia, PA: John Benjamins, 45–68.

Marsh, D., Mehisto, P., Wolff, D. and Frigols Martin, M.-J. (2011). *The European framework for CLIL teacher education*. Graz, Austria: European Centre for Modern Languages.

Martel, J. (2016). 'Tapping the national standards for thought-provoking CBI in K-16 foreign language programs'. In L. Cammarata (ed.), *Content-based foreign language teaching: Curriculum and Pedagogy for developing advanced thinking and literacy skills*. New York, NY: Routledge, 101–122.

Martens. L. and Van de Craen, P. (eds) (2017). *Klaar voor CLIL: Het CLIL Handboek voor Vlaanderen en Nederland. (Ready for CLIL: The CLIL handbook for Flanders and the Netherlands)* Leuven/Den Haag: ACCO.

Matsumoto, D. (1996). *Culture and psychology*. Pacific Grove, CA: Brooks/Cole.

Mehisto, P. (2012). *Excellence in bilingual education: A guide for school principals*. Cambridge: Cambridge University Press.

— (2015) 'Conclusion: Forces, mechanisms and counterweights'. In P. Mehisto and F. Genesee (eds), *Building bilingual education systems: Forces, mechanisms and counterweights*. Cambridge: Cambridge University Press, 269–288.

Mehisto, P. and Genesee, F. (eds) (2015). *Building bilingual education systems: Forces, mechanisms and counterweights*. Cambridge: Cambridge University Press.

Mehisto, P., Marsh, D., Frigols, M.-J. (2008). *Uncovering CLIL: Content and language integrated learning in bilingual and multilingual education*. Oxford: Macmillan.

Met, M. (2014). Conference presentation at Brazilian Immersion Conference for Educators held at Beit Yaacov school.

Mercer, N. (2008). Three kinds of talk. Retrieved on 02/02/2017 from https://thinkingtogether.educ.cam.ac.uk/resources/

Mercer, N. and Dawes, L. (2008). 'The value of exploratory talk'. In N. Mercer and S. Hodgkinson (eds), *Exploring talk in schools*. London: Sage, 55–71.

Meyer, E. (2014). *Culture map*. New York, NY: PublicAffairs.

Moon, J. (2008). *Critical thinking of theory and practice*. UK: Library of Congress.

MOSAIC (2017). Retrieved on 12/05/2017 from https://casls.uoregon.edu/mosaic/about_us.php

Moseley D., Baumfield, V., Elliott, J., Higgins, S., Miller, J. and Newton, D. P. (2005). *Frameworks for thinking: A handbook for teachers and learning*. Cambridge: Cambridge University Press.

Murphy, V. (2016). 'Research on raising achievement in English language and/or literacy in pupils with EAL', presentation at the 'Multilingual learners in context: EAL, community and international school settings' symposium held at Oxford Brookes University, Oxford, 11 June.

National Academies of Sciences, Engineering, and Medicine (2017). *Promoting the educational success of children and youth learning English: Promising futures*, Washington, DC: The National Academies Press.

Newton, P. E. and Shaw, S. D. (2014). *Validity in educational and psychological assessment*. Cambridge: Cambridge Assessment and London: Sage.

Nuthall, G. A. (2005). 'The cultural myths and realities of classroom teaching and learning: A personal journey'. *Teachers College Record*, 107 (5) 895–934.

Nuttall, C. (1996). *Teaching reading skills in a foreign language*. Oxford: Heinemann.

OECD (2016). *Education 2030: Preliminary reflections and research by experts on knowledge, skills, attitudes and values towards 2030*. Paris: OECD.

— (2013). *OECD Skills Outlook 2013: First results from the survey of adult skills*. Paris: OECD.

O'Grady, K., Deussing, M.-A., Scerbina, T., Fung, K. and Muhe, N. (2016). *Measuring up: Canadian results of the OECD PISA study: The performance of Canada's youth in Science, Reading, and Mathematics*. Toronto, ON: The Council of Ministers of Education, Canada.

Olivella, C. P., Monge, O. P. and Garriga, T. S. (2007). *The world of Math through English: To contain or to be contained, that's the question*. Barcelona: Generalitat de Catalunya, Departament d'Ensenyament.

Oxford, R. L. (1990). *Language learning strategies: What every teacher should know*. New York, NY: Newbury House.

Paul, R. and Elder, L. (2001). *The miniature guide to critical thinking concepts and tools*. Dillon Beach: Foundation for Critical Thinking Press.

Reagan, T. (2016). 'Language teachers in foreign territory: A call for a critical pedagogy-infused curriculum'. In L. Cammarata (ed.), *Content-based foreign language teaching: For developing advanced thinking and literacy*. New York, NY: Routledge, 173–191.

Rheinberg, F., Vollmeyer, R., & Rollett, W. (2000). 'Motivation and action in self-regulated learning'. In M. Boekaerts, P. Pintrich & M. Zeidner (eds), *Handbook of self-regulation*, 503–529. San Diego: Academic Press.

Riitsaar. I. (2012). Personal communication.

Ruiz de Zarobe, Y. (2015). 'The Basque Country: Plurilingual education'. In P. Mehisto and F. Genesee (eds), *Building bilingual education systems: Forces, mechanisms and counterweights*. Cambridge: Cambridge University Press, 97–108.

Rulstrum, C. (1958). *News ways of the wilderness: The classic guide to survival in the wild*. New York, NY: Macmillan.

Sadler, D. R. (1989). 'Formative assessment and the design of instructional systems'. *Instructional Science*, 18 (2) 119–144.

Sarnoff, I. (1970). 'Social attitudes and the resolution of motivational conflict'. In M. Jahoda and N. Warren (eds), *Attitudes*. Harmondsworth: Penguin, 271–282.

Schleppegrell, M. J. and de Oliveira, L. (2006). 'An integrated language and content approach for history teachers'. *Journal of English for Academic Purposes*, 5, 254–256.

Schleppegrell, M. J., Greer, S. and Taylor, S. (2008). 'Literacy in history: Language and meaning'. *Australian Journal of Language and Literacy*, 31 (2) 174–187.

Schmitt, D., Schmitt, N., and Mann, D. (2011). *Focus on vocabulary: Bridging vocabulary*. Longman Press.

Scott, D. (2010). *Education, epistemology and critical realism*. London: Routledge.

Seelye, H. N. (1993). *Teaching culture: Strategies for intercultural communication* (3rd ed.). Lincolnwood, IL: National Textbook Company.

Shaw, S. and Imam, H. (2015). *International learning and assessment through the medium of English: Supporting teachers and learners in multilingual educational contexts*. Presentation. Cambridge: Cambridge International Examinations.

Sherris, A. (2008). 'Integrated Content and Language Instruction'. *CALdigest*, September, 2008.

Sinclair, J. M., Coulthard, R. M. (1975). *Towards an analysis of discourse: The English used by teachers and pupils*. London: Oxford University Press.

Smythe, D.M. (2006). 'Research paper assignments that prevent plagiarism'. In Carless, D., G. Joughin and N.-F. Liu (ed.), *How Assessment supports learning: Learning-oriented assessment in action*. Hong Kong: Hong Kong University Press.

Snow, M. A., Met, M. and Genesee, F. (1989). 'A conceptual framework for the integration of language and content in second/foreign language programs'. *TESOL Quarterly*, 23, 201–217.

Spitzberg, B. H. and Changnon, G. (2009). 'Conceptualizing multicultural competence'. In D. K. Deardorff (ed.), *Handbook of intercultural competence*, Thousand Oaks, CA: Sage, 2–52.

Statistics Canada (2010). Retrieved on 23/03/2010 from www.statcan.gc.ca/pub/81-004-x/200406/6923-eng.htm

Stoddart, T., Pinal, A., Latzke, M. and Canaday, D. (2002). 'Integrating inquiry science and language development for English language learners'. *Journal of Research in Science Teaching*, 39 (8), 664–687.

Stobart, G. (2008). *Testing time: The uses and abuses of assessment*. London: Routledge.

Stoll, L. and Seashore Louis, K. (eds) (2007). *Professional learning communities: Divergence, depth and dilemmas*. Berkshire: Open University Press.

Swain, M. and Lapkin, S. (1982). *Evaluating bilingual education: A Canadian case study*. Clevedon, UK: Multilingual Matters.

Syed, M. (2015). *Black box thinking; The surprising truth about success*. London: John Murray.

Tedick, D. J. and Wesely, P. M. (2015). 'A review of research on content-based foreign/second language education in US K-12 contexts'. *Language, Culture and Curriculum*, 28 (1) 25–40.

Thiessen, D. and Cook-Sather, A. (eds) (2007). *International handbook of student experience in elementary and secondary school*. Dordrecht, Springer.

Thomas, W. P. and Collier, V. P. (2012). *Dual language education for a transformed world*. Albuquerque, NM: Dual Language of New Mexico and Fuente Press.

Ting, T., Bartella, C., De Cicco, T., Langellotti, Caponsacco, B. M. (2015). *Natural Science. CLIL*. Bologna, Zanichelli.

Tyler (British anthropologist) (1870), cited by Avruch, K. (1998), *Culture and conflict resolution*. Washington DC: United States Institute of Peace Press.

UNESCO (2001). *Universal Declaration on Cultural Diversity*. Paris: UNESCO.

Useem, J., Useem, R. and Donoghue, J. (1963). 'Men in the middle of the third culture: The roles of American and non-western people in cross-cultural administration'. *Human Organization*, Fall 1963, 22 (3) 169–179.

Valentino, R. A. and Reardon, S. F. (2014). *Effectiveness of four instructional programs designed to serve english language learners: variation by ethnicity and initial english proficiency*. Stanford, CA: Stanford University Center for Education Policy Analysis.

Van de Craen, P., Ceuleers, E. and Mondt, K. (2007). 'Cognitive development and bilingualism in primary schools: Teaching maths in a CLIL environment'. In D. Marsh and D. Wolff (eds), *Diverse contexts – converging goals: CLIL in Europe*. Frankfurt am Main: Peter Lang, 185–200.

Veenman, M. V. J., Prins, F. J. and Elshout, J. J. (2002). 'Initial inductive learning in a complex computer simulated environment: the role of metacognitive skills and intellectual ability'. *Computers in Human Behavior*, 18, 327–342.

Vosniadou S. (2001). *How children learn*. Geneva: International Bureau of Education.

Vygotsky, L. S. (1978). *Mind in society: The development of higher psychological processes*. Cambridge, MA: Harvard University Press.

Walqui, A. (2006). 'Scaffolding instruction for English language learners: A conceptual framework'. *The International Journal of Bilingual Education and Bilingualism*, 9 (2) 159–180.

Wesche, M. B. (1993). 'Discipline-based approaches to language study: Research issues and outcomes'. In M. Krueger and Ryan, F. (eds.), *Language and content: Discipline- and content-based approaches to language study*. Lexington, MA: D.C. Heath, 57–82.

Weston, P. (1992). 'A decade for differentiation'. *British Journal of Special Education*, 19 (1) 6–9.

Whittaker, R. and Llinares, A. (2009). 'CLIL in social science classrooms: Analysis of spoken and written productions'. In Y. Ruiz de Zarobe and R. M. Jiménez Catalán (eds), *Content and language integrated learning: Evidence from research in europe*. Bristol: Multilingual Matters, 215–234.

Wiliam, D. (2016). 'Foreword'. In D. Christodoulou in *Making good progress? The future of assessment for learning*. Oxford: Oxford University Press.

— (2011). *Embedded formative assessment: Practical strategies and tools for K-12 teachers*. Bloomington IN: Solution Tree Press.

Williams, C. (1996). 'Secondary education: Teaching in the bilingual situation'. In C. Williams, G. Lewis and C. Baker (eds), *The language policy: Taking stock*. Llangefni (Wales): CAI.

Williams, J. M. (1986). *Origins of the English language: A social and linguistic history*. New York: Free Press.

Willms, J. D. (2006). *Learning divides: Ten policy questions about the performance and equity of schools and schooling systems*. Report prepared for UNESCO Institute for Statistics.

Wink, J. (2000). *Critical pedagogy: Notes from the real world*. New York, NY: Longman.

Wolff, D. (2008). Personal communication.

Yair, G. (2000). 'Educational battlefields in America: The tug-of-war over students' engagement with instruction'. *Sociology of Education*, 73 (4) 247–269.

Zwiers, J. (2008). *Building academic language: essential practices for content classrooms, Grades 5–12* (6th ed.). San Francisco: Jossey-Bass.

Index